Rojava

Rojava

Revolution, War, and
the Future of Syria's Kurds

Thomas Schmidinger

Translated by Michael Schiffmann

PLUTO PRESS

First published as *Krieg und Revolution in Syrisch-Kurdistan: Analysen und Stimmen aus Rojava*, by Mandelbaum Verlag, Austria
www.mandelbaum.at

English edition first published 2018 by Pluto Press
345 Archway Road, London N6 5AA

www.plutobooks.com

British Library Cataloguing in Publication Data
A catalogue record for this book is available from the British Library

ISBN 978 0 7453 3773 9 Hardback
ISBN 978 0 7453 3772 2 Paperback
ISBN 978 1 7868 0254 5 PDF eBook
ISBN 978 1 7868 0256 9 Kindle eBook
ISBN 978 1 7868 0255 2 EPUB eBook

This book is printed on paper suitable for recycling and made from fully managed and sustained forest sources. Logging, pulping and manufacturing processes are expected to conform to the environmental standards of the country of origin.

Typeset by Swales & Willis, Exeter, Devon, UK

Simultaneously printed in the United Kingdom and United States of America

Contents

CONTENTS

Acknowledgements

This book would not have been possible without the many people in and from Rojava who have again and again over the course of many years told me about the situation of the Kurds in Syria, and who have also hosted me during my research trips. Among the many people to whom I have to be grateful, I especially want to thank my friend Jamal Omari and his family. I have known Jamal for over a decade. He took me with him during his first return to his home town in 2013. I will never forget how he and his brothers smuggled me across the border in the dead of the night, and how warmly I was received by his parents and siblings.

Second, I also want to express my gratitude to all my Syrian friends in Vienna, particularly to Salah Ammo, who I came to know through the longstanding friend of my youth, Barbara Husar, and who, together with his wife Rojin, has not only again and again spoken with me about Syria, but has also satisfied my longing for Syrian food and Syrian music.

Third, I want to thank my travel companion and translator Azad Ekkash, who accompanied me and my wife Mary Kreutzer – who despite her fear for me has always supported my research in Syria – on a journey to Rojava in 2014, and who was far more than merely a translator and organizer.

I also want to thank Taha Xelîl, who opened his house in Qamişlo to us and who regaled us, not only with meat and drink, but also – and even more so – with his stories and reports. It was very sad for me, immediately after the oral defence of my doctoral dissertation, to get a phone call from a friend telling me that Taha's daughter Helepçe had been killed in an act of terror – and exactly as I was in the midst of my defence. This book is devoted to her and all the others who were forced to give up their lives in the struggle for their freedom.

Preface to the English Edition

After the fourth German and the second Turkish editions I am extremely pleased to see the publication of the first English translation of this book. The English version has once more been updated with developments from spring 2017 to early 2018. Some additional interviews have also been added at the end of the book.

Simultaneously the book is also being translated into Spanish and there are talks going on regarding Arabic and Persian translations.

I want to thank especially Pluto Press and the translator Michael Schiffmann for their excellent work. Both have done a great job! I have revised the entire English translation and I am glad that my book will be available for English-speaking readers around the world.

Preface to the Fourth Edition

Since the publication of this book's third edition in 2015, there have been important changes both in the military and the political situation in Syria. When the first edition of this book came out in autumn 2014, the rapid expansion of the so-called "Islamic State" (IS) and the attack on Kobanê going on at the time were the most urgent focus of media coverage. Since then, the Kurdish self-administration in Rojava has become politically much more established. With the support of the USA, it has also been successful in the struggle against IS, primarily in the military realm. While I am updating this book, Iraqi units are attacking the Western part of the IS stronghold Mosul, and units of the Kurdish YPG and their allies are advancing in the direction of the IS capital ar-Raqqa.

For this reason, the fourth edition of this book had to be revised more thoroughly in order to remain up to date. More than in previous editions, I go into the establishment of the Kurdish autonomous regions and their political structures, and daily life under the structures of the self-administration. I will, however, also continue to describe the internal conflicts of the Kurds.

Since the publication of the third German edition, there has also been a second, updated Turkish edition. My Turkish publisher enabled me to present this new edition at the Istanbul Book Fair in November 2016. While the political situation in Turkey gets darker by the week, especially with regard to academic freedom, there continue to be courageous intellectuals and publishers in Turkey who still dare to publicly address the Kurdish question. Some of the Turkish colleagues with whom I am working in scientific cooperations have by now been dismissed from their universities, lost all pension and social security claims, and even been stripped of their passports. While I was able to present the first Turkish edition of this book in February 2016 during a guest lectureship at the renowned Mülkiye, the old civil service school of the Ottoman Empire that is now integrated into Ankara University as the faculty of political science, today, just one year later, many of the professors and lecturers who had listened to me in February 2016 are not even allowed to enter the premises of the university anymore. Given these frightening developments in Turkey, it is an open question whether another Turkish edition will be allowed to appear.

Much more gratifying is the fact that this fourth edition has now also become the basis for the first English edition, which will be published by the well-known leftist publisher Pluto Press. Moreover, a Spanish translation is also already in the works. Only the planned Kurdish edition has, unfortunately, still come to naught so far.

Even so, the book will now have a much bigger readership than ever before.

Preface to the Third Edition

When my book first appeared in autumn 2014, it immediately gained an unexpected and unwanted topicality thanks to the attack of IS jihadis on the town and canton of Kobanê that was underway at the same time. Much faster than we thought, the publisher and I had to arrange for a reprint. Reviews in various leftist magazines, as well as in big German-language papers such as *FAZ*, *Zeit*, or *Presse*, made the book widely known and also led to discussions in Kurdish circles about its core contents.

In spring 2015, the Marxist publisher Yordam Kitab published a slightly updated Turkish translation of the book. I could thus for the first time present the book at the Book Fair of Amed/Diyarbakır, and later in Istanbul. Now, not even a year later, it has already become necessary to print a third edition. How quickly the situation in Syria is changing is shown by the fact that the book had to be revised and updated only nine months after its previous printing. The book is currently also being translated into Kurdish (Soranî) and, apparently, there will soon also be an English translation.

Of course, as the book's author, I was very gratified by the many very positive reviews. But nothing has delighted me more than the award of a Kurdish journalistic prize in Rojava itself. On 22 April 2015, I was invited to Qamişlo to be awarded the Mazlum Bagok Prize for this book, together with the Kurdish journalist Kheyri Kizler from Sinjar and the team of Rohani TV from Kobanê, who were honoured for their journalistic reporting of the IS attacks on the Êzîdî of Singal and Kobanê. In my acceptance speech, I mentioned quite explicitly that this was also a sign for the political opening of the Kurdish parties themselves, because my book is not a propaganda tract, but a differentiated approach to the topic from a variety of perspectives. In my speech, I evaluated the fact that I was awarded this prize as "a hopeful sign for the determination to build a pluralistic society".

The prize is named after Mazlum Bagok, a Kurdish journalist who was murdered in the course of his work in Rabia in the Iraqi province of Mosul on 22 September 2014 by IS jihadis. For me, this award also represents a charge to continue to write for human rights and democracy in a way that is both scientific and partisan.

The Development of Kurdish Parties

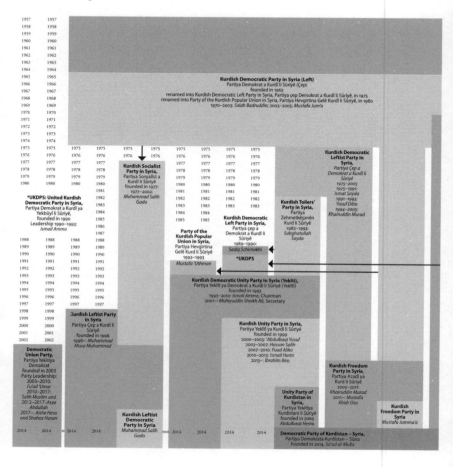

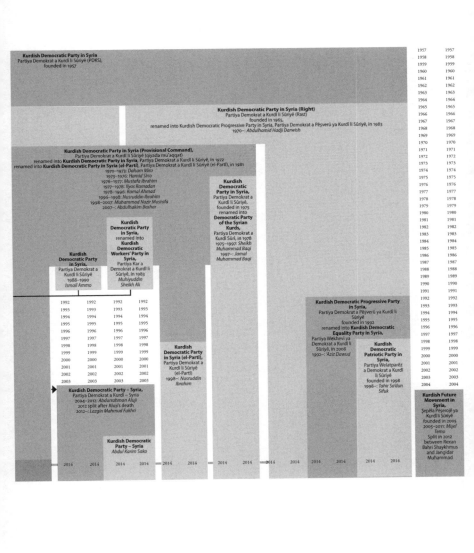

Kurdish Democratic Party in Syria, Partiya Demokrat a Kurdî li Sûriyê (PDKS), founded in 1957

Kurdish Democratic Party in Syria (Right), Partiya Demokrat a Kurdî li Sûriyê (Rast) founded in 1965, renamed into Kurdish Democratic Progressive Party in Syria, Partiya Demokrat a Pêşverû ya Kurdî li Sûriyê, in 1983
1970–: *Abdulhamid Hadji Darwish*

Kurdish Democratic Party in Syria (Provisional Command), Partiya Demokrat a Kurdî li Sûriyê (qiyada mu'aqqat) renamed into **Kurdish Democratic Party in Syria,** Partiya Demokrat a Kurdî li Sûriyê, in 1972 renamed into **Kurdish Democratic Party in Syria (el-Partî),** Partiya Demokrat a Kurdî li Sûriyê (el-Partî), in 1981
1970–1973: *Daham Miro*
1973–1976: *Hamid Sino*
1976–1977: *Mustafa Ibrahim*
1977–1978: *Ilyas Ramadan*
1978–1996: *Kamal Ahmad*
1996–1998: *Nusruddin Ibrahim*
1998–2007: *Muhammad Nazir Mustafa*
2007–: *Abdulhakim Bashar*

Kurdish Democratic Party in Syria, Partiya Demokrat a Kurdî li Sûriyê, founded in 1975 renamed into **Democratic Party of the Syrian Kurds,** Partiya Demokrat a Kurdî Sûrî, in 1978
1975–1996: *Sheikh Muhammad Baqi*
1997–: *Jamal Muhammad Baqi*

Kurdish Democratic Party in Syria, Partiya Demokrat a Kurdî li Sûriyê 1988–1990 *Ismail Ammo*

Kurdish Democratic Party in Syria, renamed into **Kurdish Democratic Workers' Party in Syria,** Partiya Kar a Demokrat a Kurdî li Sûriyê, in 1983 *Muhiyuddin Sheikh Ali*

Kurdish Democratic Party – Syria, Partiya Demokrat a Kurdî – Syria 2004–2012: *Abdurrahman Aluji* 2012 split after Aluji's death 2012–: *Lazgin Mahmud Fakhri*

Kurdish Democratic Party – Syria *Abdul Karim Sako*

Kurdish Democratic Party in Syria (el-Partî), Partiya Demokrat a Kurdî li Sûriyê (el-Partî) 1998–: *Nusruddin Ibrahim*

Kurdish Democratic Progressive Party in Syria, Partiya Demokrat a Pêşverû ya Kurdî li Sûriyê founded in 1992 renamed into **Kurdish Democratic Equality Party in Syria,** Partiya Wekhevî ya Demokrat a Kurdî li Sûriyê, in 2008 1992–: *Aziz Dawud*

Kurdish Democratic Patriotic Party in Syria, Partiya Welatparêz a Demokrat a Kurdî li Sûriyê founded in 1998 1998–: *Tahir Sa'dun Sifuk*

Kurdish Future Movement in Syria, Şepêla Pêşerojê ya Kurdî li Sûriyê founded in 2005 2005–2011: *Mişel Temo* Split in 2012 between Rexan Bahri Shaykhmus and Jangidar Muhammad

1957 1958 1959 1960 1961 1962 1963 1964 1965 1966 1967 1968 1969 1970 1971 1972 1973 1974 1975 1976 1977 1978 1979 1980 1981 1982 1983 1984 1985 1986 1987 1988 1989 1990 1991 1992 1993 1994 1995 1996 1997 1998 1999 2000 2001 2002 2003 2004 2014

1

The Long Struggle for Autonomy

The border guards do not yet dare to put their stamp right in my passport. "Komara Sûri Kantona Cizîrê," it reads in Kurdish above the Arab variant of "Republic of Syria, Canton Cizîrê," which for now is still stamped on a separate piece of paper here at the border checkpoint of Semalka. Very close to the border triangle between Iraq, Syria, and Turkey, Kurdish fighters have taken a border station under their control. Obviously, anyone entering this part of Syrian territory from Iraq is no longer coming to the "Arab Republic of Syria," as the country had called itself after its withdrawal from the "United Arab Republic" of 1961, but to a "Republic of Syria," which for now is still imaginary, but whose Kurdish cantons are already in existence.

The above snapshot given in the first German edition of the current book had already changed in 2016, when, after a few sojourns in parts of Syrian Kurdistan located further to the West, I passed the same border for a second time. Since March 2016, the traveller at this point enters the Democratic Federation of Northern Syria – Rojava (Federasyona Bakurê Sûriyê – Rojava).

Considering the war going on in large parts of Syria and the shutdown of the border by Turkey, the border with Iraq offers the only more-or-less legal way to travel to Rojava. Since January 2014, Rojava, as most of the Kurds call Syrian Kurdistan, has consisted of three cantons that in theory are directly adjacent to each other, but were in fact separated for quite some time by territories largely under the military control of the so-called "Islamic State in Iraq and Greater Syria." Only in June 2015 did the military units of the Kurds, the People's Protection Units (Yekîneyên Parastina Gel, YPG), the Women's Protection Units (Yekîneyên Parastina Jin, YPJ), and their allies succeed in unifying two of the three cantons with each other.

Finally, on 17 March 2016, the Democratic Federation of Northern Syria – Rojava was proclaimed as the joint autonomous administrative structure of the Kurdish regions and the adjoining predominantly Arab regions, which were by now also under the control of said forces.

In December 2016, the name Rojava was finally dropped. This move was strongly opposed and criticized by the Kurdish opposition parties, particularly by those close to the Kurdistan Regional Government in Iraq. They considered the dropping of "Rojava" a betrayal of the Kurdish character of the region.

The meaning of *roj* – the "j" is pronounced the same as the "s" in delusion – is both "sun" and "day." The sun has long played a central role in Kurdish national mythology. It is right in the midst of the Kurdish flag, and until its prohibition, the best-known TV station of the Kurdistan Workers' Party (PKK) also carried the name Roj TV. Literally, Rojava could be translated as the "land of the sunset." Nationalist Kurds, who often reject any terminology that reflects the division of Kurdistan among different nation states, generally translate Rojava as "West Kurdistan." Geographically, however, this concept makes little sense, as there are many Kurdish settlement zones in Turkey that are considerably to the west of Rojava. In geographic terms, Rojava is situated not in the west, but at most in the southwest of the Kurdish areas of settlement.

Even though unloved by both Arab and Kurdish nationalists, the term Syrian Kurdistan would probably be much more precise, all the more so since such terminology does not really pass judgement on whether one supports or criticizes the idea that these territories belong to Syria. Rather, the term refers to the fact that after the reordering of the Middle East after World War I, these territories were considered under international law as parts of Syria. This may be unjust and controversial, but it is no less true than the fact that Iraqi Kurdistan is a part of Iraq, that Iranian Kurdistan is a part of Iran, or that Turkish Kurdistan is a part of Turkey. For that reason, I will use the terms "Rojava" and "Syrian Kurdistan" as synonyms in this book.

The stamp that the Kurdish border guards place on a separate sheet of paper already says a lot: The "authorities" of the new Kurdish para-state in Syria, which is dominated by a sister party of the PKK, subscribe to a "Republic of Syria" and regard their canton as an autonomous region – a region that is, however, by no means an autonomous region of the Kurds only. Since the proclamation of the canton of Cizîrê (Jezira) in January 2014, people travelling there are no longer entering

Rojava but this canton. The stamp itself makes no mention of either Kurdistan or Rojava. This entry stamp thus reflects the self-conception of the cantonal authorities as a supra-national, autonomous area in a supra-ethnic Syria. The designation Rojava was added as a byname only in 2016 after the declaration of the Federation of Northern Syria. Even here, however, we still find a reference to Syria, whereas Kurdistan is not directly mentioned at all. The supra-national claim of the autonomous areas thus remained unchanged.

This change in the self-conception of the Kurdish actors in Rojava also mirrors developments in Syria, namely, from a revolution to a civil war. Over the course of 2012, hopes for a non-violent revolution on the model of Tunisia increasingly had to make room for an armed revolution, which within a year evolved into a civil war of a more and more sectarianized and ethnicized character. As the regime released high-level jihadist cadres, the character of the opposition also changed. New military actors such as Jabhat al-Nusra or the "Islamic State in Iraq and Greater Syria"[1] gained in military and political influence, thereby discrediting the Syrian opposition in the eyes of international opinion.

Syria became the destination of jihadist adventurers, among whom were an increasing number of female jihadists, and fell more and more into the hands of multifarious warlords and criminal gangs. Even among veteran oppositionists, many over time lost their belief in the possibility of success. In the depth of their hearts, more than a few now even regretted having stood up to the regime, concluding that this had thrown them from the frying pan into the fire. Since May 2014, with the re-conquest of cities in central Syria and particularly with the fall of the rebel stronghold Homs, the government's army has succeeded in retaking the offensive.

While the outcome of the Syrian civil war was still undecided when the first German editions of the present book went to print, since then the balance of forces has shifted considerably in favour of the regime thanks to its Russian and Iranian support. Many observers regard the reconquest of the rebel-held eastern part of the town of Aleppo in December 2016 as a particularly important, maybe even decisive battle. Since then, it has not only been the various rebel militias who were clearly in retreat; the same was also true for the jihadist project of "Islamic State." The reconquest of Mosul by the Iraqi Army and the liberation of the "capital" of IS, Raqqa, by the troops of the Syrian Democratic Forces (in Kurdish: Hêzên Sûriya Demokratîk; in Arabic:

Qūwāt Sūriyā ad-dīmuqrāṭya), among which the Kurdish YPG and YPJ played a decisive role, did not yet destroy the terrorist organization called "Islamic State," but it did destroy the existence in the region of a para-state called by that name. Although jihadism did not disappear from Iraq and Syria, Kurdish fighters, both in Iraq and Syria, played an important role in fighting the self-proclaimed Caliphate and liberating a territory much larger than the Kurdish-inhabited territories of Syria and Iraq.

The attack of Turkey against Efrîn and the conquest of East Ghouta by the regime indicate a second – more internationalised – stage of Syria's civil war. What seems to have been clear since early 2018 is the fact that the Syrian regime led by Bashar al-Assad will stay in power, at least in the most important parts of Syria. Whether we like it or not, the Syrian Kurds will have to negotiate and deal with the government in power in Damascus if they want to secure their autonomy within the future Syrian state.

The goal of this book is not a prognosis on the future of Syria, but rather an up-to-date portrayal of the evolution of the second Kurdish para-state. The first one developed in the Kurdish areas of Iraq after the Second Gulf War of 1991. Following the fall of Saddam Hussein and the development of sectarianized conflicts in Iraq, the "Kurdistan" region of Iraq was regarded as a haven of relative stability and economic development in an otherwise crisis-ridden country. Its economic development, however, was based on the development model of the Arab Gulf states that is rooted in the appropriation of oil rent and has little to do with a modern tax-collecting state. Furthermore, the attacks of "Islamic State" on important Kurdish strongholds since August 2014 served to show how fragile this stability continues to be. On the other hand, one effect of the successful defence of Kobanê, at the price of the complete destruction of the town, has been that it has garnered the Kurds mounting recognition at the international level.

Despite all dreams of a great Kurdish nation state, the two Kurdish para-states have so far not accommodated each other politically. On the contrary: It is exactly the existence of two Kurdish para-states that has brought intra-Kurdish rivalries and conflicts into a sharper relief than ever before. Since the takeover of Rojava by the Kurds, for the very first time there was a border *within* Kurdistan under the control of Kurds. All nationalist announcements notwithstanding, this intra-Kurdish border continued to exist until Iraqi forces took over the Iraqi side of the border once more in October 2017. But just like other border crossings, the one across the Tigris had repeatedly been closed for political reasons. While east of the Tigris, in Iraqi Kurdistan, an autonomous government led by Masud Barzani's Kurdistan Democratic Party (PDK) directs an economic boom based on a neoliberal oil rent economy, in the west a party is in charge that is still prone to revolutionary slogans. It has its roots in Abdullah Öcalan's formerly Marxist-Leninist Kurdistan Workers' Party (Partiya Karkerên Kurdistan, PKK) and, despite some ideological transformations, still regards itself as a leftist national liberation movement.

In both parts of Kurdistan, the rule of these competing power blocs is controversial and is challenged by Kurdish opposition groups. This book does not therefore present "the Kurds" as one singular actor and does not want to blind itself to intra-Kurdish political and economic conflicts. Because of this, the following narration is basically a social and political history and not a national history.

In fact, throughout their history the Kurds have never acted as a unified political subject. Yet what nationalist intellectuals and political parties often – and even, in a manner that amounts to self-orientalization, exclusively – regard as a flaw is by no means necessarily a sign of any inferiority or even subjectlessness of Kurdish society. Actually, the Kurds did not enter history as subjects of political action any later than the actors whose national states today rule over their territory or at least lay claim to such a rule. But while Turkey, Syria, and, to a certain extent, Iran constituted themselves as national states in the course of the twentieth century, the Kurds have so far been prevented from making this step. As a fragmented and strongly tribal society, to this day the Kurds have never formed a unified national movement, but have rather developed a diversity of different actors with differing loyalties and scopes of action. But this must be in no way understood as a deficiency or the lack of the capacity to build a state – it should rather be regarded as a political decision *against* the state. If there is anything detectable as a kind of a red thread in Kurdish history, it is the permanent rejection of and even rebellion against centralist state projects and the insistence on the largest possible amount of autonomy with regard to family, tribe, and region.

Attentive readers will have noticed that this last sentence didn't even mention *individual* autonomy. The modern concept of individual autonomy represents a novelty for all parts of Kurdistan, a concept that has gained ground only in recent years among certain urban elites and that often clashes with traditional family- and tribe-based collectivities, in particular when such demands for individual autonomy are raised by women.

This phenomenon is based on the fact that survival as a marginalized, politically and economically disadvantaged minority was often made possible only by very closely knit family networks. That meant that any latitude for individuals was frequently quite limited.

In all parts of Kurdistan, movements for political autonomy and independence have repeatedly looked to progressive, Marxist, and socialist ideologies that also champion freedom and equality. In some Kurdish guerilla organizations, women have actively participated in armed struggle. Others have at least regarded some amount of lip service to the equality of the sexes as a necessary element of their modernist development discourse. In the PKK and its sister parties, gender discourse has played the role of a central constant of its political ideology and practice right to this day. Yet even here, and contrary to the example of the liberal middle classes of Europe and North America who regard it as a central goal in life, individual freedom is much less of a concern than the collective emancipation of "the women" with regard to patriarchy. In the PKK and its sister parties, women have formed their own female collectives, a special women's party, and finally even a women's army, all of which are fighting collectively and separately from the men and in which the women are expected to refrain from sexual relationships. A situation where young women fight in the mountains together with their husbands and in part even with their children, as was the case in the Iraqi Patriotic Union of Kurdistan (PUK) in the 1980s, would be unthinkable in the case of the women of the PKK. Here, one collective was simply replaced by another.

Critics of the PKK/PYD draw a connection between this kind of collectivism and the authoritarianism of the PKK, which often shows itself both in the behaviour of the PYD towards other Kurdish opposition parties and its behaviour towards grassroots initiatives in Rojava. This book will also address such intra-Kurdish conflicts and authoritarian tendencies, which are of course only fostered by the war situation.

Kurdish society finds itself in the midst of a process of change in all parts of Kurdistan, a change that remains contradictory and whose final destination is by no means fixed. On the one hand, there is throughout a certain amount of urbanization, which creates, particularly for the younger generation of self-confident women, new spaces, but on the other hand, there are also patriarchal counterforces, especially within the younger generation. They manifest themselves in various currents of political Islam, some of which feature extremist young people who, for example, travel from the Iraqi part of Kurdistan to Syria in order to join the ranks of "Islamic State" in its fight against the PYD-dominated YPG.

But even among the modernist and secularly oriented parties of the Kurdish national movements in the different parts of Kurdistan, there is no unity with regard to the road to "modernity" they want to take. Most of these parties agree with an analysis according to which Kurdistan is "backward" and has to be "developed." But the goal of this developmental discourse is controversial. Whereas for the PDK ruling the Iraqi part of Kurdistan, "development" means the triggering of an economic boom conceived in accord with the ideas of neoliberal economists, the formerly Marxist-Leninist PKK has been promoting a libertarian socialism that is sometimes diffuse, but on the whole aims at collectivist forms of economy. How this socialism is supposed to look in practice, the PKK's sister party PYD will still have to prove, should it succeed in retaining the areas currently under its control.

Quite apart from these ideological differences, however, both roads to modernity will not work independently of their economic base. The model of the Iraqi-Kurdish economic miracle is for the most part based on an oil rent economy, and for that reason it is not all that unrealistic when Iraqi Kurds praise the model of Dubai as their own development model when talking to their visitors.

On which economic basis could Rojava work, and what consequences would this have for politics and society? A large part of Syria's sparse oil reserves is located in a Kurdish area, namely, in the canton of Cizîrê. But the region is also relatively rich in water and is therefore quite suitable for agriculture. The canton Efrîn in the west of Rojava has been known since ancient times for its excellent olive harvests. Vegetables are grown in the cantons of Kobanê and Cizîrê. This region used to supply half of Syria with vegetables and wheat, and even during the civil war in Syria there have been repeated attempts to export onions or tomatoes to Iraq. In the meantime, encircled by fighters of the so-called "Islamic State in Iraq and Syria" on the one side, and by an equally hostile Turkey on the other, the economy in the canton of Kobanê at one point almost came to a standstill, and in the larger cantons of Efrîn and Cizîrê the population also suffers from the consequences of the war and the economic blockade by Turkey. Under such circumstances, survival is possible only through a shadow economy and through smuggling. Although valid data for this are of course very hard to come by, the economic problems and their effects will also be topics of the present book as far as the possibilities for research allow.

After an introductory overview of the region, its religiously, ethnically, and linguistically diverse populations, and the history of Kurdistan, I will also give an overview of the Kurdish political actors in Syria, particularly their parties and political movements. In the process, Rojava is not considered in isolation, but is embedded in the histories of the Ottoman Empire, Kurdistan, and the state of Syria. In particular, it must not be forgotten that in addition to the parts of Rojava currently administered by the Kurds themselves, there are also old Kurdish districts in Damascus and Aleppo which are all the more relevant as they are the original home of several culturally and politically important Kurdish actors in Syria. The Kurdish quarter in Damascus reaches back to a colony of soldiers who went with the famous Salah ad-Din al-Ayyubi (Saladin) in the twelfth century when he promoted the liberation of the Levant from the crusaders. Salah ad-Din, himself of Kurdish origin, was accompanied by Kurdish fighters who first settled in the Suq al-Saruja in Damascus before the Kurdish quarter moved in the direction of Jebel Qāsiyūn, that is, to the foot of a mountain of a height of 1,150 metres right before the gates of Damascus. Today, the two Kurdish quarters Hayy al-Akrad (district of the Kurds) and al-Salhiyya are still located on the slopes of that mountain on which, according to the legend, Cain is supposed to have slain his brother Abel.

While these settlements in Damascus today are still under the control of the regime, the inhabitants of the two Kurdish quarters in Aleppo, Sheikh Maqsood and Ashrafieh, were able to liberate themselves in 2012 by effectively declaring their quarters a neutral zone between the Free Syrian Army (FSA) and the army of the government. Since that time, they existed as a kind of buffer zone between the frontlines and were protected by Kurdish militia. Yet even here, since autumn 2012, there have been repeated battles both with the FSA and the army of the government. Even though Ashrafieh was lost again, Kurdish units have retained control over Sheikh Maqsood since 2012. Given that background, the Kurdish districts of Aleppo cannot be entirely excluded from an analysis of Syrian Kurdistan.

Nevertheless, the real focus of the book is on the core area of Rojava and its inhabitants. They, or at least some of their representatives, will be able to speak for themselves in the second half of the book. This will make the various perspectives of political and social actors in Rojava visible – a necessary addition, as the ultimate goal of this book is not to offer a closed narrative or analysis of the situation in Rojava, but rather, an attempt at a multi-perspectival approach to a current conflict.

2

Background and Methods of Social Science Research in War

This book is based not just on an extensive literary study, but also on interviews and my own field research in Rojava. Under the existing conditions of war, such field research is no simple matter. Moreover, the security conditions do not allow for a longer sojourn in the region: The risks of western observers attracting attacks against themselves – and therefore also against their escorts – or becoming kidnapped are just too great. Therefore, at present field research is possible only for brief periods and when accompanied by local people. Of course, in a highly politicized society this also means being in constant danger of adopting the particular views and perspectives of some concrete actor, for example the respective escort, and therefore to end up pursuing, in analogy to embedded journalism, "embedded research." I was particularly conscious of this danger during my five research trips between January 2013 and September 2016. I cannot exclude the possibility that I have occasionally fallen into that trap because, just like other researchers, I, too, could travel only in the company of Kurdish activists. However, I have tried to minimize that danger to the best of my abilities.

For one thing, in 2013 and 2014 I travelled with different political actors. In 2013, I had the opportunity to travel to Rojava via Turkey, together with my Syrian-Kurdish friend Jamal Omari, who has lived in Austria since 2001 and whom I met in 2004 when he was looking for support for protests against the Syrian regime. At the time of our trip, Omari, whose brother took us secretly across the border and to his home town Amûdê under the cloud of night, belonged to Mustafa Oso's Partiya Azadî ya Kurdi li Sûriyê, one of the four parties that would go on to found a unified sister party of the Iraqi-Kurdish governing party PDK in 2014. Already in 2013, his party strictly opposed the Partiya Yekîtîya Dêmokrat (PYD) that had assumed control over most Kurdish areas in 2012 and that at present rules these areas as the sister party of the PKK. Thus in 2013 I was able to talk mostly to opponents of the PYD who belonged to various parties and initiatives, and to interview them. In February 2014, however, I travelled to Rojava on the invitation of Salih Muslim, the party leader of the PYD, which put me in a position to mostly interview politicians, fighters, and functionaries of the PYD and organizations close to it. For security reasons, I was accompanied by an old cadre of the party, who not only served as a driver, but also always carried his Kalashnikov with him and who told us very much about a region that he knew like the back of his hand. In 2014, I succeeded only once, for a couple of hours, to escape the watch of the PYD and to meet oppositionists from other Kurdish groups, among them a couple of men who had been arrested and tortured by PYD fighters in 2013. Yet even our escorts from the PYD were quite prepared to bring us in contact with persons who were not exactly representatives of the party line, such as the members of the Naqshibandi order of the Khaznawi, whose representatives, as far as they have remained in Syria at all, are often regarded as friends of Turkey.

Since the publication of the first German edition of this book, I have undertaken additional trips under the protection of the YPG/PYD to Efrîn and Kobanê, as well as one journey organized individually without any help from any party to Cizîrê, Kobanê, and the town of Tal Abyad – which is located between the two cantons – in September 2016, where I met people from different political currents. This should serve to further round out the picture and bring up to date the information garnered previously.

The information gathered directly from the scene was time and again supplemented by telephone conversations and Facebook chats with different politically active persons both in Rojava and in exile. Quite independently of the various political perspectives of my escorts, all this yielded a multi-perspective picture of the situation in Rojava that I try to reflect in this book. In order to make the original voices of some of my interview partners immediately accessible to the reader, interviews with different Kurdish activists constitute a substantial part of this book. These interviews provide a direct introduction into the various views of the interviewees of the conflict and their own commitment.

This publication is a snapshot of a development happening in real time. Such a snapshot can, however, never be up-to-the-minute. Writing the history of the political development of Rojava must thus remain a project of the future. The aim of this publication is to enable readers to understand current developments. Therefore, the book is consciously not conceived as a detailed scientific study, but was written with the goal of being as intelligible and accessible as possible. Nevertheless, it also claims to satisfy scientific criteria. I have tried to the best of my abilities to include only verifiable facts in the book, to analyse them from the perspective of social and political science, and to refrain from writing a piece of propaganda. Therefore, the various Kurdish readers will probably find only a small part of their own respective perspectives reflected one-to-one in the book. The reason is again that my goal was not to write a propaganda tract in any form for any party or group, but to retain a critical gaze from the outside, one that is not only politically committed and interested, but also aloof enough to avoid being co-opted by any particular political party.

3

Kurds, Arabs, Armenians, and Assyrians
Rojava as Part of the Ethnic Diversity of Syria

Contrary to the Arab-nationalist ideology of the Ba'ath party, Syria was a country that was both religiously and ethnically diverse. Syria is inhabited not just by Arabs of different religious-confessional origin, but, apart from the Kurds, also by Armenian, West- and East-Aramaic, Turkmen, Circassian, and Chechen minorities. Even the Kurds in Syria are not as linguistically united as it might seem at first glance.

Different from other parts of Kurdistan, in Rojava there is a clear dominance of the main variety of Kurdish, namely, Kurmancî. It is also the most important variety in Turkish-Kurdistan and is spoken in the north of both Iranian and Iraqi Kurdistan. Among the Syrian Kurds, there are also – smaller – minority variations that were brought to Syria by migration from other parts of Kurdistan. In Serê Kaniyê (Arabic: Ra's al-'Ain), there are several hundred families who speak Zazakî (Kirmanckî/Dimilî), which is otherwise spoken in Turkey, and in Hesîçe (Arabic: al-Hasaka), there is a similarly-sized group of Kurds whose mother tongue is Soranî and who once immigrated from Iraqi Kurdistan.

Whereas Syria's Turkmen, Chechen, and Circassian minorities are the descendants of immigrants during the Ottoman Empire, most Armenians descend from the survivors of the genocide of 1915, whose deportation trails led into the steppes and semi-deserts near Deir az-Zor in today's Syria. The Armenian enclave of Kesab at the Mediterranean, bordering on Turkey, and the close-by village of Yakubiyah are exceptions; the Armenians living in the small town of Kesab and the surrounding villages are descendants of a Cilician-Armenian enclave around the Musa Dagh that has existed for about 1,000 years. Their struggle for survival against the genocide of 1915 was documented by the Austrian Jewish writer Franz Werfel in his world-renowned novel *The Forty Days of Musa Dagh*. After World War I, the Armenians who had offered resistance at the so-called "Moses mountain," until the French marines came to their rescue, returned to their home. When France, after the interlude of a short-lived formal independence, once again ceded the province of Antakya/Hatay to Turkey, the Armenians of Kesab resisted the planned annexation to the state of the descendants of their former tormentors. While the northern Armenian villages of the Musa Dagh indeed fell to Turkey and most Armenians again left their villages, the inhabitants of the southern villages succeeded in being allowed to remain under the French protectorate. Today, north of the border there is only a single Armenian village (Vakıflı). On the other hand, until its capture in 2014 by jihadi militias (with Turkish help), Kesab was considered the last safe remainder of Cilician Armenia, characterized by a special variety of Armenian that is very different from the other Armenian dialects in Syria. In the meantime, the Syrian army has been able to reconquer Kesab, and many of the inhabitants who had fled have returned. Yet the future of the enclave remains uncertain.

The Aramaic-speaking minorities of Syria consist of the descendants of those Christians who represented the majority population of the whole region when Syria was conquered by the Muslim Arabs. Even before the Roman conquest, Aramaic dominated the Middle East right into Iran as the language of trade and commerce. In the course of the last two and a half thousand millennia, it has split into different varieties that are mutually unintelligible and are regarded as different languages today. Up to the conquest of Syria by the Muslim Arabs, Jews, Mandaeans,[1] and many Christians in Greater Syria and Mesopotamia spoke different varieties of Aramaic as their mother tongue, which were then only slowly replaced by Arabic. Three of these varieties are still in daily use and spoken as a mother tongue in today's Syria: Western Neo-Aramaic, spoken in the Christian town of Ma'alula and in two adjacent Muslim villages (Bach'a and Ǧubb'adīn) in Anti-Lebanon to the north-west of Damascus, and two Eastern Neo-Aramaic varieties whose speakers today lead a life as minorities, particularly in the canton of Cizîrê in Rojava.

The Eastern Neo-Aramaic variant of Turoyo (ISO 639-3: aii), which is also spoken in the adjacent Tur Abdin in Turkey, is the mother tongue of most Syriac Orthodox Christians in Rojava, who represent a substantial part of the population of Qamişlo and Dêrik as well as of some villages close to the Turkish border.

In the south of the canton of Cizîrê, around the provincial capital al-Hasaka (Kurdish: Hesîçe) – which was itself at the beginning only partially taken over by the Kurds – and in the wake of the massacres of 1915, thousands of Assyrian Christians settled in the 1920s under the rule of the French protectorate. In the 1930s, these refugees were joined by survivors of the massacre of Semile in 1933 during which 60 out of 64 Assyrian villages in Northern Iraq were destroyed and almost 10,000 Assyrians were murdered. After the massacre of 1933, parts of this Assyrian-Nestorian population that had primarily lived in the Turkish province Hakkâri (Kurdish: Colemêrg) until 1915 and whose survivors had been resettled north of Mosul by the British after World War I fled further to the west, where they enjoyed the protection of the French. There, they built new villages on the river Khabur or joined the Assyrian community already living in al-Hasaka. Alongside Turoyo, the variety spoken today by these Assyrian and Chaldean Christians (ISO 639-3: aii) is the most important minority language in the canton of Cizîrê.

Under the Arab-nationalist Baʿath regime, there was never any serious survey of the number of speakers of these minority languages. But a raw estimate suggests that more than half of the 80,000 native speakers of Turoyo and some further 40,000 to 50,000 speakers of Assyrian-Aramaic live in the canton of Cizîrê and the areas around al-Hasaka.

While the Christians speaking the two Eastern Neo-Aramaic varieties represent the largest non-Kurdish minorities in the canton of Cizîrê, they are almost totally absent in the other two Kurdish cantons. Yet in all three cantons, there are Arabic-speaking minorities who in part belong to tribes that have lived in the region for a long time, but who are partly also the descendants of ideologically motivated resettlement projects of the Baʿath regime, a fact that turns them into the subjects of political controversy. The more than 20,000 members of the relatively large Arabic tribe of the Tai who dominate the Arabic district of Qamişlo belong to the historically oldest inhabitants of the region. Other Arab villages were brought to the region by the regime only in the 1960s.

In the canton of Cizîrê, there are also a few Armenian communities operating their own church communities and schools in the towns of Qamişlo, Dêrik, Serê Kaniyê, al-Hasaka. Both in the elementary schools in Qamişlo, Dêrik, Serê Kaniyê, and al-Hasaka, and in the secondary school in Qamişlo, classes are taught in both Arabic and Armenian. This, however, does not extend to Kurdish.

Turkmens, Chechens, and Circassians represent three additional small minorities in the canton of Cizîrê. The Circassians are the descendants of those Caucasian Muslims who fled to the Ottoman Empire following the advance of Russia and the brutal colonization of the Caucasus, and who have left their traces from Israel to Kosovo to this day.

Another ethnic minority present both in the Arab and the Kurdish areas of Syria are the Nawar who, as a sub-group of the Dom, or Dūmī, live in Syria, Lebanon, Israel, and Jordan. Their language, Nawari, is a dialect of Domari and undoubtedly belongs to the Indo-European languages. However, most of them are at least bi- or tri-lingual and today also speak Kurdish and Arabic. Partly on account of cultural and social similarities, the Dūmī are often regarded as a sub-group or a "branch" of the Roma. There are, however, some linguists who advocate the hypothesis of an earlier autonomous migration of the Dūmī from India to the Middle East and who trace the relationship between the languages back to earlier commonalities in India (see Matras 2012: 20 ff.). Even though all Nawar in Syria are bi- or tri-lingual, are mostly members of the Sunni majority religion, and are by no means the only nomads in Syria, they have remained isolated from both Arabic and Kurdish societies. To this day, the more than 30,000 Nawar, or Dūmī, remain a highly marginalized group whose members mostly live an

Languages of the respective majority populations in Syria[2]

Semitic languages:

 Arabic

|||| Western Neo-Aramaic

≡ Eastern Neo-Aramaic

Indo-European languages:

 Kurdish

Armenian

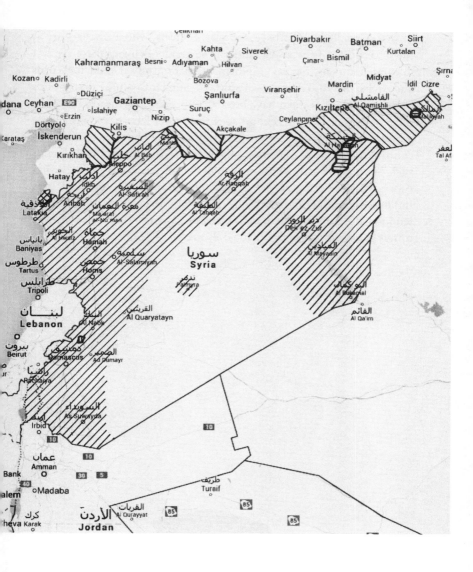

isolated life in miserable settlements of huts and tents on the outskirts of towns and villages, held in contempt by the majority population. There is one such Nawar settlement on the periphery of Qamişlo, consisting of shacks made from garbage and plastic sheets, whose dwellers are at the lowest end of the social ladder. The residents living there are not integrated into any regular employment relationships. Unlike the Kurds and Arabs, they also do not own any land. Similar to some Roma groups in Europe, most of them have been able to keep their heads above the water as musicians. In recent decades, the Nawar have been particularly popular as musicians at weddings, and they have certainly also contributed to the preservation of Kurdish music. Certain instruments such as the Ottoman Zurna, a double-barrel reed instrument with a cone-shaped bell, are played almost exclusively by Nawar musicians. But in economically and politically difficult times in which the weddings tend to be less opulent than before, the musicians of the Nawar, whose misery is anyway glaringly obvious, also suffer.

4

Muslims, Christians, Jews, Alevi, and Êzîdî

Religious Pluralism in Rojava

But Syria is not just ethnically and linguistically diverse; the same is also true of its religions. The Sunni majority population is supplemented by a number of minorities who largely originate in Shiite Islam. Among the largest heterodoxies are the Alawis (Nusayris) – not to be confused with the Anatolian Alevi – and the Druze. The minority of the Alawis who had been discriminated against for centuries and were able to survive only in their retreat areas in the western coastal regions and in the Turkish province Hatay/Antakya, but from whose midst the family of President Assad originates, currently finds itself in a dilemma. If it sides with the regime, it will turn itself even more into an object of the hate of extremist jihadis. During the Ba'ath regime, many Alawis gained important positions in the military and the intelligence services. If they drop President Assad, they have to fear the revenge of the Sunni majority population. Apart from them, there are also the members of the "Twelver Shia" (Imamites) and Ismaelites who, in the current conflict, are also subjected to attacks by the Sunni-jihadist groups, as well as a small group of Alevi.

The exact number of the Alevi among the almost 8,000 inhabitants of the small town Mabet in the canton of Efrîn is not known. Yet even so, the Kurdish Alevi there, although one of the smallest religious minorities in Syria, play a quite important social and political role in the canton. The fear of jihadist violence against religious minorities has driven many Alevi into the arms of the secular and well-armed PKK sister party PYD – and Hêvî Ibrahim Mustafa, an Alevi from Mabet, has even become the first administrative head of the canton of Efrîn. In Efrîn, which is anyway regarded as relatively secular and detribalized, the Alevi are seen as an integral part of the Kurdish population and are not subjected to any hostility, except that coming from jihadist groups.

Apart from the Alevi, the Êzîdî (Yazidi) are the second religious minority within the Kurdish population. After being denounced – and often persecuted – by both Christians and Muslims as "devil worshippers," today they are again regarded as a group that is particularly endangered, this time by jihadist violence. The numbers given for the Êzîdî still living in Syria today vary from 3,000 to 50,000 persons. In the current situation, their real number is impossible to determine, but given emigration and flight, it should be at the lower end of the estimates. The Turkish historian Birgül Acıkıyıldız, who is a specialist on the Êzîdî and the Ottoman Empire, thinks that the presence of the Êzîdî in Rojava goes back to the twelfth century AD (Acıkıyıldız 2010: 65). On the other hand, in his investigation of the Êzîdî in Syria and Iraq carried out in the 1930s, the famous French orientalist and Kurdologist Roger Lescot (who secured for himself a lasting name in Kurdology both with the foundation of the professorship for Kurdish at the École Nationale des Langues Orientales Vivantes and his grammar of Kurmancî jointly developed with Celadet Alî Bedirxan) came to the conclusion that the first Êzîdî did not come to the region and settle around Efrîn before the thirteenth century (Lescot 1938: 205).

There is no doubt that the Êzîdî community in Efrîn is several hundred years older than the one in Cizîrê. Lescot dates the arrival of the first group of Kurdish Êzîdî in Cizîrê only to the eighteenth century, when the first Êzîdî settled close to the then still mostly Aramaic town Amûdê (Lescot 1938: 199). But many Êzîdî only came to Syria, together with Muslim Kurds, after the collapse of the Sheikh Said uprising in Turkey, that is, after 1925 (Lescot 1938: 200), and then again around 1930 from the Iraqi region Jebel Sinjar (Kurdish: Şingal) (Acıkıyıldız 2010: 65).

Since 2013, fighters of the "Islamic State in Iraq and Greater Syria" have repeatedly attacked villages of the Êzîdî and committed massacres among Êzîdî civilians. In Rojava, the Êzîdî for the most part live in the cantons of Efrîn and Cizîrê. But particularly in recent years, because of the specific threat posed by IS, but also because of the danger emanating from other jihadist groups, many Êzîdî have chosen the difficult path into exile.

The situation of the Êzîdî becomes even more difficult because of the fact that many of their villages are located at the fringe of the Kurdish settlement area and are therefore particularly prone to attacks from not only ISIS, but also Jabhat al-Nusra. In the canton of Efrîn, most of the Êzîdî villages are located between the towns of Efrîn and A'zaz – the latter of which was conquered by ISIS, Jabhat al-Nusra, and other more or less Islamist opposition groups on 18 September 2013 – and, turning to the south, the mountain range of the Jebel Siman (Mount Simon) west of the actual Kurd Dagh. This mountain range, named after Simon Stylites the Elder, with its villages of Beradê, Bircê Hêdrê, Basûfanê and Kîmarê, and which is called Çiyayê Lêlûn in Kurdish and is separated from the actual Kurd Dagh (mountain of the Kurds) by the Efrîn valley, is the core area of the Êzîdî in the canton of Efrîn. The 26 Êzîdî villages in total in the region are often located directly on the frontline between competing Arab and jihadist opposition groups. In 2017 Turkish forces and their allies finally encircled most of Efrîn including the Êzîdî villages of Jebel Siman. The Êzîdî in the canton of Cizîrê have experienced a similar frontline situation. Many of the Êzîdî villages (such as al-Asadia, Tileliya, al-Qonjaq, or Cefa) lie south of the town Serê Kaniyê (Arabic: Ra's al-'Ain), in a region that was repeatedly contested between Kurds, FSA, Jabhat al-Nusra, and the "Islamic State in Iraq and Sham" from 2013 to 2015. In the process, some of the Êzîdî villages fell victim to targeted jihadist attacks and massacres.

In fact, the persecution of the Êzîdî is based on a misunderstanding handed down over the centuries. This religion, which emerged from various pre-Islamic roots and in its present form goes back to the Sufi-Sheikh Adī ibn Musāfir (Kurdish: Şêx Adî) who lived in the twelfth century and was born in Lebanon, worships, apart from God, the angel Tausî Melek (Angel Peacock) who is regarded as God's first and most faithful angel. Since Tausî Melek venerated God particularly faithfully, he also remained true to God's first commandment to worship no one but God. Therefore, he refused to follow God's order to prostrate himself before man after the creation of Adam. In this episode, Tausî Melek was tested by God, and he passed the test. This view is contrary to the Christian and Islamic conception of hell according to which this angel was *punished* and turned into the devil. Unlike these two religions, the Êzîdî have no conception of hell as a place of eternal condemnation. For the Êzîdî, God is so omnipotent that there cannot be any second force representing personified evil. But the similarity of the story of Angel Peacock to that of the Christian and Islamic devil, who refused to prostrate himself before man *out of arrogance*, was used for centuries to accuse the Êzîdî of being "devil worshippers." This is all the more absurd once one considers the fact that this kind of personified evil doesn't even exist in the Êzîdî worldview.

The problems of this minority are enhanced by a political-religious conflict with a current close to the PKK/PYD that is trying to reconfigure the religion of the Êzîdî as a variety of Zoroastrism and, at the same time, to reform it, something many traditional Êzîdî regard as an attack on their religion. Additional conflicts within the Êzîdî communities are rooted in its extremely strict marriage rules and rigid caste system, both of which are no longer accepted by many younger Êzîdî.

The religious identity crisis of many Êzîdî also has to do with the fact that many of them, particularly in the Kurd-Dagh region, have had hardly any access to the religious centres of the Êzîdî in today's Iraq, have produced few religious scholars, and, unlike the Êzîdî in Jebel Sinjar (Kurdish: Şingal) or in the Sexan region around their religious holy place in Lalish (Lališ), have been much more integrated into the Sunni population. Even in the 1930s, Lescot already described the Êzîdî in the Kurd-Dagh region as a group that was difficult to distinguish from its compatriots (Lescot 1938: 202). The orientation of these Êzîdî towards a form of Yazdânism (which the PKK has declared to be a variety of Zoroastrism) is also rooted in this far-reaching oblivion of the old religion. In a way, it is the remaking or reinvention of a religion whose adherents in the Kurd-Dagh region may still have constituted a separate group, but who had already largely forgotten their religious traditions.

Unlike many other religious minorities in Syria, the Êzîdî were never a recognized religious community. The secular-authoritarian Ba'ath regime may have occasionally held a protecting hand over the Christians, Druze, or Alawis, but this was never true for the Êzîdî or Alevi. Both religious communities used to lead a shadowy existence in private refuges. Only after the retreat of the Syrian regime from the Kurdish areas have these two religious minorities also become able to organize. Since that time, new umbrella associations of the Êzîdî have vigorously raised their voice and have been actively participating in shaping Rojava's future.

On 15 February 2013 and supported by the new Kurdish self-administration, the first Êzîdî organized themselves in local councils in the region of al-Hasaka, soon to be followed by further villages in different parts of Cizîrê (see Maisel 2017: 147). These associations then merged into an umbrella organization close to the PKK, the Union of the Êzîdî of West Kurdistan and Syria (Komela Êzdiyên Rojavayê Kurdistanê û

RELIGIOUS PLURALISM IN ROJAVA

Sûriye, KÊRKS). Competing with it are two additional newly established organizations, the Union of the Êzîdî of Syria (Hevbendiya Êzîdiyên Suriyê, HÊS) and the Council of the Êzîdî of Syria (Encûmena Êzdiyên Sûriyê, EÊS), both of which are, respectively, close to different currents of the Kurdish opposition.

Just as in most parts of Kurdistan, the majority religion of the Kurds in Rojava, Sunni Islam, is strongly influenced by Sufism. Among the Kurds themselves, the orders of the Qadiriya and the Naqshibandiya are dominant, particularly the latter's Khalidi branch, which reaches back to Diya al-Din Khalid, who was born in 1779 AD in the Qaradagh mountains in today's Iraqi Kurdistan (see Weismann 2007a: 88). After its founding it competed with the Qadiriya order, which until then had dominated in Kurdistan. The centres of these Sufi orders did not just represent religious focal points, but also cultural, and occasionally political ones, a fact which turned the Naqshibandi order in particular into an important backbone of the Kurdish national movement. But the regional centres of these orders often acted very autonomously and did not always pursue the same line. As a consequence, the well-known Kurdologist Martin van Bruinessen in his important standard work *Agha, Shaikh and State* confessed that "[m]y expectations were rather disappointed during my research in that the orders seemed to play no appreciable role in nationalism now, and that in the cases where the orders took a position in class antagonisms they chose against the interests of the underprivileged, instead of serving as a medium for their protest" (Bruinessen 1992: 212).

Yet Bruinessen, who carried out most of his field research in Iran and in Turkey and who, because of the collapse of the Kurdish uprising in Iraq, could stay for no more than six weeks, himself concedes that the Kurdish Sheiks might have behaved very differently from one region to the next. The fact that only a few Sheiks took a social-revolutionary stance is easily explained by the observation that most of them functioned themselves as feudal lords and often ruled over several villages inhabited by landless peasants who worked for them. Nevertheless, some of them in Iraq (e.g. the Sheiks of Barzan) played an extremely important role in the Kurdish national movement there – even though they represented the conservative-feudalist wing of that movement. In the Iraqi Kurdistan of the 1930s, the heterodox Sheik Ebdulkerîm Shadala and his Haqqa movement also played an important role as an anticolonial and social-revolutionary movement (see Schmidinger 2014).

In Syrian Kurdistan, most of the Sheiks tended to refrain from political activity. One important exception, however, is the Naqshibandi Sheikh Murshid Maʿshouq al-Khaznawi, who made an attempt to unify the Kurdish party landscape in the early 2000s.

The Sheiks and the Ulamā (the Islamic religious scholars) were just as unable to be politically active in Syria as other social forces. Even so, through their connections with the new economic actors, Sunni Sheiks and Ulamā played an important role in the economic liberalization of the Syrian economy in the 1990s. Private businessmen who had gained wealth during the previous 20 years or so funded charity organizations run by the Sheiks and the Ulamā. They, in turn, conferred a certain moral-religious legitimacy on the nouveau rich operators (see Pierret 2013: 144 ff.).

Yet Syria is also home to the other two monotheist world religions. As a core region of the Bible, Syria is inhabited by Christians of the most diverse variety, and by no means only by the Western and Eastern Aramaic- or Armenian-speaking minorities already mentioned above. Of the course of the centuries, very many Syrian Christians were Arabized and now generally use Arabic in their daily life, a use that often even also extends to religious service. Another reason for the great complexity of the many finely grained confessions of the Syrian Christians is that Syria harbours both a whole series of diverse ancient Near-Eastern Christian confessions that fell out with each other in the fourth and fifth centuries over the question of the nature of Christ, *and* break-aways from these factions that go back to Catholic and Protestant attempts at proselytizing among the Christian churches in the Middle East. The oldest example for such a Uniate church is the Maronites, who emerged in the seventh century and, apart from their centre in Lebanon, are also represented in Syria. In addition, apart from the Armenian-Apostolic church, there also is an Armenian-Catholic church united with the Catholic church, and apart from the Syrian-Orthodox church there is a Syrian-Catholic one. The Holy Apostolic Catholic Assyrian Church of the East – which is falsely designated as "Nestorian" in the West – also has a break-away, the Chaldean Catholic Church, which is united with Rome. In Syria, the latter two are actually only represented in Rojava, particularly in al-Hasaka and in the Assyrian villages built in the 1930s on the shores of the river Khabur. Even the Greek Orthodox Church, which is also relatively well represented in Syria, has a counterpart united with the Roman Catholic Church in the form of the "Melikite" Greek Catholic, or Byzantine-Catholic Church. In addition to the Catholics, Protestant missionaries also proselytized among the ancient Near-Eastern churches of Syria, and thus, by analogy to their Catholic counterparts, today we also have an Armenian-Protestant Church and an Assyrian-Protestant Church. The whole picture is completed by several Evangelical Free Churches that have emerged only in recent years and which, with their strongly missionary line of work, also contribute to conflicts with the Muslim population.

All traditional members of the Christian churches in Rojava happen to belong also to ethnic minorities. Within their families, they speak a variety of either Eastern Neo-Aramaic or of Armenian. Kurdish Christians are only rarely found in the new Evangelical Free Churches. It is worth mentioning that the latter have translated the Bible into the various varieties of Kurdish to promote their missionary work among the Muslim Kurds.

Like Christianity, Judaism has also been an integral component of Syria's religious diversity for centuries. In fact, the Jewish communities in Damascus and Aleppo have been important sites of Jewish scholarship for more than two millennia. In addition, there has been a smaller community in Tadif, the location of a shrine of the prophet Ezra. Qamişlo is yet another place where, after the founding of the town in 1926, a lively Jewish community emerged, which was partly composed of emigrants from Turkish Kurdistan. In his travel notes, Carsten Niebuhr, who travelled from Mosul to Nusaybin through the destroyed town of al-Hasaka in 1764, described a Jewish pilgrimage site "a quarter of an hour to the west of the present Nissabin" (Niebuhr 1778: 381), that is, today's Nusaybin, near Qamişlo and immediately north of the national border, whose Christian and Jewish population founded Qamişlo in 1926.

Even though, like everywhere in Kurdistan, there existed a great cultural closeness and adaptation of the Jewish population to the Kurds in general, the Muslim and Jewish Kurds mostly lived endogamously (Ammann 1991: 12). Mixed marriages occurred – if at all – between a Jewish woman and a Muslim man, but were frowned upon within the Jewish communities (Ammann 1991: 12).

In the 1930s the Jewish community in Qamişlo already comprised approximately 3,000 persons. Jews were active primarily as goldsmiths and traders as well as civil servants, and operated a synagogue in the city centre that still exists today. But the pogrom in Aleppo in 1947 and the mass dismissal of Jewish civil servants in the same year did not only lead to the emigration of a part of the Jewish population in Aleppo and Damascus; the same was also true in Qamişlo. All the same, the Syrian Jewish communities held out for longer than those in many other Arab states because Syria refused to cooperate in the emigration of Jewish citizens and, under the Ba'ath regime, did not even hand out passports to Jews anymore. Before the Six Day War of 1967, around 800 Jews still lived in the town and were still a functioning community. However, the increasing anti-Semitism under the Ba'ath regime and the fury of Arab nationalists sparked by the defeat in the Six Day War led to a renewed wave of emigration. After 1967, only about 150 Jews continued to live in the town.

After the Six Day War, the authorities tried to stop the Jewish emigration in all of Syria for fear of strengthening the "Zionist enemy." Journeys abroad were now only possible on condition of depositing high "guarantee sums" in the country. Between 1967 and 1977, Jews were even singled out as the only religious community whose religion was highly visibly stamped into their passports (see Bunzl 1989: 78).

Religions of the respective majority populations in Syria

Islam:
Sunni
Twelver Shia
Ismailis

Alawis
Druze

Christians

Êzîdî

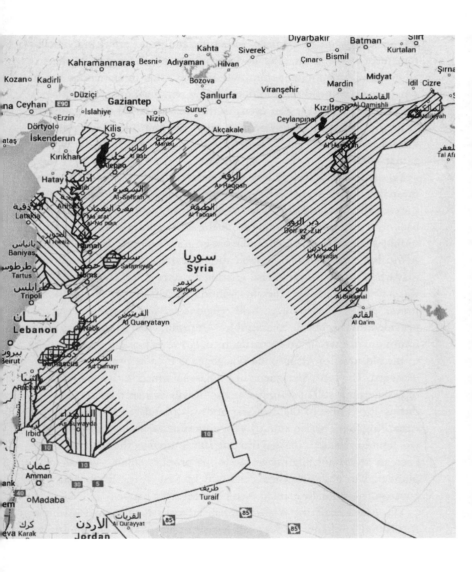

The remaining Syrian Jews were allowed to emigrate only in 1992. The whole community still present in Aleppo, about 4,000 community members in Damascus, and a large part of the remaining Jews in Qamişlo emigrated at that time. In 1994, the chief rabbi left the country together with the last group. Only 300 older community members continued to stay in Damascus. In Qamişlo, only one family and a few individuals remained in the town. The Jewish community in Qamişlo came to an end as a functioning community in 1992. Only in Damascus has a synagogue continued to be in operation; it remained open even during the civil war. The year 2011 even saw the restoration of the synagogue al-Raqi in the town's old Jewish quarter. But the elderly Jews still in Damascus now represent a disappearing minority of hardly more than a dozen persons.

Yet the disappearance of Syria's historical Jewish communities doesn't mean that their synagogues have also disappeared. Until the beginning of the civil war, the large al-Bandara synagogue in Aleppo – which reaches back to a predecessor building from the fifth century AD – still stood, unmolested, in the old town, and it has even survived the war in Aleppo. A Muslim historian who showed me the synagogue in 1999 told me that when the historical Jewish quarter was torn down, the synagogue was saved not least by the intervention of Muslim intellectuals. At times, Jewish travellers even held religious services in the synagogue, provided they were able to assemble a "minyan," that is, the prescribed minimum of ten religiously mature men. However because of the battles in the old town of Aleppo, the synagogue is by now probably severely damaged. The Jobar synagogue in Damascus, which in the end was the only synagogue still operating, was also heavily damaged by the fighting during the course of the civil war and was plundered in the process. According to the Syrian authority for antiquities, the synagogue – which was built in 720 AD, is located in a district captured by the rebels and has been an important pilgrimage site to the prophet Elijah – was already plundered in 2013 and then destroyed in May 2013. Rebels and the government mutually blamed each other for what happened.

The pressure of the Arab-nationalist Ba'ath regime on (Muslim) Kurds and Jews and the Kurdish-Jewish origin of the community in Qamişlo, which also expressed itself in the community's mastery of the Kurdish language, together served to bring the two groups closer to each other. Thus the remaining Jews sometimes cooperated with Kurdish smugglers in order to escape across the border into Turkey and to go on from there to Europe, America, or Israel. In the 1970s and the 1980s the community in Qamişlo also became an intermediate station for many Jews from Damascus and Aleppo who were brought across the border from here by experienced Kurdish smugglers. In this, they were in part aided by Muslim clerics such as the Naqshibandi Sheikh Murshid Ma'shouq al-Khaznawi. In 2013, a close collaborator of the Sheikh (who was critical of the regime and was murdered in 2007 under circumstances that haven't been entirely clarified to this day) told me that he had personally smuggled a number of Syrian Jews across the border and into Turkey. The Jews smuggled by him and his colleagues were brought across the border into Turkey near Qamişlo under the protection of the night and then travelled on from there to Europe, to the USA, or to Israel.

After 1992, basically just one family and a couple of individuals had remained in Qamişlo. Yet in 2006, the *Jerusalem Post* was still able to run an extensive article in which it reported on the last three Jews in Qamişlo, who stressed that they did not intend to leave the town. The last of them, a well-known personage in the town, lived through the beginning of the uprising against the regime before dying in his home town Qamişlo in autumn 2013. The now empty synagogue in the inner city testifies to the once numerous Jewish community just as much as some businesses in the inner city that are still named after their former Jewish owners, but have long since been managed by Muslims and Christians. Above the entrance to the synagogue itself a picture of the late President Hafiz al-Assad is still on display. A bit further away, there are still stores in the bazaar on whose top one can read signs with Jewish names such as "Ezra." Some of them are said to still be in the possession of Jews once living in Qamişlo who supposedly continue to receive rent from their current operators.

But Syria was not just home to a diaspora of the main current of Judaism. Up until the seventeenth century, Samaritan[1] diaspora communities existed in Damascus and Aleppo whose survivors returned to the only remaining community in Nablus after the conquest of Syria by the Ottomans (Schur 2008: 3). Unlike the Jews, in the conflict between the Mamelukes and the Ottomans they had sided with the defeated Mamelukes, which meant the end of their Syrian diaspora communities. Up until then, Damascus had been one of the centres of Samaritan intellectual activity, where important scholars such as Abu al-Faradj Munadjdja b. Sadaka and his son were active (Gaster 1925: 160).

Moreover, in Damascus there existed a community of Karaites, a Jewish sect that emerged, at the latest, in the eighth century AD in today's Iraq and that only recognizes the Thora and not the other books of the Bible, such as the Holy Scripture. In the seventeenth century, a traveller from Geneva wrote about a Karaite community of 200 persons in Damascus (Henderson 1826: 319). According to reports, apart from Damascus there had also been a Karaite community in Aleppo (Olszowy-Schlager 1997: 46), whose members had probably dissolved into the respective Jewish communities or had emigrated to the Karaite communities in Cairo and Jerusalem.

5

Kurdistan

Country without a State or Country against the State

The term "Kurdistan" is considerably older than the national states that divided up the territory of the Kurds after World War I and has been documented at least since the Middle Ages – and it may actually even be much older. The conjunction of "Kurdi-" with the Persian suffix "-stan" for "location of" or "home of" really boils down to no more than "the country of the Kurds." Today, we find a similar combination both with respect to national states under the influence of the Persian language (Turkmenistan, Uzbekistan, Afghanistan, etc.) and with respect to other regions basically named after ethnic groups (Lasistan, Lorestan, Nuristan, Dagestan, Baluchistan, etc.).

Exactly which region was considered as Kurdistan has, however, historically been variable. Until 1915, the historic, closed settlement area of the Kurds had been both smaller and more intermingled with other – mostly Christian – groups than it is today. Since it is impossible to convey here a detailed history of Kurdistan, as my goal is simply to give an introductory overview as a background for the description of the current situation and the more recent history of Syrian Kurdistan, the reader should not expect an overall presentation of Kurdish history. All the same, some historical developments are still important for the present, and these will be sketched at least in broad outlines.

After the Islamicization of the Kurds and the disintegration of the Islamic empire into various smaller domains only nominally belonging to an Islamic Caliphate, Kurdistan experienced the emergence of semi-autonomous principalities and tribal dominions on a regional level. All these regional power centres were, of course, not modern states, but pre-modern systems of rule that, on the one hand, enjoyed a substantial internal autonomy, but, on the other, were dependent on bigger centres of government in various ways. At that time, individuals were always incorporated into an extended family and a tribe (Kurdish: Eşiret) that offered them and their core families protection. At the fringes of these dominions, there emerged retreat areas for heterodox religious communities such as the Êzîdî, the Alevi, the Ahl-e Haqq (Yaresan, Kakai), and the Shabak. The few urban centres, however, became in most cases sites of Sunni orthodoxy. In many parts of Kurdistan, there emerged a symbiosis between an ethnically pluralist urban population and a nomadic or semi-nomadic Kurdish population. Many of the towns that are now overwhelmingly Kurdish had a completely different ethnic composition until the beginning of the twentieth century. Thus, Van and Kars were overwhelmingly Armenian towns. In Diayarbakır (Kurdish: Amed), Armenians, Aramaic-speaking Christians, Jews, Kurds, Arabs, and Turkish-speaking Ottomans lived together. Even today, the old town is characterized by a great number of Armenian, Syrian-Orthodox, and Chaldean churches, even though by now only few of them still fulfil their original functions. At the southern edge of today's Kurdish settlement area, it was often Arabs who dominated the towns, while the Kurds dominated the countryside. To this day, Mardin, Urfa, or Mosul are good examples for towns with an Arab majority in a partially Kurdish-speaking environment.

At times, Kurdish political and military leaders played a political role far beyond Kurdistan, in which cases they didn't act as Kurds, but as Islamic rulers. Probably the best-known example of this is Salah ad-Din Yusuf ibn Ayyub ad-Dawīnī, the famous Saladin, who, in 1187, reconquered Jerusalem for Islam from the Christian crusaders and who founded the dynasty of the Ayyubids. Even though he was thus one of the most famous and successful Islamic rulers of Kurdish origin of all times, Salah ad-Din did not act with a Kurdish political entity in mind. Centuries before the emergence of nationalisms and national states, Islam represented the central unifying element of his empire.

For the Ayyubids, the Kurdish settlement areas also remained a peripheral issue. For centuries, these areas were never centres of political power, but rather represented the periphery of the big political systems of government. This peripheral status of Kurdish history continued for centuries, a status that was politically characterized by the partial absence of a centralized power and a division of political power between different regional and tribal structures. The political power of the centres of the empires did play a role, but the Kurdish Aghas and Sheiks simultaneously used it for their own purposes and tried to keep it at a safe distance.

The various local rulers were repeatedly opposed to each other in bitter rivalry and also used the political centres of the empires to get resources from them for their fight against their competitors. At the same time, however, they opposed all attempts to curtail their interior autonomy and refused any stronger integration into the various empires. This was also true for those times when Kurdish areas became part of the Ottoman Empire in the sixteenth century, or when, with the treaty of Qasr-e Shirin, the border between the Safavid Iran and the Ottoman Empire was drawn in 1639 and the spheres of influence in Kurdistan were thereby fixed (see Barfield 2002: 74).

However, Kurdistan remained a de facto peripheral border area of two great empires, neither of which controlled their border regions in a spatially inclusive manner like modern territorial states do, but rather limited themselves to a symbolic presence in the towns. The Kurdish feudal lords, in turn, limited themselves to the occasional payment of taxes and, if required, the delivery of troops. Their – often varying – loyalty to the centres of the respective empires was also quite limited. In reality, the Eşiret continued to be the backbone of the Kurdish social order and its political and economic power, both of which have to be regarded as one.

Yet in some parts of Kurdistan, non-Kurds were also integrated into the Kurdish tribal system. Thus, there were Christian-Assyrian tribes in today's Turkish province Hakkari whose way of life was, apart from their Christian religion and their Eastern Neo-Aramaic language, no different from that of the semi-nomadic Kurdish tribes of the region, with whom they frequently formed alliances and tribal federations but with whom they were at loggerheads just as often. In the sixteenth century, the emirs of Hakkari, who traced their origins back to the Abbasid caliphs, ruled over a complex power structure of Assyrian and Kurdish tribes (see Brentjes and Günther 2001: 10).

The period of the rule of the Safavids is also the time of the adoption of the Shia in Iran, the turn of many Southern Kurds to the Twelver Shia as the new religion of the empire, and the settlement of mostly Shiite Kurds in Khorasan at the border with Central Asia under Shah Abbas I

(Rezvani 2013: 157). To this day, the descendants of Kurds who had once settled there form an enclave of more than 500,000 mostly Kurmancî-speaking citizens of Iran and today's Turkmenistan.

In the heartland of Kurdistan, different varieties of Iranian emerged that are described as Kurdish today, but which are actually so different from each other that many linguists regard them as different languages. In both Kurdistan and among intellectuals of the diaspora it is one of the most controversial questions whether, for example, the variety Zazakî belongs to Kurdish or whether it is a language of its own. Yet this is a question that only really began to pose itself with the development of the nationalist movements of the twentieth century. Because there still is no Kurdish national state that could enforce a particular variety as the national language, and because it is well known that a language – according to Max Weinreich's *bon mot* – is no more than a "dialect with an army and a navy," the passionate debates about the question of whether there is a Kurdish language, which Zazakî, Gûranî (Hawrami), the South Kurdish varieties (Feyli, Kermanshahi, Kelhuri), or – for many Kurdish nationalists – even Lorī, despite its closer relationship with Persian (Farsi), are a part of, are anyway based more on political than linguistic points of view.

Be that as it may, in the midst of a mostly nomadic environment the semi-independent principalities of Kurdistan developed regional urban centres that also became places of education and the nursery of Kurdish culture and language(s). Some of these principalities lasted for several centuries, enjoying changing spheres of influence in the process. Thus, from around 1200 to 1832 the princes of Bahdinan ruled over the larger part of the province Dohuk of today's Iran from their base in the town of Amediye before they were overrun by the principality of Soran. From the fourteenth century to 1867, the princes of Ardalan ruled over a large part of the Kurdish areas of Iran and extended their rule to the South Kurdish areas of Iraq. The court of Ardalan experienced the development of a high culture and literature, the latter of which was written down in the dialect of Gûranî. Poems and songs were certainly the most important literary form. Historical works were in part also written in rhymed form and always functioned simultaneously as songs of praise for the regional rulers of the day. Interestingly, the history of the dynasty of the princes of Ardalan was written by a female poet and historian by the name of Mastūray Ardalān (1805–1848), a fact that points to the important position of women in the region. While Gûranî was dislodged by Soranî from its former core area around the capital of Ardalan, Sanandaj, in the eighteenth and nineteenth centuries, the poems by Parishan Dinawarî (fourteenth century), Mustafa Beseranî (1641–1702), Xana Qubadî (1700–1759), and particularly Mewlewî (1806–1882) are still read in the mountain region of Hewraman to this day.

Yet it was not only the development of Gûranî into the oldest Kurdish literary language that was closely connected to a princely court; the same was also true of the establishment of Kurmancî. In the fifteenth century, the princely court of Cizîra-Botan (Cizre) evolved into the cultural centre of the Kurmancî-speaking Kurds, yet it was also the home of Jewish and Christian communities in a remarkably multicultural town. It was a place for doctors, scientists, religious scholars, and, not least, poets, whose works are still considered the classics of Kurmancî literature. At this court, Melayê Cezîrî (1570–1640) created a substantial Diwan. Ehmedê Xanî (1651–1707), who was born in today's Hakkari and wrote the most famous Kurdish love poem *Mem û Zîn*, was also active here at the court of the princes of Cizîra-Botan. In Cizre, one can still visit the graves of several major classical poets of Kurmancî. Even today, the building of the Medreseya Sor (Red School) where the classical Kurdish poets and intellectuals taught their students still gives impressive testimony to the intellectual life at the centre of Cizre in the sixteenth and seventeenth centuries.

The Kurmancî spoken in the region is still regarded as the "most beautiful" variety of this sub-group of Kurdish. Even after decades of Turkish assimilation policies and even during the high phase of the war between the Turkish army and the guerrillas of the PKK, Kurmancî continued to be almost the only language spoken in the town of Cizre in today's tri-border region Turkey/Syria/Iraq. There is no better place than here to learn Kurmancî in an everyday context. Since the larger part of today's canton of Cizîrê in Rojava once also belonged to the principality of Cizîra-Botan, the historical, linguistic, and cultural connections between the northern – now Turkish – and southern – now Syrian – part of the old principality are especially close. Just like the citizens of Cizre, the inhabitants of the canton of Cizîrê owe their reputation of speaking a particularly beautiful form of Kurmancî to this heritage.

After the last ruler of the princedom Bedirxan Beğ put the Ottoman Empire in diplomatic distress following massacres of Assyrian Christians and Êzîdî Kurds, the government of the Empire, which was already aiming to centralize its rule, crushed a rebellion in the region and in

1847 sent the last prince of Cizîra-Botan into exile. The town and its surroundings became a part of the Vilâyet Diyarbakır.

Yet in contrast to the urban centre of the princedom Botan, Cizre, which today is located in Turkey directly at the Syrian border, the part of Cizîrê that today belongs to Syria was overwhelmingly characterized by nomads, not urban settlements. Today's largest towns in the region, al-Hasaka and Qamişlo, were only (re)founded under the French protectorate following World War I. In the nineteenth century, only today's much smaller town Amûdê, which is inhabited mostly by Syro-Aramaic Christians, and a few villages were inhabited on a permanent basis. Until the beginning of the twentieth century, the population of the region, particularly the Kurds, overwhelmingly led a nomadic life. This nomadic population was dominated by the powerful Kurdish tribal confederation of the Mîllî. Apart from the Mîllî, there were also smaller tribes such as the Dakkuri, the Heverkan, or the Hasenan present in the region. It was only the partition of the country by a new state border that cut through families and pastures, and the settlement policies of the administration of the French protectorate after World War I, that forced many Kurds to settle permanently in villages.

Until the twentieth century, the other two cantons of Rojava that are Kurdish today also functioned merely as the rural hinterland of urban centres that are today located in Turkey and Syria. As towns, both Efrîn and Kobanê (Arabic: Ain al-Arab) have their origins in the beginning of the French protectorate. The region around Efrîn, the so-called Kurd Dagh (Arabic: Jabal al-ākrād, Kurdish: Çiyayê Kurmênc) was a mountain region in the Vilâyet Aleppo, or to be more precise, in the Sandjak Aleppo within the Vilâyet; that is, the region was administered from the predominantly Arab town of Aleppo. This was, however, also one of the core reasons why Aleppo emerged as the urban and cultural centre of the Kurds of the Kurd Dagh, a centre where Kurds formed their own districts outside of the old city. The town Kilis served as the regional administrative centre, but since 1921 has lain on the Turkish side of the border.

The Kurd Dagh's character was shaped by five different Kurdish tribes (Kurdish: Eşiret): the Amikan, Biyan, Sheikan, Shikakan, and Jums. Inferior to these in terms of influence were the smaller tribes of the Robariya, Kharzan, Kastiyan, and others. The twenty-six Êzîdî villages with their total 1,140 inhabitants (in the 1930s) were subordinate to the Muslim Robariya (Tejel 2009: 9).

Yet the importance of the tribes had already begun to dwindle by the turn of the century. Compared to the other Kurdish regions of Syria, in today's canton Efrîn at least parts of the population settled down pretty early, since this low mountain range was excellently suited for the cultivation of olives. Thus, a sedentary peasant population emerged for whom the production of olives and olive oil became the central source of income. Today, the region is host to more than 13 million olive trees (Allsopp 2014: 19). In this rural society of the Kurd Dagh, affiliation to the Kurdish tribes played much less of a role than it did for the nomadic and semi-nomadic Kurds. In a society in which the land was cultivated continuously and in which, therefore, the possession of land became an important resource, territorial affiliation represented a function that was increasingly more important than the affiliation to a tribe. Already at the beginning of the twentieth century, the village (Kurdish: gund) played a role for the population of the Kurd Dagh that was at least as central as the tribal affiliation. To this day, the canton Efrîn, which is still characterized by smallholder olive cultivation, is the part of Rojava in which the affiliation to a tribe plays the slightest role and which is inhabited by a largely detribalized peasant society.

Kobanê, the smallest of the three Kurdish cantons, is certainly also the poorest and most isolated part of Rojava. Not until after World War I were there any permanent settlements here. The region represented no more than the southern offshoot of a settlement to which Kurdish nomads used to descend from the higher regions of Kurdistan during the winter and which became more intensely settled only in the seventeenth century. The region was dominated by the tribal confederation of the Barazi, which included both Kurdish and Arab tribes. Administratively, the sparsely settled region belonged to the Sandjak Urfa within the Vilâyet Aleppo. The closest small-town settlement was Suruç (Serugh) in today's Turkey, a once predominantly Christian-Aramaic town in which, during the turn from the fifth to the sixth century, the Syrian-Orthodox Saint Jacob of Serugh (Mor Yakub) was active. However the hinterland, which by now belongs to Syria, was almost entirely nomadic. The only town to this very day got its Kurdish name because it accommodated a "company" under German command for the construction of the Baghdad Railway, the railroad line along which the border between Turkey and the French protectorate Syria was drawn in the 1923 Treaty of Lausanne.

Joined by Arab rebels, allied troops occupied Damascus on 1 October
1918. After Feisal I from the dynasty of the Hashemites was proclaimed
king on 7 March 1920, it took the European victorious powers of World
War I only until April 1920 to agree, in San Remo, on a French League
of Nations mandate for Syria based on the Sykes-Picot Agreement of
1916. Yet in the Treaty of Sèvres, concluded in August 1920, and which
from the Turkish-Ottoman perspective was no more than a dictated
peace enforced by the victors of World War I, the borderline between
the Ottoman Empire and the new protectorate was not yet fixed along
the Baghdad Railway, but was located further to the north. According
to the decisions of Sèvres, not only were the northeastern provinces of
Turkey, with Kars, Trabzon, Erzerum, and Van, to become part of the
new state of Armenia, but there was also to be an autonomous Kurdistan
that was to include Diyarbakır, Dersim, and a strip of land south of Van
up to the Iranian border. The border between the French mandated
territory in Syria and the Ottoman Empire had been drawn considerably
further to the north than was to be the case later on. Cizre, Nusaybin,
Mardin, Urfa, Kilis, and Antep – which was renamed Gaziantep after its
reconquest by the Turks in 1921 – were at first occupied by the British
and then, together with today's Syria, handed over to the French. It was
only with the agreement of Ankara of 20 October 1921, later confirmed
by the Treaty of Lausanne on 24 July 1923, that the border of the French
protectorate was relocated further to the south along the current
national border between Syria and Turkey.

The fact that there is any Syrian Kurdistan at all today thus goes back
to this delineation of the border following a railroad line, and not to
any ethnic or linguistic criteria. Both France and Turkey wanted access
to this rail line, which at the beginning of the twentieth century was
regarded as the main supply line to the region. Thus, the rail line itself
was turned into the new boundary, and trains could roll both into the
east of Syria and the east of Turkey. Yet this left behind Arab-speaking
settlement areas on the Turkish side and Kurdish settlement areas on
the Syrian side. Syrian Kurdistan was thus actually born as a "waste
product" of the colonial division of the Middle East.

For the overwhelming majority of Kurdish intellectuals, the failure
after World War I to create a Kurdish state still represents the core
problem of the Kurdish question. In this connection, they accuse the
West of having prevented the formation of a Kurdish state. On the other
hand, they also reproach their own population for having been too

"backward" or tribally divided, or, at any rate, having suffered from the lack of an organized national movement able to enforce the creation of a Kurdish state. Indeed, at the beginning of the twentieth century the idea of an autonomous Kurdish national state was no more than an extremely marginal concept entertained by just a few urban intellectuals, many of whom did not even live in Kurdistan themselves. The first Kurdish-language magazine (*Kurdistan*) was published by intellectuals in Cairo. In nationalist discourses of all stripes, the Kurdish society of the time is conceived of as deficient and backward. In the tradition of Edward Said's critique of Orientalism (see Said 1978), Wendelmoet Hamelink and Hanifi Barış describe this stance, which actually denies the Kurdish actors any agency, as "self-orientalising," a description that certainly has some justification. Against this position, they counterpose the idea that Kurdish actors consciously refrained from developing any nationalism, but rather tried to keep the state at bay as far as possible instead. On the basis of a highly interesting study of traditional Dengbêjs, that is, very extensive narrations from Kurdish history that were also often sung, they conclude that these traditional texts revolve around local spaces and alliances and not around a national Kurdish project. According to them, in these texts borders are described as disturbing factors imposed from the outside. In the specialist journal *Kurdish Studies*, which was founded only in 2013, the two authors come to the conclusion that the Kurdish society of the time did not simply *lack* the wish or will to have a national state, but that it actively fought *against* the very conception (Hamelink and Barış 2014). There is indeed a lot of evidence in Kurdish history indicating that the Kurds actually did participate in the making of history, but that the idea of the national state was more than simply alien to them. They argue that well into the twentieth century, the overwhelming majority of the Kurdish actors did not regard the concept of the "state" *as such* as an adequate form for the organization of political rule. This does not mean that Kurdistan consisted of spaces free of domination or represented a utopia of "noble savages," as is suggested by some romanticizing descriptions of the Kurds as a "freedom-loving" people. Kurdish society was permeated by a myriad of structures of dominance. Ağas, Sheikhs, and regional princes formed the backbone of authority. They remained, both locally and in many other respects, opposed to a centralization of power in the form of a state.

Many of the actors that Kurdish nationalists today regard as predecessors of the Kurdish national movement, such as Bedirxan Beğ

(1802–1868), the last prince of the principality of Cizîra-Botan, or the Iranian-Kurdish tribal leader Simko Ağa (1887–1930), did not regard themselves as Kurdish nationalists, but stood in the tradition of self-defence against the state. From the middle of the nineteenth century, they were confronted with an increasingly statist Ottoman Empire that provided less and less space for vassal rulers and tribal territories.

For this reason, it is not particularly surprising that, since the beginning of the rise of the Ottoman and Iranian states and the successive transformation of both the Ottoman and the Persian Empires into modern territorial states, not only were these defensive battles lost, but also in the end, the national state descended on the Kurds in the form of "alien" territorial powers. In the case of the Syrian Kurds, this took the form of the French protectorate.

6

Syrian Kurdistan under the French Protectorate

With the takeover by France and the displacement to Iraq of King Faisal I, who had been defrauded of his Great Arabic Empire, France proceeded to establish different states on the territory of its mandate. They were meant to enable not only a regional federalization, but also a certain amount of self-rule for the religious minorities. The protectorate as a whole was divided into the states of État de Grand Liban, État des Alaouites, État de la Montagne Druze, État d'Alep, and État de Damas. In addition, the Sandjak d'Alexandrette enjoyed autonomy within the State of Aleppo. Thus, the Alawis with their État des Alaouites – and in a way, also with the Sandjak d'Alexandrette – the Druze with their État de la Montagne Druze, and the Christians with the État de Grand Liban all possessed their "own state." The last of these later indeed became a state in the form of Lebanon.

But the Kurds and the Aramaic-speaking Christians of Cizîrê gained no autonomy at all. All Kurdish areas became part of the State of Aleppo (État d'Alep), which was created on the territory of the old Vilâyet Aleppo in September 1920. (Takla 2004: 80). Within the State of Aleppo, the Sandjak of Alexandrette was granted administrative autonomy and a "régime special" (Takla 2004: 81), but the same was not true of the Kurdish or Christian-Aramaic regions.

Actually, the State of Aleppo was a "state" dominated by Sunni Arabs, even though the Sunni-Arab majority in it was less pronounced than in the State of Damascus (and even though it was actually anyway under French control). Apart from the Kurds, the State of Damascus was inhabited by large Christian, Shia, and Alawite minorities. But since the time of the Ottomans, various Muslim minorities from the Caucasus

(Chechens, Circassians) as well as Turks also settled in the region. The State of Aleppo was thus surely the ethnically and religiously most heterogeneous of all Syrian partial states under the administration of the French protectorate.

Different from the Sandjak of Alexandrette, the Kurds were not granted any rights of self-rule within the State of Aleppo, a fact that led to the first demands for autonomy. Interestingly, the first such demands were not raised in the later centre of Kurdish political activities in Cizîrê, but emanated from the Kurd Dagh. From May 1924, the Kurdish representative Nuri Kandy promoted the idea of an administrative autonomy for all regions with a Kurdish majority population, by which he meant an autonomous region along the whole border with Turkey. He also held the view that the Kurds could help fight back Arab nationalism and could thus also be of use to the French administrative authorities. A second early demand for autonomy is known to have come from the tribes of the Barazi, who demanded an autonomy exclusively for their own region around today's Kobanê (Tejel 2009: 27).

Generally, the Kurdish actors cooperated with the French colonial administration because to them, the Arab-nationalist ambitions in Damascus seemed a greater danger than the French administrators. The latter were thus at least partially regarded as allies. And among the French officers and administrators, there developed a certain interest in Kurdish questions, which in the case of Pierre Rondot and Roger Lescot also led to an academic occupation with the Kurds. Lescot's cooperation with Kurdish intellectuals later resulted in a grammar of Kurmancî jointly written with Celadet Alî Bedirxan, which is still of enormous importance for the standardization of Kurmancî as a literary language.

However, a large part of early Kurdish nationalism played itself out primarily outside of Rojava, namely, among Kurdish intellectuals and exiles in Damascus and Beirut. The wave of refugees after the suppression of the Sheik Said rebellion in Turkey in 1925 in which Sunni Kurds under the leadership of a conservative Sunni Sheik fought for a degree of autonomy in Turkey supplied the already exiled intellectuals in Damascus and Beirut with new activists from Turkish Kurdistan.

In October 1927, Kurdish intellectuals, supported by the left-nationalist Armenian Revolutionary Federation also known as Daschnaktsutiun (Tachjian 2003), met in the Lebanese mountain town Bhamdoun, where they founded the political movement Khoybun ("Independence"). As their first president, they elected Celadet Alî Bedirxan, one of the leading intellectuals of the time who, moreover, came from the dynasty of Botan and thus also had traditional influence among Sunni Kurds in Turkey and in Syria. In addition, earlier Kurdish political movements such as the Kürdistan Teali Cemiyeti founded in 1918 in Istanbul, the Kürt Teşkilat-ı İçtimaiye Cemiyeti founded in 1920 by Ekrem Cemil Paşa, the Kürt Millet Fırkası, and the Comité de l'Independence Kurde united with previously independent intellectuals and tribal leaders. Apart from Celadet Alî Bedirxan, Mehmet Şükrü Sekban, Memduh Selim, Haco Agha, Ramanlı Emin, Ali Rıza, Bozan bey Shahin, Mustafa bey Şahin, and Süleymniyeli Kerim Rüstem Bey were members of the first central committee of the new organization.

Khoybun saw itself as an all-Kurdish National Liberation Movement, which, however, intended to learn from previous military defeats and rejected any premature spontaneous uprisings. Khoybun decided to establish a permanent headquarters in Aleppo (McDowall 2004: 203). Together with Damascus, the town became a centre for Kurdish nationalist activities which, however, were primarily directed at Turkey and Syria. Thus, Khoybun actively supported the second and the third Ararat uprisings of 1927 and 1930 by sending the former Ottoman officer Ihsan Nuri Pasha to function as military leader of the "Republic Ararat" led by Ibrahim Heski. In Syria, however, the Khoybun activists focused on cultural work and cooperated with the French authorities on a continual basis. The fruitful scientific cooperation of Celadet Alî Bedirxan and Roger Lescot also goes back to this phase of intense contact between the French authorities and the Kurdish national movement.

Politically, Khoybun saw itself as a progressive movement that countered the Kemalist disparagement of the Kurds as "backward" and "barbaric" with a description of the Turks as "barbaric." But unlike the Sheik Said uprising a couple of years earlier, a cooperation with the anti-Kemalists who strived for a reestablishment of the Caliphate was rejected. Instead, Khoybun sought friendly relations with the Soviet Union, Iran, and Iraq in order to at least obtain their neutrality (Tejel 2009: 19).

Even though the Treaty of Lausanne of 24 July 1923 had fixed the new border line between the area of the French protectorate – and therefore, also the State of Aleppo – with Turkey, in the following years both sides tried to instrumentalize the tribal leaders of the respective other side of the border for themselves and to manipulate the controversial boundary line. The exact final border line was only fixed in 1929 in a new international agreement (Dillemann 1979: 33 ff.).

Already since 1920, Kurdish refugees from Turkey had come into the Kurdish regions of Syria, where they preferentially settled in Cizîrê, encountering a mixed Christian-Kurdish population there. After the suppression of the Sheikh Said uprising in Turkey in 1925, thousands of followers of the Sheikh fled across the border to Syria. In Cizîrê, this also changed the majority situation in favour of the Kurds. At any rate, in the late 1920s the Aramaic-speaking Christians, many of whom had themselves fled into the region only ten years before, were already in the minority.

Since the previous trading centres of the region were all located north of the new state border and, in addition, thousands of new Kurdish and Christian refugees had to be settled, the French administration had to plan for additional new towns that were to serve as regional administrative and trading centres of the region.

In 1922, the French built a military camp on the site of what would become the city of al-Hasaka, and where under the Ottomans there had been no more than an insignificant and largely deserted settlement. In 1764, Carsten Niebuhr still saw only the ruins of an earlier town. "Haskne", he writes, "also seems to have been a town." He suspected that there had been a fortress on a hill where, as he reported, there were still some remnants of buildings. "Half a mile to the south," he believed to have noticed the remnants of a small church. "The whole building is just 13 double-steps long and 9 double-steps wide, all built from big hewn stones" (Niebuhr 1779: 378). Between the eighteenth century and the time of the French protectorate, al-Hasaka had never been rebuilt. It was only with the construction of the French military outpost that development into a town began again. Members of the Syrian Legion were promised land so as to make settling in the garrison towns attractive for them.

In 1926, Assyrian and Aramaic-speaking Christians created the town of Qamishli, which was directly at the border and adjacent to Nusaybin. In the following years, about two thirds of the population of Nusaybin went across the border to resettle in Qamishli, which soon became more populous than the old Nusaybin. The whole Christian population as well as many of the Kurds moved into the town, whose Kurdish name was Qamişlo. To them, we need to add the Jewish community of Nusaybin and the Arab tribe of the Tai. The new town within just a few years grew into a multi-ethnic and multi-religious commercial town in which people spoke Arabic, Kurdish, Aramaic, and Armenian, and in which Christians, Muslims, and Jews cooperated under French suzerainty.

Finally, the Comité Central des Réfugiés, which aided Armenian refugees in the 1920s, resettled Armenian, Syro-Aramaic, and Kurdish refugees in the garrison towns such as al-Hasaka, Qamishli, Dêrik, or Ra's al-'Ain (Serê Kaniyê) (Velud 2000: 77 f.).

But it was not only Armenian, Syro-Aramaic, and Kurdish refugees who came into Cizîrê in the 1920s. Probably the most incisive change in the region was the settlement of the region's hitherto nomadic and semi-nomadic Kurdish population. The French administration wanted the fertile agricultural land to be cultivated more intensely and so the former nomads were turned into sedentary peasants who lived in rural settlements.

Thus, in Cizîrê, there emerged a rural and small-town population of various ethnic origins that, however, had little in common with the population of Western Syria. The regions that – unlike the rest of the State of Aleppo – had never been part of the Vilâyet Aleppo, but belonged to the Vilâyet Diyarbakır, barely had any connection with the Syrian heartland. The "Upper Jezira," as today's Cizîrê was called at the time, formed a region of its own that also increasingly strived for political autonomy.

These aspirations for autonomy in the 1930 were supported not only by the Kurds living in Cizîrê, but also by a Christian-Kurdish coalition whose goal was a regional, not an ethnic autonomy.

Apart from a large part of the Kurdish elite, the movement for autonomy was primarily supported by Christians from the churches united with the Catholic Church. Among the most important protagonists of the autonomy movement were the Syrian-Catholic Archbishop of Aleppo and Patriarch of Antioch, Ignatius Gabriel I. Tappouni, and his vicar general for the Jezira, Msgr. Hanna Hebbé, as well as Michel Dôme, the Armenian-Catholic mayor of Qamishli. The autonomy movement was furthermore supported by the French Dominicans who were active in the region from 1936 and served as an important link to the French authorities.

However, as well as the Christian and Kurdish inhabitants of the region, some Arabs also took part in the efforts to achieve autonomy. Thus, the Shammar, who were relatively strongly represented in the region, were divided with regard to the question of autonomy. While one part of the tribe cooperated with the protagonists of Arab nationalism, another part supported the movement for autonomy (Tejel 2009: 31).

Such splits were by no means only to be found in the Arab population of Cizîrê. And the Kurds also did not all support the demands for autonomy. While a part of the Kurdish tribes hoped to use the French to escape their marginalization within an Arab national state, others strived for cooperation with the Arabs in order to mobilize against the French "Christian occupiers" in the name of a common Muslim identity. Even though the adherents of the "Bloc national," which was founded in 1928 and rose to become the most important anticolonialist political force in the 1930s, were to be found primarily amongst the Arab population, among the Kurds there were also allies for this collective movement of Arab nationalists and conservative Sunnis who primarily came from the most influential and wealthy families of the country. According to Nelida Fuccaro's estimate, in 1936 about one third of the Kurdish population supported the Arab coalition in Damascus (Fuccaro 1997: 320).

In the Jezira, however, the allies of the National Bloc did not only display an anti-French direction, but also an anti-Christian one. A Pan-Islamic orientation was supposed to secure a Kurdish-Arabic unity under a Sunni flag. Since the French were not easily available as targets for these anti-Christian activities, some of the local Christian communities became the victims of this political current. The sad climax of the anti-Christian alliance of pro-Arab Kurds and some Sunni Arab-nationalist groups in Cizîrê was the so-called Amûdê affair, which also dealt a heavy blow to the Christian-Kurdish cooperation, and thus, to the autonomy movement.

In 1937, conflicts in all of Syria between champions of a centralization of power in Damascus and of Syrian independence on the one hand, and adherents of a strengthened autonomy for the ethnic and religious minorities on the other were coming to a head (Yildiz 2005: 26). In the summer of 1937 there was an open uprising in Cizîrê, when the Kurds in al-Hasaka began violently resisting the appointment of Arab senior civil servants. But with the aid of French troops, the uprising was suppressed just as violently as had been the protests of Christians in Qamishli and other towns of the region (Jweideh 2006: 146).

Against the background of these violent protests, in August 1937 members of the Arab Shammar and pro-Arab Kurds jointly attacked the predominantly Assyrian small town of Amûdê and organized a pogrom of local Christians, who were forced to seek refuge in Qamishli and al-Hasaka (Joseph 1983: 107). The fact that even though Amûdê today still has two Christian churches in its old town, but unlike other towns in the region is no longer host to any Christian community goes back to this pogrom of 1937, which "Kurdicized" the town. For many Christians in Cizîrê, this pogrom lastingly shattered the hope of a joint struggle with the Kurds for autonomy. Afterwards, many of them turned towards Damascus and away from joint efforts aimed at autonomy. The defeat of the autonomy movement in 1937 also marked the slow end of the Christian-Kurdish coalition in Cizîrê – even though the actors of the autonomy movement tried to jointly commemorate the pogrom and to continue the Christian-Kurdish cooperation. However, the Christians began to gravitate more and more towards the central government and the option of a joint Syrian state, and thus to defect from the previous alliance with the Kurds.

With the beginning of World War II, like other countries Syria found itself between the frontlines of the warring parties. At the time, German agents tried to forge contacts with the Kurdish nationalists in Syria (Tejel 2009: 20). In the context of the present book, it would lead us too far afield to give a precise picture of the various coalitions and – frequently short-lived – alliances engaged in by the Kurdish actors in the region. With the defeat of France in 1940, Syria came under the administration of the Vichy regime, but was already reconquered in summer 1941 by British troops and troops of Free France during their Syrian-Lebanese campaign. The independence of Syria, which was proclaimed in 1941, was not recognized, but the promise of Syrian independence after the war was an essential part of the strategy of the new administration to keep the country quiet. At the same time, even though Kurdish efforts to achieve autonomy continued, they no longer resembled the strong movement of the 1930s.

7

Kurds in Independent Syria

With the withdrawal of the last French troops in April 1946, Syria was finally released into independence as an integral state, without, however, Lebanon (and the Sandjak of Alexandrette, which had been handed over to Turkey in 1938 and 1939). The new entity formed a central state in which Pan-Arab and Syrian-patriotic political groups competed with one another, but in which there was no room for the autonomy demands of ethnic or religious minorities anymore. On the contrary, the detachment of Lebanon and the transfer of the Sandjak of Alexandrette (which was never recognized by Syria), made it easy from then on to taint all demands for autonomy with the suspicion of separatism. After the disastrous military defeat of Syria and the other Arab states in the Israeli War of Independence from 1948 to 1949, this domestic state of siege only intensified. In such a political climate, demands for territorial autonomy would have been interpreted as high treason.

All the same, the Kurds represented an integral part of the new Republic of Syria as long as they eschewed any specifically Kurdish demands. Kurds had already made up a relatively large share of the French colonial army, and thus the increasing importance of the military after independence was quite advantageous for the Kurds, or at least for those who relinquished their demands for autonomy and actively participated in the Syrian state. Finally, on 11 April 1949 the Kurdish officer and participant in the war with Israel, Husni az-Za'im, took power in a coup and thus triggered a long series of subsequent military coups in the country. Even though az-Za'im publicly de-emphasized his Kurdish identity and did not put any Kurdish demands into practice, he still surrounded himself with relatively many Kurdish advisors and ministers. Thus, under his government yet another Kurd, Muhsen al-Barazi, became prime minister. Accordingly, Arab nationalists and followers of the Muslim Brotherhood accused him of creating a "Kurdish Republic" and of favouring the Kurds and Circassians (Tejel 2009: 45). The Kurdish activist and poet Cigerxwîn recounts that after the overthrow and execution of az-Za'im by Sami al-Hinnawi of the Syrian Social Nationalist Party, the Syrian media cheered the event as the downfall of a "Kurdish government" (Cigerxwîn 1995: 280).

However, the Arab Sunni al-Hinnawi also did not remain in power for long and was soon replaced in a third military coup in December 1949 by yet another Kurdish officer. Yet unlike az-Za'im, no one expected Adib ash-Shishakli to bring about any improvement of the situation of the Kurds in Syria. Adib ash-Shishakli not only did not pursue any policy friendly to the Kurds, but also explicitly allied himself with the Arab nationalists, presumably trying to "offset" his Kurdish origin. Moreover, Adib ash-Shishakli and his Pan-Arabist propaganda and defamation campaign against the Druze (Tejel 2009: 41) created a political climate characterized by hatred of minorities and paranoia that was also directed at the Syrian Kurds. It was thus a Kurd who prepared the way for a spiritual climate that was to create massive problems for the Kurds under the various Arab-nationalist regimes in the decades to come.

During this phase, Kurds could essentially choose between three different political camps: They could join the Arab nationalists, follow the Pan-Syrian forces, or support the Communist Party. Social upheavals brought about by the mechanization of agriculture, which drove thousands of Kurdish agricultural workers to the cities where they formed a new Kurdish proletariat (Zaza 1982: 137 f.), led to deep social and political changes. For many of these new proletarian Kurds, the Communist Party in particular became a political home. Founded in 1924 as the Syrian-Lebanese Communist Party, the organization was led by Khalid Bakdash following his return from Moscow in 1937 (Ismael and Ismael 1998: 25). He was a Kurd from the Hayy al-Akrad district of Damascus and managed, despite all sorts of different splits and factional struggles within the Communist Party, to remain the autocratic ruler of his party until his death in 1995.

Bakhdash's Kurdish origins may have contributed to his popularity among the Kurds, but primarily, communism offered a modern ideology by which one could separate oneself from Arab nationalism without courting the old conservative tribal chieftains, posing instead the social question that was so important for the new urban proletariat.

Even the persecution of political parties or the policy of ash-Shishakli could not subtract from the political appeal of the Communist Party. To this day, one can meet old men in Syrian Kurdistan who still have the pictures of Khalid Bakdash hanging on the walls of their houses. Because Khalid Bakdash's Communist Party cooperated with the Ba'ath Party during the whole existence of the latter's regime, this type of confession remained – different from the membership in one of the oppositional Communist Parties – without punitive consequences even in Ba'athist Syria. Between 1946 and 1957, autonomous Kurdish parties beyond the regional level simply didn't exist in Syria. Yet in the second half of the 1950s, the younger Kurdish activists around and within the Communist Party increasingly realized that they could expect no support whatsoever in the struggle for the rights of the Kurds from Khalid Bakdash's strictly Stalinist Communist Party. Inspired by the younger generation of the Kurdistan Democratic Party (PDK) in Iraq, from the mid-1950s on thoughts were aired about the founding of a separate Kurdish party in Syria. An important impulse for this had been the sojourn in Syria of Jalal Talabani, the later founder of the Patriotic Union of Kurdistan (PUK), who in the 1950s was still active in the PDK in Iraq. The initiative for founding the party came, for the most part, from the circles of Kurdish intellectuals of Hayy al-Akrad in Damascus. Among the first activists to deliberate about the founding of the party in 1956 were the Damascus-based Kurds Osman (Arabic: 'Uthman) Sabri, who had already been active in Khoybun, Abduhamid Hadji Darwish, and finally Hamza Niweran, whose origins were in Cizîrê.

Even though in the beginning the Kurds from Hayy al-Akrad dominated the effort, there was a conscious attempt from the start to integrate the Kurds from Aleppo and the three Kurdish enclaves. The group from Damascus was supplemented by a group around Muhammed Ali Khodsha, Khalil Muhammad, and Shawkat Hanan Na'san, as well as Rashid Hamo who came from Afrîn (Kurdwatch 2011a: 5).

In Cizîrê, the establishment of the party successfully integrated two Kurdish organizations, the Jam'iya wahidat ash-Shabab al-dimoqratiyin al-akrad (Organization of the United Democratic Kurdish Youth) and the Azadî group around the Kurdish poet Cigerxwîn and Muhammad Fakhri, which had its origins in the Communist Party (Allsopp 2014: 75). The exact circumstances that surrounded the founding of the Kurdistan Democratic Party of Syria (PDKS) have not been clarified to this day.

While some of the founding members claim that the party was founded already in 1956, others give 1957 as the founding date, a date that coincides with the one given in the official party history. It is not in doubt that the party held its first congress on 14 June 1957 and elected Osman Sabri as its first secretary general. In 1958, Nur ad-Din Zaza became the first president of the party.

The PDKS was not active under its later name from the beginning, but constituted itself at first as the Democratic Party of the Kurds in Syria (Partiya Dêmokrat a Kurd li Sûriyê). When and under which circumstances it changed its name to the later one, Partiya Demokrat a Kurdistanê li Sûriyê, is controversial, not just among the actors of the time, but also within the small circle of scholars who occupy themselves with this topic today. Jordi Terel writes that the renaming only occurred in 1960 (Tejel 2009: 49). Harriet Alsopp leaves the question open and gives both 1958 and 1960 as possible dates for the renaming (Allsopp 2014: 76). Be that as it may, the use of term "Kurdistan" represented one of the early conflictual issues within the party, since it implied that the territories of the Kurds in Syria were part of a greater Kurdistan. The question of whether the party should strive for a Kurdish national state that integrated the Kurdish regions of Syria or whether it should fight for the rights of the Kurds as a minority within Syria was part of the debates within the party right from the start. It seems only logical that different political and social interests with regard to this question were also reflected in the party base. The Kurds from the Hayy al-Akrad district of Damascus or from Aleppo had a big stake in strengthening their position as Kurds in Syria, and not in a secession of Cizîrê, the Kurd Dagh, or Kobanê. A large number of these Kurds have to this day remained focused on Syria as the frame of reference, but in Cizîrê in particular, things have been different. For the Kurdish population living there, the proximity to Turkey, the distance from Damascus, and most of all the proximity to Iraqi Kurdistan and the autonomy movements of the Kurds in that country, which are in part even militarily active, opened totally different perspectives.

Another conflict that followed the party right from the start was the one between left and right. Many of the party founders came from the Communist Party or its environment and were either progressive intellectuals or belonged to the increasingly self-confident Kurdish working class that had developed since the late 1940s. Some of them had their origins in the progressive peasant movement in Cizîrê that had defended itself against the old tribal notables and their feudal system of large estates since 1952 with the support of the Communist Party. At the same time, however, the party also tried to tie these very same old elites to the party and to form an alliance with them based on Kurdish nationalism. Yet in the long run, nationalism was unable to overcome the real conflicts of interest between the old Aghas and Sheiks and their (former) landless peasants, who flocked in increasing numbers to the cities to become workers. With the various land reforms of the 1950s and 1960s, the conflicts of interest between the large landowners and the peasants also evolved and became an important aspect of the relations within the Kurdish community itself.

From the mid-1960s onwards, the original PDK Syria split, at first, into a "Left" (Çep) and a "Right" (Rast) party. Interestingly, the PDKS Çep remained connected with the tribal and conservative PDK Iraq, whereas the PDKS Rast entertained connections with the more leftist split from the PDK Iraq under Jalal Talabani and Ibrahim Ahmed, the later Patriotic Union of Kurdistan (PUK). In the following decades, both ideology and personal relations and loyalties as well as intrigues by the Syrian secret service, and beyond that, the influence of Iraqi-Kurdish and Turkish-Kurdish parties, led to an increasingly splintered landscape of Kurdish parties in Syria that was extremely difficult to understand even in comparison with the political landscape in other parts of Kurdistan. Additionally, many parties carried identical names for many years and could be distinguished only by the names of their respective chairpersons. Most of the parties still in existence today – with the important exception of the sister party of the PKK, the PYD – have emanated from one or the other of the splits from the historical PDKS founded in 1956/57. A simplified graphic representation of the splits and fusions of the Kurdish parties can be found in the front matter of this book. I devote a later chapter to the landscape of the political parties of the Syrian Kurds.

Be that as it may, the historical PDKS – just as all its successor parties – was never legalized and was never able to participate in a Syrian parliamentary election. All of its activities took place illegally, that is, more or less underground. Nevertheless, the holders of power in Syria regarded the party as a threat.

8

In the Crosshairs of Pan-Arabism
From the United Arab Republic to Ba'athism

After Syria – under its president Shukri al-Quwatli who had been democratically elected in 1954 – entered a union with Egypt in 1958, the long-running conflict between Pan-Arabists and leftists was, for the time being, decided in favour of the Pan-Arabism of the Nasserist variety. The former Egyptian military ruler, Gamal Abdel Nasser, became president of the new republic, with al-Quwatli as his vice president. Even though the United Arab Republic was de jure conceived of as a union of both states, de facto it was tantamount to an accession of Syria to Egypt. As early as 1959, al-Quwatli fell out with Nasser and had to flee into exile. Both the Kurds and the non-Nasserist Arabs began to distance themselves from the new regime. The government was almost completely composed of Egyptians. Cairo was chosen as the capital. The nationalization of Syrian firms also often worked to the benefit of Egypt. Though the land reform carried out under Nasser was popular among the poorer small farmers, the middle class and the old elites soon felt colonized by Egypt.

Yet under Egyptian rule there was also one of the most intense waves of repression of Kurdish political activists. On 20 September 1960, Nasser appointed the Pan-Arabist officer Abd al-Hamid as-Sarraj, born in 1925 in the Syrian town of Hama, as chairman of the Executive Council of the Northern Region of the United Arab Republic, which made him the de facto prime minister of Syria. Yet even before this, he had been, as minister of the interior, Nasser's man in Syria and had been responsible for the repression of political opponents. From 1958 to 1960, he reconstructed Syria into a police state, which contributed to the lasting destruction of Nasser's positive image in Syria. During his time as minister of the interior, the repression was at first primarily directed against the Communist Party and the Syrian Social Nationalist Party, which favoured a greater Syrian state over a Pan-Arabic state (Moubayed 2006: 325).

On 12 August 1960, as-Sarraj finally began his "Big Campaign" against the Kurds, during which more than 5,000 members and sympathizers of the Kurdistan Democratic Party – Syria were arrested in just a few days, including the majority of the party leadership. With the arrest of Osman Sabri Nur ad-Din Zaza and Rashid Hamo, the central committee of the party was hit heavily. In captivity, the tensions between Nur ad-Din Zaza and Osman Sabri came to a head. While Nur ad-Din Zaza urged not even mentioning the liberation of Kurdistan as a goal, but to regard the Kurds as a minority within Syria, Osman Sabri rejected this stance and demanded the admission that the Kurds were a separate nation (Allsopp 2014: 78).

In the midst of this wave of persecution, on 13 November there was an event in the small town of Amûdê that many Kurds still observe as a day of remembrance. During the screening of an Egyptian film that the mayor of the sub-borough had ordered all primary schoolers to attend, the movie theatre burnt to the ground. At that moment the cinema's 250 seats were packed with about 500 children. The overheated film projector had begun to burn. Because of the poor escape routes and the mass panic sparked by the fire, at least 152 children died.[1] The fact that the town had only 14,000 inhabitants meant that almost every extended family had to mourn at least one dead child. Among the Kurdish population, there were very soon widespread rumours that the fire had been consciously started by the regime or other anti-Kurdish forces. There is no evidence whatsoever for this. The fact that a town of this size didn't even have a fire brigade and that therefore the fire service had to be ordered from Qamişlo, and the fact that the movie theatre was hopelessly overcrowded both surely contributed significantly to the high number of victims. We can thus certainly diagnose a neglect of Kurdish infrastructure in the Kurdish regions. That this tragedy happened during a time of extreme repression against the Kurds also contributed to the view among many Syrian Kurds of the movie fire as a national tragedy and a crime by Arab nationalists. To this day, a much honoured memorial site in Amûdê recalls the memory of the children and of Mohamed Said Daqori, a well-known personality of the town who saved children from the fire by his own hand and who himself perished in it. There are annual celebrations there commemorating the fire.

Even though it was very likely no more than an accident, the fire in the movie theatre still plays a significant role in the cultural memory of Syrian Kurds. Thus, in 2013 a Kurdish website in Germany described the first commemoration in Amûdê after the withdrawal of the Syrian security forces in the following way:

> According to the official version, the overheated film projector caught fire, which quickly spread because the movie theatre was built of wood, clay, and straw. There was never any investigation on the part of the state. The fire brigade and the security forces arrived only hours later. Many Kurds still believe that the regime or other dark powers within the state started the fire. They therefore call the movie theatre fire the "Massacre in the Cinema of Amûdê." Amûdê can now for the first time recollect the memory of its children in freedom and without repression on the part of the regime.[2]

The intense wave of persecution directed against the PDKS ended only with Syria's withdrawal from the United Arab Republic in 1961, when a broad popular movement in alliance with the military brought the rule of Egypt to an end. Abd al-Hamid as-Sarraj had already resigned on 26 September. On the following day, the military overthrew the government, and on 28 September it declared Syria's departure from the United Arab Republic.

But the contrast between political parties that had a Syrian agenda, such as the Communist Party and the Syrian Social Nationalist Party, and the parties with a Pan-Arabist orientation remained. Even though the old conservative elites were now once more in power, that did not mean that Arab nationalism was now dead. Its traces were even left in the new name of the state. The newly reconstructed state no longer called itself "the Republic of Syria," but rather "the Arab Republic of Syria," which meant that it had pushed ethnic minorities, most of all the Kurds, out of the nation on even a nominal level. Moreover, the various currents of Arab nationalism also reorganized themselves in terms of party politics. Apart from the now discredited Nasserists, the Ba'athists were the most important force.

Ba'athism emerged in the 1940s around a group of Syrian students, the Christian Michel Aflaq, the Sunni Salah ad-Din al-Bitar, and the Alawi Zakī al-Arsūzī. But the official founding year of the "Socialist Party of the

Arab Reawakening" (Hizb al-ba'th al-'arabī al-ištirākī) is considered to be 1947, when the former Ba'athist clubs officially merged into a single party at a party congress. During their studies in France, the three founders had been inspired by both Marxist and Fascist European models, and they pursued an Arab nationalism infused with state socialism that was supposed to overcome confessionalism and to bring about a strong and unified Arab national state. But the party's nationalism remained diffuse and contained both ethnic and cultural elements. On the one hand, the Ba'athists defined the Arab nation entirely as a *völkische* nation determined by ethnic descent and thus advocated, as far as citizenship was concerned, a legal conception strictly based on the *jus sanguinis*. On the other hand, even Aflaq, al-Arsūzī, and al-Bitar knew quite well that the Arab nation could not have historically developed as a community of common descent, but was the result of the assimilation of extremely varied population groups under the dominance of the Arabic language, which was in turn closely connected to Islam. Therefore, the relation to Islam also remained ambivalent. On the one hand, the party advocated a strict secularism that was quite attractive for religious minorities; on the other, it understood Islam as a culturally important element of the Arab nation. There are even reports that Aflaq converted to Islam towards the end of his life, but these should be regarded as rumours rather than facts and they have always been denied by his family. It is, however, a fact that Aflaq and al-Bitar conceded Islam a central role in the formation of the Arab nation. Under the roof of this Arab nation, the existence of minorities could indeed be acknowledged, provided that they committed themselves to the Arab nation. In the Ba'athist ideology, Syrian Kurds, Turks, Circassians, or Aramaic-speaking Christians could therefore be regarded as "potential Arabs" if they saw themselves as part of the Arab nation, assimilated themselves culturally and linguistically, and transformed themselves into Arab nationalists.

But the three founders of Ba'athism were repeatedly in conflict with each other right from the beginning. Apparently, Zakī al-Arsūzī fell out with the two other founders early on. He became the co-founder of the Arab National Party (Hizb al-qawmī al-'arabī) and started, after the latter's failure, yet another Ba'athist group that remerged with the group around al-Bitar and Aflaq only in 1947 (Mahr 1971: 26 f.).[3]

From the outset, members of religious minorities were represented, and not just among the founders. By stressing the importance of the Arab nation, they hoped to become a part of the ruling national collective.

The only religious minority that was largely absent were the Jews, who were deterred by the anti-Semitic orientation of the party that was present from the start, and who were seen as something like the "enemy within" of the Arab nation. Although the anti-Semitic elements within the nationalism of the Ba'ath Party were also an expression of the Arab-Israeli conflict, which came to a head in the party's founding year with the UN partition plan in November 1947, they were not simply an exaggeration of the anti-Zionism that was also widespread among other Arab parties. Rather, this was another aspect where the party had taken its cue from Fascist models in Europe and in particular from German National Socialism. After all, the Ba'athists entertained friendly contacts to German National Socialists even long after the end of the "German Reich." The best known example for this is certainly SS-Hauptsturmführer Alois Brunner, who, as the right hand of Adolf Eichmann, was one of the top persons responsible for the deportation of the Jews from Austria, Germany, France, Greece, and Slovakia to the concentration and annihilation camps, who probably came to Syria already in the 1950s and who is reported to have been active as a consultant of the Syrian secret service (in, among other things, "Jewish questions") after the Ba'ath Party came to power. The Syrian regime for a long time denied that he was in the country, but Brunner himself felt carefree enough to give an interview datelined from Damascus to a German magazine. It is certain that he was still in Damascus in the 1980s (Schröm and Röpke 2002: 52 ff.), which is also where he probably died sometime in the course of the last ten years.

A detailed investigation of the anti-Semitism and ethnic nationalism of Ba'athism would lead us too far afield. Of primary relevance for the present book is the fact that Ba'athism actually defended a religious pluralism within the Arab nation and was thus quite attractive for religious minorities (with the exception of the Arab Jews), but that it positioned itself simultaneously against all non-Arab minorities, particularly those who were suspected of harbouring territorial demands and claiming areas the Ba'athists saw as "Arab land." In the view of the Ba'athists, "Arab land" was not just land where the Arabs formed a majority population, but the territory of all Arab states. Ba'athist ideology was thus directed not only against the Jews, but also against the ethnic minorities of Syria, particularly against the Kurds, who, apart from Israel, were seen as the greatest danger to Syria's territorial integrity. Of course, under Ba'athist rule, other minorities, especially the Syro-Aramaic minorities, were also persecuted, if these minorities insisted on an autonomous ethnic and cultural identity and refused to simply be turned into "Arab Christians." However, these kinds of persecution should be seen in the context of the repression of all opposition movements under an extremely authoritarian regime. For the Ba'ath Party, the most important danger to the territorial integrity of the country probably emanated from the Kurds, who had indeed managed to create a relatively strong, competing national movement.

In the 1960s, Ba'athism was not the only Arab-nationalist current in Syria. There also continued to exist Nasserist currents even though they had lost support after the experiment of the fusion with Egypt, and the Arab Liberation Movement (Harakat al-tahrir al-'arabī) founded by Adib ash-Shishakli. But the influence of this latter group could not compete with that of the Ba'ath Party after its leader was driven into exile. In the first free election after the recovery of independence from Egypt held in December 1961, the Ba'ath Party gained 20 seats, while the Arab Liberation Movement won only four.

Overall, however, these elections constituted a defeat of the Arab nationalists. The victors were the two old big parties, the ideologically varied, more or less liberal People's Party (Hizb ash-sha'b) with 33 seats, and the conservative Syrian-national National Party with 21. The Muslim Brotherhood achieved an unexpected success, winning ten seats, a success that was also due to the anti-Nasserist mood in the country. Because no Kurdish parties had run in the elections, all seats in the province of al-Hasaka – and therefore, also the canton of Cizîrê – fell to independent candidates of various ethnic origins. The two seats in the district of 'Ayn al-'Arab (Kurdish: Kobanê) also went to independent candidates, whereas the three seats in the district of Afrīn (Kurdish: Efrîn) were won by three Kurdish candidates of the People's Party. Another independent candidate won in Jarābulus, a mixed district with an Arab, Kurdish, and Turkish population (Oron 1961: 503 ff.).

Ma'rūf ad-Dawālībī became prime minister and Nazim al-Qudsi the new president. Al-Qudsi remained in office until the coup of the Ba'athists and their allies on 7 March 1963 and was thus the last democratically elected president of Syria. But the governments appointed by him turned out to be more short-lived. In March 1962, Bashir al-'Azma became the successor of Ma'rūf ad-Dawālībī. Already in September 1962, he was in turn succeeded by Khalid al-'Azm. The new system remained unstable and soon made itself unpopular through its restorative economic policy. The government tried its best to restore the status quo before the unification with Egypt, and in the course of doing so also reversed the redistributive measures that had actually been very popular among the lower strata of society. The nationalization of banks and various industries was reversed, and there was an attempt to rescind as many as possible of the Nasserist land reforms (Hinnebusch 2001: 43).

Even though the new government was by and large dominated by pro-Western liberal politicians, which pushed the Arab nationalist into the opposition, this democratically elected government undertook one of the most fatal measures against the Syrian Kurds, which has had severe repercussions to this very day. On 23 August President al-Qudsi, influenced by the military, issued decree No. 93, which ordered the execution of a special census in the Jezira.

9

Special Census and Statelessness

Although this special census was ordered by the al-Qudsi government, Sa'id as-Saiyid is generally regarded as its driving force. Unlike the president, the governor of the province of al-Hasaka was regarded as an ardent Arab nationalist who continued to have free reign in the border province even after the preliminary political end of Nasserism. During the special census in the Jezira of November 1962, which had the explicit aim of finding out how many presumably illegal migrants from Turkey lived in the region, 120,000 Kurds were stripped of their citizenship. Apparently, the government in Damascus, which was subject to the strong influence of the military, was too weak or disinterested to intervene against this policy. According to observers,

> [Sa'id as-Saiyid's] justification for the denaturalisations that followed the census was that the "illegal invasion of the Kurds into Syria" was a "conspiracy with the goal of establishing non-Arab ethnic groups within the Syrian crude-oil triangle."
>
> (Kurdwatch 2010a: 6)

The census must be seen in both an intra-Syrian and a regional context. On the one hand, the Syrian authorities tried to use this limitation of Syrian citizenship to as few Kurds as possible to manage the land reforms executed during the United Arab Republic in a way that made it possible to strip as many Kurdish small farmers as possible of the land that the reforms had just given to them. On the other hand, the year 1962 was also a critical one in a regional context. In September 1961, armed insurrections led by Mulla Mustafa Barzani had begun in Iraq. At first, Barzani retreated into the mountain regions of his tribal home in the Barzan valley, but in spring 1962, he went on the offensive and together with 5,000 Peshmerga conquered[1] large parts of today's Kurdish province of Dohuk in Northern Iraq. The government in Damascus was afraid that this region with its close linguistic and historical ties to Cizîrê would be seen as an example by the Syrian Kurds. This is probably one of the reasons why it gave Arab nationalists such as Sa'id as-Saiyid so much leeway in the region.

But the exclusion of the Kurds was not limited to distant Cizîrê. The government of Khalid al-'Azms itself also described the Kurds as a security risk and disqualified them as "infiltrators." The public agitation against the Kurds and for the struggle for the "Arab character" of the Jezira also led to consequences in Damascus itself, where some of the houses in the Hayy al-Akrad were defaced with anti-Kurdish graffiti (Vanly 1992: 151).

Yet the Berlin-based human rights organization Kurdwatch, which is active on behalf of the rights of Syrian Kurds, points out that Sa'id as-Saiyid could also count on local allies, namely, the big landowners, for whom the expatriation of Kurdish small farmers "provided the opportunity to avoid or reverse the confiscation of their estates as envisaged by the land reform. If Kurdish small farmers were to be discredited as 'invaders' and hence lose their claim to a share of the estates, this could work in favour of large landowners" (Kurdwatch 2010a: 6).

However, at first probably *both* Arab and Kurdish big landowners benefitted from the expatriation of Kurdish small peasants. After all, during the land reforms stateless Kurds not only were not assigned any land, but they could also neither buy nor inherit any land and were thus altogether excluded from landownership.

It was the declared goal of the census to find out which Kurds were Syrian citizens and which ones could be categorized as refugees and could thus be deprived of their political and civil rights. In the event, all Kurds in the Jezira had to prove that they or their ancestors had already lived in Syria before 1945, a task that was often impossible to fulfil in a region in which a large number of people still didn't hold certificates of birth. Moreover, the authorities often acted arbitrarily and in some cases conceded Syrian citizenship to certain siblings while rescinding that of their brothers. It is difficult to give an exact number of Kurds who actually lost their citizenship in the process. One number that is generally quoted is 120,000 (Yildiz 2005: 33 f.).

Kurds who were stripped of their citizenship received no more than a white slip of paper that noted that the owner was not on the registration list of Syrian Arabs of the province of al-Hasaka (HRW 1996: 15).

In addition to this group of "foreigners" (*ajnabi*, plural: *ajānib*), there was the group of the "non-registered" (*maktum*, plural: *maktūmīn*), whose status was even lower than that of the *ajānib*.

The status of the *ajānib* and *maktūmīn* was transmitted over decades, which is why statelessness proliferated in Syria. Normally, the status a person had was transmitted via the family's father. Yet in addition, a whole number of marital combinations were not recognized, with the resulting consequences for the status of the children. The only way to pass one's citizenship on was essentially for "a male with Syrian citizenship to marry a stateless female Kurd or a female Kurd with Syrian citizenship" (Wierzbicka 2011: 214).

The children of male *maktūmīn* always also became *maktūmīn*. If the fathers were *ajānib*, their children would also be. But if an *ajnabi* married a *maktuma*, the marriage was not recognized and the status of the mother was transmitted, meaning that the children also became *maktūmīn*. This explains the rise in the number of persons with that status, which was the worst of all.

The current number of *ajānib* and *maktūmīn* is controversial, but it is certainly far larger than the number of persons who were stripped of their citizenship in 1962. Serious estimates for the year 2011 arrive at a number of, altogether, about 300,000 persons categorized as either *ajānib* or *maktūmīn*, which amounts to more than 10 per cent of the whole Kurdish population of Syria. It was only in the context of the protests of 2011 that decree No. 49 of 7 April offered the *ajānib* – but not the *maktūmīn* – the resumption of their citizenship. This measure was probably designed to keep the Kurds away from the opposition's uprisings. With it, the *ajānib* could indeed regain their citizenship, but now they were also, right in the midst of an impending civil war, subject to the draft. The *maktūmīn* are prevented from getting the Syrian citizenship to this very day.

10

The Kurds under Ba'athist Rule

As described above, the relatively liberal period of a multiparty system in Syria did not bring about an inclusive policy vis-à-vis the Kurds. Rather, it excluded them and was, despite formal democracy, characterized by the strong influence of the army. Moreover, on 8 March 1963 it came to an abrupt end. The old Pan-Arabist nationalists who had been overthrown by a regime that was later described as "secessionist" or "separatist" regained power through a coup staged by the army. However, this time, the alliance of the Arab nationalists was not led by the Nasserists, who had been discredited by the period of the United Arab Republic, but rather by young Ba'athist officers, with the later president, Hafiz al-Assad, among them. The Ba'ath Party itself remained in the background at the outset, but was later on able, as the best-organized Arab-nationalist force, to emerge as the strongest faction within the coup coalition. Yet that didn't mean at all that the resulting regime was stable. From July 1963, the Ba'ath Party was the sole power centre in Syria, and, after the destruction of the Nasserists and their influence on the army, did not have to fear any serious competition. However, now there was a period of internal power struggles *within* the Ba'ath Party, which led to a succession of different regimes. From an ideological point of view, these regimes were all Ba'athist, but they belonged to different factions of the party with different economic and social programmes; moreover, they differed with regards to the strength of their roots within the army (Rabinovich 1972: 75 ff.). What did not change, however, in the course of these power struggles was the basic anti-Kurdish and Arab-nationalist orientation of these regimes.

One of the first important anti-Kurdish measures of the new regime was executed in 1965 on the initiative of the director of the security apparatus of the province of al-Hasaka, Muhammed Talab Hilal, namely, the construction of an "Arab Belt" (*al-hizām al-ʿarabi*) in the Jezira. Already in 1963, Hilal had suggested a deportation of Kurds from the border region. In a study that was characterized by anti-Kurdish and anti-Semitic resentment, Hilal had argued that the Kurds were to be regarded as a group that would do everything to create its own homeland, which was why they had to be regarded as enemies despite religious commonalities. There was, supposedly, no difference between Israel and the Kurds, since "Jewishstan" and "Kurdistan" were entities of the same sort (Vanly 1968: 22).

At first, Hilal's suggestion remained secret, but in 1965 it became official policy. It included the creation of a border strip that was 350 kilometres long and 10 to 15 kilometres wide and within which Kurdish villages were to be dismantled and replaced by loyal Arab settlers. According to the original plans, altogether 140,000 Kurds from 332 villages were to be deported to desert regions further in the south (McDowall 2004: 475), a plan that bore an uncanny resemblance to the deportation of the Armenians and the Assyrians in 1915 by the Young Turks, which had a deadly ending for most of them in the deserts around Deir az-Zor.

Even though the original plans were never fully carried out and did not end in genocide, the construction in 1973 of the Taqba river dam across the Euphrates in the ar-Raqqa Governorate did offer the opportunity to transfer the Arab population there to the Jezira.

All this meant that the "Arab Belt" was realized only under President Hafiz al-Assad, who finally turned out to be the winner of the party-internal power struggles in the Baʿath Party in 1970 and formalized his position by having himself elected as president in 1971. With him in power, both the "leftists" and the pro-Iraqi forces had lost the power struggles within the Baʿath Party, which, on the Pan-Arab level, had split into an Iraqi and a Syrian wing in 1966. Whereas Aflaq and Saddam Hussein in Iraq represented the Baʿathist "orthodoxy," Assad was more or less regarded as a pragmatist who reconstructed the Baʿath government in Syria into a regime that was primarily based on the religious minorities, in particular the Alawis. Under Assad, the key positions in the secret service and the military especially were filled with loyal Alawis – mostly those with kin relations to his own family – while in the government itself as well as in the administration and the economy, the Sunni, Christians, Shiites, and Druze quite often also got a fair shot.

Despite – or perhaps precisely because of – the favoured treatment of the religious minorities, Syria under Assad was an extremely repressive regime that tolerated no opposition whatsoever and reacted with extreme brutality to all its opponents. Former Nazi war criminals such as SS-Hauptsturmführer Alois Brunner reportedly passed their knowledge on to the Syrian secret service, and the same was apparently true of the secret services of the GDR and the Soviet Union, countries that Syria under the Ba'athist rule had turned to during the Cold War.

The plan for an "Arab Belt" that went back to the very beginning of Ba'athist rule was resurrected with the completion of the Taqba river dam under the Assad regime. This led to the construction of a total of 41 Arab model villages on Kurdish territory (HRW 2009: 11). Between 1973 and 1976, about 25,000 Arab families were resettled in the province of al-Hasaka (Kurdwatch 2009a: 13).

Even though the Kurdish landowners were expropriated, most Kurdish peasants refused to leave the area. The new Arab villages thus existed in parallel with the Kurdish villages of the region, but they were equipped with far better infrastructure than their neighbouring Kurdish villages and had the reputation of being extremely loyal to the regime. Even today, many inhabitants of the then newly created Arab villages still side with either the regime or the jihadist opposition. At any rate, since 2012 many Kurds have regarded these villages as a security risk within Rojava. The Kurdish parties cannot agree on whether these villages should remain within Rojava or whether the status before the resettlements should be re-established, meaning that the Arab population that immigrated in the 1970s would have to leave. While the PYD is in favour of integrating the Arab settlers into the political system of Rojava, the parties connected to the Iraqi PDK agitate for their resettlement.

Like all oppositional activities, Kurdish political activity was greatly suppressed by the regime. The state of emergency in existence since the coup of 1962 (Galehr 2011: 203) allowed for Syria's reconstruction into a state largely ruled by the secret services, which were in turn directly subservient to the president. But even Assad could not govern by means of repression alone. The regime actually succeeded in economically and politically integrating large parts of the population into a system of patronage and clientelism that was beneficial for many Syrians.

Parts of the Kurdish population were also included in this system of patronage and clientelism. After the Ba'ath Party opened itself to non-Arabs after the so-called "correction movement" of 1970, both individual Armenians and individual Kurds were given important positions. The price for this was strict abstention from any mention of Kurdish identity and particularly from any commitment to each and any kind of "Kurdish cause." Using this strategy, certain Kurds succeeded in attaining high public offices. Thus, from 1972 to 1976 a Kurdish member of the Ba'ath Party, Mahmud al-Ayyubi, even held the office of prime minister.

In the religious realm im particular, the Kurds were able to get important posts. Thus, Ahmad Kuftaru (1921–2004), the Syrian head of the Khalidi branch of the Naqshibandiya, which is widespread in all of Kurdistan, first became the Grand Mufti of Syria and was then, under Assad, totally coopted into the political system. A Kurd was thus able to dominate official Sunni Islam in Syria for 40 years. Ahmed Kuftarus's influence was based not only on his support by the regime, but also on a family tradition that goes back – via his father – to 'Isa al-Kurdi (1831–1912), who played an important role in the reanimation of the Khalidi-Naqshibandiya in Damascus and whose order – which in Syria is also called Kuftariyya after the Kuftari family – formed the religious centrepiece of the Hayy al-Akrad district in Damascus. Quite apart from these factors, however, Ahmad Kuftaru's cooptation by the regime meant that he had a function that went far beyond his tasks as a Mufti. After Assad's ascension to power, Kuftaru was appointed as a member of parliament. His mosque became the centre of the religious charities of the government, and he himself became the mouthpiece of a secular Islam (Weismann 2007b: 118). For the regime, this arrangement was doubly useful: On the one hand, it could thus use a respected proponent of a moderate form of Islam as a mouthpiece against its most dangerous political adversary, the Muslim Brotherhood. On the other hand, it tried to use Sunni Islam as a unifying tie between Kurds and Arabs and thereby to Arabize the Kurds. To a certain extent, what was just said about Ahmad Kuftaru is also true of another Kurd, Shaykh Muhammad Sa'id Ramadan al-Būtī, a theologian of the Ash'aritic school who was born in Turkey and had relations to the Nurculuk movement of the Turkish-Kurdish religious scholar Sa'id Nursi. Shaykh Muhammad Sa'id Ramadan al-Būtī was appointed as the Imam of the Ummayad mosque in Damascus in 2008 and from then on played a role quite similar to that of Ahmad Kuftaru before him. In 2011, Al-Būtī remained loyal to the regime and publicly turned against the protests. In 2013 he was killed in a mosque under circumstances that remain unclear.[1]

Yet all these cooptations of individual Kurds into the power system of the regime were tied to the condition that they didn't insist on their Kurdish identity and didn't pursue any Kurdish interests. In 1973, Assad had Arab nationalism enshrined in the constitution as a basic principle. Under the Ba'athists, Arabic, which was already Syria's only official language, was also to become Syria's only educational language. In 1970, even the Armenian and Assyrian private schools that had up to then been tolerated were either closed or, like all other schools, nationalized. In 1971, however, some of them were allowed to reopen as bilingual schools (Armenian/Arabic) (interview with Thomas Thomasian, 20 February 2014).

Even before the Ba'athists, there had been no Kurdish schools in Syria, and unlike the Armenian and Assyrian schools, now they were not even allowed in a bilingual form. The public schools were designed to be the central location of the Arabization of the Kurdish population (Tejel 2009: 63). Kurdish lessons were organized only privately by the Kurdish parties or by private persons and remained illegal. Moreover, a whole series of decrees were used to suppress the mere use of the Kurdish language. Publications in Kurdish were criminalized, and Kurdish place names were Arabized. The singing of Kurdish songs at weddings, Kurdish concerts, and any other public presentations in the Kurdish language were all banned, and businesses with Kurdish names were forced to Arabize them (McDowall 1998: 47 ff.).

How the regime dealt with rebellions was clearly shown by the armed uprising of the Muslim Brotherhood in Hama, when President Assad simply ordered a bombardment of the city that razed the historical inner city to the ground. According to different estimates, up to 20,000 people were killed in this operation.

On the one hand, the regime counted on the integration of the population into Ba'athist mass organizations, particularly the party itself, but on the other, it also counted on the massive expansion of a security apparatus based on the secret services. Political prisoners were tortured on a regular basis. At least eight different forms of torture were in regular use, among them the tearing out of fingernails, electric shocks on the genitalia or other sensitive areas of the body, or the method of the "black slave" (*al-'abd al-aswad*), in which the victims are stripped naked and placed on a machine, which then rams a heated metal lance into the anus (George 2003: 13).

With its powerful security apparatus and the ruthlessness with which it persecuted any organized opposition, the Syrian regime undoubtedly belonged to the most repressive regimes of the region. At the same time, however, the expansion of the educational system and of a relatively well-functioning welfare state with a high public spending ratio actually garnered it a certain amount of sympathy among the population. Authoritarian regimes can never remain in power by pure repression, but also need some support on the part of the population. What is often described in political science as the *authoritarian bargain* de facto represents the exchange of political rights for greater economic security and the promise of enhanced prosperity (Desai, Olofsgård, and Yousef 2009). In Syria under the Assad regime, this *authoritarian bargain* worked: For a long period the regime was able to undergird the economic rise of a broad middle class. The political and world-economic leeway that the regime needed for "catch-up" development was provided not least by the Cold War. In this, Syria sided with the Soviet Union, securing for itself the military and economic support of Moscow.

Even though, compared to the first phase of the Ba'ath regime, a certain ideological pragmatism found its way into policy under Assad, Arab nationalism still remained its ideological backbone. Kurdish parties and organizations rooted in civil society did not have any place in such a system. Yet unlike the first phase of the radical persecution of Kurdish activities after 1963, under Assad there was a certain normalization of the situation. Kurdish parties were still not legalized and were not allowed any official activities. However, a well-informed secret service that was well aware who held the leading positions in which party refrained from destroying them. Rather, the illegal Kurdish parties were conceded a certain low level of activity, accompanied by informal contacts between the regime and the leaders of the parties. The latter were thereby legitimized to a certain degree as "go-to persons" for the Kurdish population. To what extent the various parties cooperated with the regime remains unclear to this day. But these informal contacts, which some parties entertained more intensely than others, also led to a certain amount of suspicion on the part of the population. The secret service itself also had its own informants within the parties, who were partly known as such and who sometimes held differing loyalties vis-à-vis the secret service and their parties. With regards to the parties, the basic concern of the state was that they would not cross certain "red lines," that none of them would grow too strong, that none of them would demand the independence of Syrian Kurdistan, and that none would dare to sympathize with an open or even armed rebellion. If the parties kept to these red lines, they would remain supervised, but tolerated. If they crossed them, their leading cadres would be arrested, tortured, and brought into line.

At the end of the 1970s, a Kurdish party in the neighbouring state of Turkey brought a series of changes for the Syrian Kurds: In June 1979, that is, even before the military coup in Turkey, the chairman of the Workers' Party of Kurdistan (PKK), which had been founded in Turkey in November 1978, Abdullah Öcalan, fled to Syria, where he found the support of the regime for his struggle against Turkey. After the military coup on 12 September 1980, additional cadres of the party followed him into exile in Damascus, from where Öcalan led his party.

In 1980, the PKK was far from the only leftist group to find a safe haven in Syria. However, it was the one that had been present in the form of its chairman Öcalan since before the coup and thus had better contacts than the groups that arrived only later. Because of the historical quarrel over Hatay, Syria had been in conflict with Turkey since its independence. Yet at this moment the main reasons for supporting armed opposition groups were different. For one thing, Syria and Turkey stood on different sides in the Cold War. Even more importantly, however, Turkey was threatening to increasingly deprive Syria of its scarce water resources with its so-called Southeast Anatolia Project (Güneydoğu Anadolu Projesi, GAP). This development project in the Kurdish regions of Southeast Anatolia, which had been in the making since the end of the 1970s and was begun at the start of the 1980s, accounted for a total of 22 river dams and 19 hydroelectric plants along the Euphrates and the Tigris, both rivers that flow into Syria and Iraq. Turkey thus secured for itself control over Syria and Iraq's two most important sources of water. Even apart from the ecological problems connected with the project, from the outset Syria regarded it as a strategical threat that it then countered with, among other measures, the support of leftist opposition groups in Turkey.

At the end of 1979 or the beginning of 1980, Öcalan arranged for a meeting with Nayef Hawatmeh's Democratic Front for the Liberation of Palestine (DFLP), which, just like the PKK itself, at the time subscribed to a Marxist-Leninist ideology and had been supported by the Syrian regime for a number of years. After a further meeting, the two sides agreed that the DFLP would train some PKK militants in guerrilla warfare in its camps, a form of training that had already been given to Sandinistas from Nicaragua and to Iranian and Greek communists. Even before the military coup in Turkey, the first militants arrived at the Helwe camp in the Lebanese Bekaa valley to receive military training by the DFLP (Marcus 2007: 56).

In Lebanon, the PKK was also able to gain its first battle experience alongside Palestinian armed groups in the course of the latter's resistance to the June 1982 Israeli invasion of Lebanon. From August 1984, this newly acquired military experience was finally brought back into Turkey with attacks on police posts and military installations in the provinces Siirt and Hakkâri. The guerrilla war against the Turkish state had begun. Even though the Syrian regime demanded a certain amount of discretion from the PKK leadership, it supported the latter's armed struggle in Turkey. In 1986, it placed the Helwe camp in the then Syrian-controlled Lebanese Bekaa valley at the disposal of the PKK as its central educational and training facility (Gunes 2012: 99).

A full description of the checkered history of the PKK would go far beyond the scope of this book. Decisive for the Syrian Kurds is the fact that the regime supported the PKK and also tolerated its activities in Syria, because they were directed against Turkey and not against the regime in Damascus. In return for its support by Damascus, the PKK steered clear of any meddling in intra-Syrian affairs. Other Kurdish parties in Syria also accepted the regime's red lines and, in the 1980s, adopted the position that even though there were Kurds in Syria, there was no Kurdistan there. But the PKK went much further than this and adopted the Syrian position "that actually, there were no Syrian Kurds, but only Kurdish refugees from Turkey" (Yalçın-Heckmann and Strohmeier 2000: 166).

All the same, the party managed to attract many younger Syrian Kurds. On the one hand, in the 1980s a certain dissatisfaction developed among younger Kurds with regards to the role of the traditional parties, which many of them now thought were incapable of achieving anything. On the other hand, in the same decade the Marxist-Leninist orientation of the PKK offered an attractive ideological reorientation for leftist Kurdish students and young people in Damascus.

Thus the Kurdish poet Taha Xelîl (Khalil) joined the PKK during his days of study in Damascus together with his boyhood friend Lukman Shekhe. Before, the two had sympathized with Fateh Jamus's Communist Workers' Party, an oppositionist break-away from the Syrian Communist Party that, unlike the latter, was committed to the struggle against the Ba'ath regime and tended towards less dogmatic forms of Marxism.[2] For Xelîl, the combination of the Kurdish question and a clearly Marxist orientation made the PKK an attractive alternative to the existing Kurdish parties. Yet the party leadership of the time found the young intellectuals more difficult to deal with than its supporters from the rural areas. At the beginning of the 1980s, the party chairman Abdullah Öcalan's brother, Osman Öcalan, and some other high-ranking functionaries carried out an anti-intellectual campaign within the party to which Taha Xelîl almost fell victim. Even today, Taha Xelîl still vividly remembers how he was accused of Trotskyism during his training sojourn in Lebanon, and feared for his life. In the camp, he was stripped of his weapons. He and Lukman Sheke were placed under de facto arrest. Yet party proceedings against the two friends were not carried through to the end. The anti-intellectual campaign was stopped at the third party congress in October 1985, and with it the proceedings against Xelîl and Sheke. Both were now given the choice to be rehabilitated and to remain within the party or to depart without further molestation. While Taha Xelîl, after his experience with the proceedings, took the opportunity to leave the party and drew nearer to it again only after years in exile and on his return to Syria, Lukman Sheke remained in the party and was killed in 2002 during the party's armed struggle in Turkey (interview with Taha Xelîl, 20 February 2014).

The biographies of Xelîl and Sheke are but one example for many young people who found their way into the PKK in the 1980s. Many others also ended up fighting with the guerrillas in Turkey and were killed while in the ranks of the PKK. The Syrian regime actually seemed to support this because it served to divert attention from the Kurdish question in Syria itself. The political potential of young, more radical Kurds was thus redirected to Turkey, a country with which the Syrian Ba'ath regime was anyway in conflict.

Even though the regime's primary plan was to use the PKK against the neighbouring country Turkey, it could not thereby prevent the emergence of a new Kurdish self-confidence in Syria itself, with which the regime now had to cope as a "side effect" of the presence of the PKK. Thus, the Kurdish New Year's festival Newroz that up to then had had significance only for a few intellectuals now became an important event for the Kurdish population. In 1986, the regime finally banned the Newroz celebrations, a step that only led to an enhanced participation in them and to an even stronger political character for the spring festival.

On 21 March, thousands of young Kurds wearing Kurdish costumes came together in the Hayy al-Akrad district of Damascus. When the police moved in and proclaimed that the Kurdish festive clothing was forbidden, fighting broke out. The security forces fired into the crowd, leaving one young Kurd dead. His body was later brought back to his family in Qamişlo where 40,000 people participated in his funeral, which thus turned into a political demonstration against the regime. In Efrîn, three Kurds lost their lives and 80 were arrested (Vanly 1992: 128).

On the political level, the regime's close cooperation with the PKK presented it with the danger of partially losing control over some Kurdish areas. In the Kurd Dagh in particular, the PKK in part functioned as a parallel state. In some offices, pictures of Assad were replaced by portraits of Öcalan, and at times, the PKK acted as a kind of para-state. In the early 1990s, the regime felt strong enough to submit a few Kurdish candidates to the parliamentary elections. In the elections of May 1990, the number of independent deputies rose from 35 to 84. In the Jezira, three leading members of Kurdish opposition parties managed to be elected as independent candidates. Kemal Ahmad of the Partiya Demokrat a Kurdî li Sûriyê, Fuad Aliko, who today is active in the Partiya Yekitî ya Kurdî li Sûriyê founded in 1999, and Abdulhamid Hadji Darwish of the Partiya Demokrat a Pêşverû a Kurdî li Sûriyê were elected there. At that time, the Jezira was still dominated by parties that had emerged from the old PDKS, but the Kurd Dagh had long since been controlled by the PKK. In that area, as many as six deputies from the PKK were elected to parliament as independents (Tejel 2009: 67).

The good relationship between the PKK and the Syrian regime only began to change in 1998, when Syria, pressured by Turkey, ordered the expulsion of Abdullah Öcalan. While the Syrian regime still wanted to use the PKK, not least because of the conflict around the water from the Euphrates that was endangered by the Turkish GAP project, Turkey now threatened with a military attack on Syria. This apparently led to a quick decision to sacrifice the PKK. On 21 October 1998, two days of secret negotiation between the two governments began in the Turkish town of Ceyhan. At them, Syria committed itself to cracking down on the PKK and to ending all support of the guerrillas (Hochmüller 2011: 223). But Öcalan had already left Syria on 9 September 1998, and with that, his odyssey through Rome, Athens, Moscow, and Nairobi began, finally ending with his abduction by Turkish agents and his conviction in Turkey. After this the PKK was occupied with internal factional struggles and with processing the loss of its leader. It was thus only in 2003 that the PKK cadres in Syria founded an autonomous Syrian-Kurdish sister party of the PKK, the Partiya Yekitîya Demokrat (PYD). The latter, however, no longer had the support of the regime, and was at times subjected to even more vicious repression than the old Kurdish parties.

11

Between Two Brief Springs
Rojava under Bashar al-Assad

The death of Hafiz al-Assad and the ascent to power of his young, European-educated son Bashar al-Assad in June 2000 at first inspired hope for a liberalization of the political system. And indeed, there was a new activism in civil society, and some long-term political prisoners were released. But the brief "Damascene Spring" ended just one year later with a new wave of arrests of oppositionists, and, particularly from 2003 on, with an even more repressive course of action against the Kurds. As early as 1991, the Syrian regime had been afraid that the autonomy won by the Kurds in Iraq might offer a model for the Kurds in Syria, even though it was simultaneously pleased by the weakening of its intra-Ba'athist rival in Baghdad. With the overthrow of Saddam Hussein, the citation of Syria in George W. Bush's speech on the "Axis of Evil" and the safeguarding of the autonomy of Kurdistan in Iraq in 2003, however, fear of a similar development in Syria turned into one of the central motives for the actions of the regime with regards to the Kurds. With the securing of an autonomous Kurdish entity in Iraq, Syria also seemed to confront the "danger" that in the future, Kurdish demands would carry a greater weight and would aim for a territorial autonomy similar to the Iraqi model.

This background explains the overreaction of the regime that led to the hitherto largest Kurdish rebellion against Ba'ath rule in 2004. The trigger for the unrest was a football game in the 10,000-person capacity stadium "April 7" in Qamişlo, between the teams of al-Futuwa from Deir az-Zor and al-Jihad from Qamişlo on 12 March 2004. The successful club al-Futuwa ("Youth"), which had won the national professional league and the Syrian Championship several times, was known for its Arab-nationalist fans, who included not only followers of the ruling Syrian branch of the Ba'ath Party, but also – probably in part because of the proximity of Deir az-Zor to Iraq – fans of Saddam Hussein. In contrast, the fan base of the club al-Jihad from Qamişlo, which was founded only in 1962, was primarily Kurdish.

The fans of al-Futuwa were allowed to enter the stadium without security checks, even though they were known to be prone to violence. Even before the start of the game, they attacked the fans of al-Jihad with stones and bottles. The false rumour that three children had been killed in the melee triggered a free-for-all both inside and outside the stadium, during which the fans of al-Futuwa shouted anti-Kurdish slogans, hurled insults against the Iraqi-Kurdish leaders Barzani and Talabani and gave cheers to Saddam Hussein. On the other side, the Kurdish fans shouted Kurdish slogans, and both sides attacked each other with stones. In this situation, the Syrian security forces began to shoot with live ammunition, killing nine people. Afterwards, all the Kurdish opposition parties agreed to conduct a joint funeral as a political cortège the next day. The leaders of the parties were assured that the funeral procession would be allowed to take place, provided that it was peaceful. At first this was indeed the case. However, after a few demonstrators began to shout pro-American slogans and started to throw stones at an Assad statue, the security forces started to shoot into the air. Then, at the end of the procession, men in plainclothes fired targeted shots at the demonstrators. Now the situation escalated. There were demonstrations and riots not just in Qamişlo, but also in Amûdê, Dêrik, Serê Kaniyê, and Kobanê, during which offices of the Ba'ath Party were attacked and statues and pictures of Hafez al-Assad were destroyed. On the following day, the riots continued and increasingly also included the Kurdish neighbourhoods of Damascus and Aleppo. The PKK-affiliated TV station Roj TV openly called for rebellion and thus made sure that the protests would continue to spread. The Syrian security forces used live ammunition and fired deadly shots at the demonstrators, which escalated the situation even further. After talks between Kurdish, Christian-Aramaic, and Arab groups on 15 March, during which the Kurdish representatives vowed that the course of action was to be exclusively directed at the regime and not against the other ethnic groups, on 16 March Kurdish parties and Arab human rights organizations jointly called for an end to the violence. Altogether, 33 people were killed by the security forces, and many more were wounded (Commins and Lesch 2014: 275).

In the course of the following days and weeks, between 1,000 and 2,000 people were arrested and tortured. Additional military were stationed in the Kurdish regions. Most parties cancelled their Newroz celebrations and instead summoned their followers to express their mourning for the martyrs with black flags and lapel pins. Only the PKK's sister party the PYD insisted on carrying out its Newroz celebrations.

The repression against this Kurdish uprising led to criticism of the parties by younger Kurdish activists and to a radicalization of young people who were no longer satisfied with the occasional protests of the parties. With the founding of the Partiya Yekîtî ya Dêmokrat a Kurd li Sûriye in 1993, which took a far more aggressive stance than the older parties, and with the end of the cooperation of the PKK with the regime and then the founding of its sister party in 2003, two parties had already gone on the offensive. But it was only the protests of 2004 that sparked hope in a new generation of Kurdish adolescents for a revolutionary solution to their problems. Youth groups independent of the parties emerged in the underground. For the first time, some of these young people even thought about starting an armed struggle against the regime on the model of the Kurds in Iraq, Iran, and Turkey.

In the weeks after the uprising, adolescents in Qamişlo and other Kurdish cities assembled and, on 12 March 2005, clandestinely founded the Kurdish Youth Movement in Syria (Tevgera Ciwanên Kurd, TCK). The new group consciously dissociated itself from the parties and discussed a strategy that included acts of sabotage and an armed struggle against the regime. The founders of the TCK were between 13 and 16 years old and thus represented the youngest generation of activists at the time. Unlike most other parties apart from the PKK and the PYD, the TCK's activists included not just boys, but also girls.

Yet some of the activists of the TCK also became active in a group that, for the first time in the history of the Syrian Kurds, was preparing for a military struggle against the regime, the Liberation Movement of Kurdistan (Kurdish: Tevgera Azadiya Kurdistan; Arabic: Haraka Hurriya Kurdistan). However, these militants were either infiltrated by the Syrian secret service or their existence was uncovered by the PKK – or this is at least the claim of the group's most important founding personality, Hisen Ibrahim Salih, a former PDK Peshmerga who had already been active in Iraq and in Turkey. The mere name of the group, which was founded on 23 March 2005 demonstrated a clean break from the existing parties. As a territorial point of reference, Syria didn't play any role anymore. But most importantly, the group broke with the tradition of partial cooperation with the regime and non-violent forms of political action. The new movement was the first Kurdish grouping in the history of Syria that did not only explicitly call for an armed struggle on Syrian territory, but that also actually executed it. On 10 March 2008, the group began with its armed actions. Hisen Ibrahim Salih, who acted under the *nom de guerre* Tirej Kurd[1], claims that his group murdered a total of 120 members of the Syrian secret service of the police (interview with Hisen Ibrahim Salih, 25 August 2014).

However, quite soon after the beginning of the military operations in 2008, 42 fighters of the organization were arrested in a single blow. Unlike many younger members, however, the much older and experienced Hisen Ibrahim Salih managed to flee. At the time, 16-year-old Munzur Eskan, one of the adolescent founders of the group, was arrested and tortured. Even today, he only reluctantly talks about the details of his torture. When I got to know him in 2013, the torture had left both psychological and visible physical traces. Since his release in 2012, he has had to wear glasses. After his arrest, his family were not informed about his whereabouts for 15 months. In 2013, he told me the following about his experiences in jail:

> All in all, more than 40 of our members were arrested. Even though we were all still teenagers, we were all tortured. Torture is actually par for the course in Syrian prisons. We were tortured by means of electricity, beatings, and waterboarding. But the psychological forms of torture were just as terrible as the physical ones.
>
> (Interview with Munzur Eskan, 11 January 2013)

In 2010, the regime struck a further blow against the remaining members of the organization, as part which Haymat, Munzur Eskan's brother, was also arrested. But Munzur Eskan refused to be broken by arrest and torture. Almost immediately after his release, he started once more to congregate with his friends and participate in the activities of the TCK in protests against the regime.

Even though the TCK was the largest of the political youth groups that began organizing underground after 2004 as a consequence of the regime's repression, it was far from the only one. However, until the beginning of the mass protests of 2011, it was by far the biggest and best-organized youth group, and in 2011, it became one of the most important protagonists of the protests in Rojava.

Quite apart from the founding of various organizations, we can say of the years after 2004 that the repression of young people, particularly in the Jezira, led to the radicalization of a new generation of young Kurds and a crisis in the old Kurdish parties. While the PKK and the PYD remained the dominant forces in the Kurd Dagh and in Kobanê, new political groups emerged both in the Jezira and in Aleppo and Damascus, and increasingly competed with the old party that originated in the PDSK. Moreover, some forces particularly in the Jezira again started to refer favourably to the experiment with autonomy in Iraqi Kurdistan.

After the popular Naqshibandi Sheikh, Muhammad Ma'shouq al-Khaznawi, was abducted on 10 May 2005 and found dead three weeks later, a further wave of protests by Kurdish activists in Syria followed. In the months before his abduction, this progressive cleric, who had been active in the inter-religious dialogue between Jews, Christians, and Êzîdî for years, had also gained increasing prominence as a political mediator between the Syrian Kurdish parties and had clearly gained in political standing. As a respected religious personality, Al-Khaznawi had successfully interlinked Kurdish intellectuals, parties, and religious movements, and was probably regarded as a danger for the regime after 2004. In any case, both his son Mufid al-Khaznawi and most Syrian Kurds attribute his still largely unsolved murder to the regime, and the murder triggered new protests against the regime both in Syria itself and in the Syrian-Kurdish diaspora.

Yet even these protests demonstrated the divisions within the political landscape of Syrian Kurdistan. While the Kurdish Freedom (Azadî) Party, Ismail Ammo's Kurdish Democratic Unity Party in Syria, and Ismail Hami and Hassan Salih's Kurdish Unity Party in Syria organized protests within Syria despite warnings from the regime, most other Syrian Kurdish parties turned against the protests. Particularly active in this was Abdulhamid Hadji Darwish, the party leader of the PUK's sister party, the Kurdish Democratic Progressive Party in Syria, who publicly condemned the demonstrations of the three other parties and tried to organize the other Kurdish parties against Azadî and particularly against the two unity (Yekîtî) parties.

12

The Kurdish Party Landscape

No other part of Kurdistan is home to such a confusing diversity of Kurdish parties and groups – who are often difficult to tell apart from each other – as Syrian Kurdistan. Nevertheless, in order to understand the topical developments since 2011 and 2012, I must at least try to give an overview of this landscape of parties from a present as well as a historical perspective. In the front matter of this book, there is a simplified presentation of the development of the Kurdish parties in Syria.

A large number of the Kurdish parties active in Syria today have developed out of the Kurdistan Democratic Party of Syria (Partiya Demokrat a Kurdistanê li Sûriyê, PDKS) already described. Beginning in the mid-1960s, the party first split into "Left" (Çep) and "Right" (Rast) wings, with the interesting twist that the PDKS Çep remained allied with the tribal and conservative PDK Iraq, while the PDKS Rast entertained connections with the more or less leftist secession of the PDK Iraq under Jalal Talabani and Ibrahim Ahmed, which later called itself the Patriotic Union of Kurdistan (PUK). One reason for this connection was certainly the personal friendship of Abdulhamid Hadji Darwish with his schoolfriend Jalal Talabani.

On the initiative of Mulla Mustafa Barzani in Iraq, in 1970 the two currents decided to reunite, but this attempt at reunification could not be realized and in fact ended with the founding of a third political force that, like the other two parties, called itself the PDKS, but used the addition el-Partî, that is, the definite article el- (al-) in front of the Kurdish term Partî ("party"), trying to make the claim to be "the" party itself. This new party, which was sort of centrist, now became the official sister party to the Iraqi PDK, that is, Barzani's party, a role that it would continue to play, despite various splits, until its unification with the two Azadî parties and the Unity Party of Kurdistan in Syria (Partiya Yekîtîya Kurdistani li Sûriyê) in the spring of 2014.

From the start, the Syrian Kurdish parties' proximity to and even dependence on various Kurdish parties in Iraq and in Turkey has been a feature of the history of the parties of Syrian Kurdistan and has had various consequences for the processes of party development. On the one hand, the Syrian Kurdish parties could thus build on the prestige and probably also the resources of the larger parties in the neighbouring states. On the other hand, they became dependent on them and political decisions and developments in the neighbour states, and were forced to pursue a policy that was not exclusively oriented on Syria (or Rojava). For parties that cooperated closely with the Iraqi PUK and PDK or the Turkish PKK, the latter of which could count on the support of the Syrian regime, this translated into the need to set aside certain goals within Syria itself. Moreover, party splits within the "mother parties" had large consequences for the Syrian Kurdish parties, which more or less emulated these splits. This is one reason for the complex landscape of the political parties in Syrian Kurdistan, which is extremely fragmented even in comparison to other Kurdish contexts.

The remarkable fragmentation of the Syrian Kurdish party landscape is, however, also based on other factors. Unlike the Iraqi, Turkish, and Iranian parts of Kurdistan, in Syria there had never been, with the exception of the brief, failed attempt of the Freedom Movement of Kurdistan (Tevgera Azadiya Kurdistan), any armed struggle by the Kurdish parties. The geographical conditions in Syrian Kurdistan alone[1] would have made an armed guerrilla struggle impossible from the outset. While centralist party structures around charismatic leader personalities were able to develop in Turkey, in Iraq, and in Iran in the context of such military struggles, the Syrian Kurdish parties had to stick to a symbolic policy that put it in a difficult position of mediator between the Kurdish population and the regime.

However, even though this mediating role between the regime and the Kurdish population softened the repression and brought certain advantages for both the regime and the Kurds, it always remained precarious. Since all parties remained illegal and the Syrian secret service always knew about the leadership of the various parties, the parties constantly lived under the Damoclean sword of repression. The existence of the parties was thus predicated on their agreement not to cross the regime's unspoken "red lines" of the regime. Certain activities of the parties were accepted, provided they were not too aggressive and did not demand the overthrow of the regime or the independence of Kurdistan. As long as the parties disseminated their underground literature or provided Kurdish lessons discreetly, such activities were tolerated by the regime. Yet as soon as a party became too aggressive, the regime responded with harsh measures of repression, arresting and torturing party leaders and, if thought necessary, not even refraining from murder. This precarious mediating position was made even more difficult by the fact that these red lines were also subject to change – that is, what was tolerated at one point in time would not necessarily be tolerated one year later. The parties thus had to continually sound out the limits of what was possible. The leftist parties in particular, which pursued a more aggressive policy vis-à-vis the regime, had a harder time with the repression of the secret service than those parties that entertained a closer cooperation with the regime. According to reports, the Kurdish Democratic Progressive Party in Syria was particularly willing to cooperate. It was led by Abdulhamid Hadji Darwish, who was known for his close connections to the boss of the secret service of Qamişlo, General Muhammad Mansourah (Allsopp 2014: 115). On the one hand, he was thus for a long time able to hold the role of an informal speaker for Kurdish parties vis-à-vis the regime, but on the other hand, he was repeatedly accused of being a collaborator.

Criticism on the part of party members of the cooperation of party leaders with the authorities – a cooperation that was by no means only practised by the sister party of the Iraqi PUK, the Kurdish Democratic Progressive Party in Syria – was repeatedly the reason for party splits. Again and again, splinter groups would explain their dissent with their party leaderships with the latter's "collaboration" with the regime.

Another factor in the fragmentation of the Syrian Kurdish party landscape was the direct intervention of the secret service. Even though interventions by the secret service are by their very nature hard to prove and can for the most part be thoroughly evaluated only by future historians, it is quite obvious that the Syrian regime had an interest in the splintering of the Syrian Kurdish party landscape, and that the Syrian Kurdish parties were thus again and again infiltrated by members of the secret service. In many parties, it is even an open secret who is working for the Syrian secret service. Sometimes, such people also take on a function in which they work more or less openly as "double agents," mediating between the secret service and the parties themselves.

It is reasonable to assume, but so far impossible to prove, that the Syrian secret service saw to it that no single party grew too strong but would rather occupy itself with party-internal fights and splits. Foolproof evidence for this will probably be found only after the overthrow of the regime. But Syria's Kurdish population generally assumes that at least some of the parties are infiltrated by the Syrian secret service, an assumption that led to an increasing scepticism vis-à-vis the parties in the years before the uprising of 2011. Many intellectuals and artists who had earlier been active in parties have distanced themselves from them in recent years. The fact that more and more independent youth groups and initiatives have emerged since 2011 can also be seen as a consequence of this increasing trend within the population to turn away from the parties.

Yet another factor in the strong diversification of the party landscape that needs to be mentioned is the structure of the parties themselves. Due to their illegality, all Syrian Kurdish parties are characterized by an extremely weak party structure. Almost all parties are organized in a clandestine system of party cells in which only the members of small groups even know each other. No larger meetings are held, and it is impossible to create permanent structures that are transparent to members. The parties therefore very strongly depend on individual people who are located at certain junctions and who maintain contacts with other party cells. Such a structure leads to a lack of opportunities for discussing the political orientation and strategy of a party and creates many predetermined breaking points that become particularly pertinent when, for example, a long-term party leader dies. In Syrian parties, successor questions are almost always "solved" by party splits. In addition, such a structure hardly enables any change in leading positions. The party bosses of the Syrian Kurdish parties often hold their positions for many decades. Thus, the Kurdish Democratic Progressive Party in Syria and its predecessor party, the PDKS (Rast) have been led from 1965 until today by Abdulhamid Hadji Darwish. Salih Gado first led the Kurdish Socialist Party in Syria from 1977 to 2002 and has then been the leader of the Kurdish Leftist Democratic Party in Syria since 2012. The PDKS chaired by Abdurrahman Aluji had been led by him until his death in 2012 and then split. Only a few parties can boast of any real rotation in their leadership.

Be that as it may, the confusing diversity of the Kurdish parties in Syria cannot really be explained by political and ideological differences. Actually, it is striking how similar the political demands of the various parties have been over time. Even though there were different emphases in their programmes, before 2011 hardly any party demanded autonomy for Syrian Kurdistan. Even today, no single party is demanding the independence of Kurdistan and its secession from Syria. The differences between "rightist" and "leftist" parties are often of more of a stylistic than a substantive nature. Right into the 1990s, a precarious coexistence with the regime had developed among most of the Syrian Kurdish parties that became more and more unattractive for the younger generation of activists. This drove many Kurds either into the arms of the PKK, whose activities were directed towards Turkish Kurdistan (a trend that was approved by the regime), or towards new forms of political practice. Already in 1993, with Ismail Ammo's Kurdish Democratic Unity (Yekîtî) Party in Syria, a party had emerged that was politically much more aggressive and that, together with its break-away parties, brought a new style to Kurdish politics in Syria. The demonstrations organized by these parties and their far more aggressive behaviour also increasingly changed the performance of some other parties.

Even though all traditional parties are actually products of the historical PDKS, since 2003 several significant exceptions have emerged that can be regarded as an expression of a crisis of this traditional party system. In 2003, Syrian members of the PKK who had remained in the country after the break of the regime with the PKK and the expulsion of Abdullah Öcalan founded their own Syrian sister party. With the founding of the Democratic Union Party (Partiya Yekîtiya Demokrat, PYD), the old PKK members for the first time truly entered the framework of Syrian politics. In the following years, the regime's repression was particularly strongly directed against these erstwhile allies. On the model of the party it came from, the PKK, the PYD adopted a relatively strong party structure, but even this could not prevent it from being affected by the propensity to split so common to almost all Syrian Kurdish parties. Even in the very year of its founding, a group seceded from the PYD and founded the Syrian Kurdish Democratic Reconciliation (Rêkeftina Demokrat a Kurdî ya Sûri).

Yet another new creation outside of the tradition of the parties coming out of the PDKS was represented by the Kurdish Future Movement (Şepêla Pêşerojê ya Kurdî li Sûriyê) started by Mishal at-Tammu (Kurdish: Mişel Temo) in 2005. This movement sought increased cooperation with Arab oppositionists and was already focused on the overthrow of the regime at the start of the "Arab Spring" in 2011. But the fact that this movement, which was particularly strong in Qamişlo, strongly depended on its charismatic leader showed itself after the latter's murder in 2011, which dealt a heavy blow to the group and led to its split into two factions.

The various parties sharply differ with regard to their presence in the three Kurdish enclaves. The historical PDKS had its base primarily in the Cizîrê, in the Kurd Dagh, and in the Kurdish neighbourhoods of Damascus and Aleppo, but was barely represented in Kobanê. The successor parties of the PDKS were mainly concentrated in Cizîrê. The political vacuum in Kobanê was then filled in the 1980s by the PKK, whose sister party, the PYD, to this day has its stronghold in this city, which is also the hometown of the party's chairman, Salih Muslim.

In the Kurd Dagh region in today's canton of Efrîn, the PKK superseded el-Partî, the Kurdish Left Party in Syria, and the Kurdish Popular Union Party in Syria as well as the other PDKS successor parties in the 1980s. But the latter organizations never completely disappeared from the region. Both the two Yekîtî parties and the new PDKS, which was reunited in 2014, are still represented in the canton of Efrîn, even though they are weaker there than in Cizîrê. After the PKK had already temporarily carried out government functions in the region in the 1980s, the area is now dominated by its successor organization, the PYD.

Without democratic elections, it is of course impossible to give any serious estimates on the majority relations among the Syrian Kurds. It is, however, remarkable that the parties coming out of the PDKS and the Kurdish Future Movement are much stronger in Cizîrê than in the two other cantons, and that in Kobanê hardly any other party is present than the PYD.

The excessive party splits in the Syrian Kurdish party landscape have been regarded as problematic not just by the Kurdish population, but also by the parties themselves. This led to the founding of the first party alliances in the form of umbrella organizations already in the 1990s. In 1992, Abdulhamid Hadji Darwish's Kurdish Democratic Progressive Party, Ismail Ammo's Democratic Unity Party, Muhammad Musa's Leftist Party, and Nusruddin Ibrahim's PDKS founded the Hevbendi ya Dêmokrat a Kurdî li Sûriyê (Hevbendi) with Abdulhamid Hadji Darwish as its speaker. This was followed in 1996 by the Eniya Demokrat a Kurdî li Suriyê (Eniya). In these two alliances, the influence of the neighbouring states on Kurdish parties was once again visible. While Hevbendi acted under the leadership of Abdulhamid Hadji Darwish's sister party of the PUK, the Eniya parties came together under Abdulhakim Bashar's sister party of Barzani's PDK Iraq. The relaxation of the conflict between the PUK and the PDK in Iraq after the overthrow of Saddam Hussein eased the way for an accommodation between the two alliances. This enabled the joint signing of the Declaration of Damascus by the parties of the Hevbdendi and the Eniya in 2005.

Following these developments, in 2006 the parties that belonged neither to Hevendi nor to Eniya, namely, the Kurdish Freedom Party (Azadî), Ismail Hami and Hassan Salih's Kurdish Unity Party (Yekîtî), and the as Kurdish Future Movement formed the Komîta Tensîqê ya Kurdî (Komîta Tensîqê).

The PYD and its break-away Rêkeftina remained outside of these party alliances, which themselves remained relatively stable until the beginning of the protests in Syria.

13

From Revolution to Civil War

As is well known, the protests that spread to Syria following the revolutions in Tunisia and Egypt in the spring of 2011 at first had their origin in Dar'ā in the south of Syria and then fanned out primarily to the Arab parts of Syria. Even so, the impression – also spread by many Arab oppositionists – that the Kurds at first abstained from the protests is deceptive. In fact, Kurdish political actors reacted in very different ways to the protests in the Arab parts of Syria. In Amûdê and Serê Kaniyê, protests that explicitly echoed protests in other parts of Syria were already taking place in the spring of 2011. In Amûdê, spontaneous protests happened as early as 27 March, meaning that the city began to rise up against the regime almost simultaneously with the protests in Dar'ā in Southern Syria that today are regarded as the beginning of the protests in Syria. After prayers on the following Friday, 1 April 2011, Amûdê saw the first organized demonstration against the regime (group interview with Tansiqiya Amûdê, 12 January 2013). Serê Kaniyê and other cities in Cizîrê followed suit.

In the meantime, the regime tried to appease the situation, at least in Kurdistan. At the beginning of April, President Assad proclaimed that the stateless Kurds would get their Syrian citizenship back. Decree No. 49 of 7 April 2011 gave all *ajānib*, that is, all those who were regarded as foreigners, but not the non-registered *maktūmīn*, the right to citizenship.[1] This measure may have weakened the protests in the Kurdish areas at first and may have been seen by many Kurds as a sign that change within the regime might be imminent. It was, however, insufficient to prevent the protests more permanently.

The organization of the first demonstration in Syrian Kurdistan did not originate in a Syrian Kurdish party, but from young men who organized in small groups and soon began to call themselves *Tansiqiya*

(Arabic for coordinating committee), like their counterparts in other Syrian cities. While participation in the protests was relatively strong from the outset in Amûdê, and the parties of the Komîta Tensîqê (Future Movement, Azadî and Yekîtî) supported the protests from the start, participation in other cities at first remained fairly weak. The other Kurdish parties likewise seemed to be in a mode of wait and see and did not yet participate in the spring protests of 2011. When the Syrian National Council (SNC) constituted itself as the umbrella organization of the Syrian opposition at a national salvation conference in Istanbul in July 2011, the only Kurdish party to participate was the Kurdish Future Movement. Its leader Mishal at-Tammu was elected as a member of the executive council of the SNC and thus took over a central mediating position between the Arab and the Kurdish opposition.

This key position was probably also the undoing of this party leader, who was very popular among the younger Kurds in Qamişlo. Mishal at-Tammu had already been convicted to three years in prison in May 2009 on account of paragraphs 285 and 286 of the Syrian penal code ("undermining of the reputation of the state" as well as "weakening of the national sentiment" and the "morals of the nation"), but this repressive measure only enhanced his credibility in the eyes of young Kurds. On 8 September 2011, he became the target of a first assassination attempt, and on 7 October he was finally shot and killed in his hometown Qamişlo by four unknown assailants. The crime has never really been solved. Some functionaries of the Future Movement accused the PYD of having been responsible for the murder (interview with Siamend Hajo, 10 August 2014), an accusation the PYD vehemently denies. For its own part, the PYD accused either Turkey or the regime in Damascus of having been behind the murder. In fact, the regime had a lively interest in the elimination of an important mediator between the Arab and the Kurdish opposition, but of course it could also have used Kurdish perpetrators for the deed.

During his lifetime, Mishal at-Tammu had not succeeded in convincing other Kurdish parties to join the SNC. Instead, intense activities developed among the other parties to found their own comprehensive umbrella associations of the Kurdish opposition. After the murder of Mishal at-Tammu, the protests in Syrian Kurdistan turned into a mass movement. His funeral became the biggest anti-regime demonstration ever in Qamişlo, a development that put the other Kurdish parties increasingly under pressure to finally act if they didn't want to lose their connection to the quickly developing protest movement.

On 26 October 2011, after long negotiations and under the mediation of Masud Barzani, the parties that came out of the historical PDKS agreed on the founding of a Kurdish National Council (Encûmena Ni timanî ya Kurdî, KNC) in Erbil. The KNC was certainly the hitherto most extensive alliance of Syrian Kurdish parties. After the accession of three member parties of the Union of the Kurdish Democratic Forces in Syria founded by the Future Movement – namely, the Yekîtî Kurdistani, the Rêkeftin, and one of the PDKSs – at the beginning of 2012 the KNC consisted of 16 different parties in total.

There were, however, two significant exceptions: the Future Movement, weakened by the death of its leader, remained a member of the SNC and stayed away from the KNC; the PYD also refused to participate. In fact, the important mediating role that Masud Barzani had played in the establishment of the KNC only served to increase the distance between the PYD, which was anyway in rivalry with the Kurdistan Regional Government, and the parties in the KNC. Indeed, the reconfiguration of the Kurdish party landscape occurred at the time of an intensified intra-Kurdish power struggle between the PDK party bloc led by Masud Barzani and the PKK party bloc, both of which laid claim to the leading role in all of Kurdistan.

The PYD increased its activities to create its own administrative structures and competing oppositionist alliances. At an all-Syrian level, the PYD had already founded a National Coordination Committee for the Forces for Democratic Change (NCC) in September 2011, which comprised 12 smaller leftist Arab and Syro-Aramaic opposition parties[2] and took a relatively pragmatic stance towards the regime right from the beginning. Led by Hassan Abdel Azim of the Democratic-Arab Socialist Union and the human rights activist Haytham Manna, the NCC negotiated with the regime of Bashar al-Assad and tried to bring about change by means of non-violent protests. Unlike most other opposition groups, the NCC rejected both a violent rebellion and an international military intervention. For this stance, the NCC was harshly criticized by the other opposition groups and was repeatedly accused of being a kind of front organization for the regime. The NCC in turn accused the other opposition alliances of plunging the country into a civil war and being dependent on Turkey or other foreign suppliers of funds. Because of the militarization of the conflict that had indeed taken place since 2012, the

NCC lost its importance outside of Rojava, but even so, with hindsight, its criticism of the militarization of the revolution seems to have been vindicated.

Be that as it may, at least since the founding of the Syrian Democratic Forces (Hêzên Sûriya Demokratîk, SDF) in October 2015, the NCC seems to have lost its significance for good. Though the alliance was never formally dissolved, it was de facto replaced by the military alliance of the YPG with its Arab, Turkmen, and Christian allies, that is, by the SDF.

Even though the negotiations of the NCC with the regime did not lead to any systemic change, they brought about at least some smaller reforms. Thus, in the course of the year the regime released a whole number of political prisoners of different orientations. Apart from jihadist prisoners who belonged to the core of the armed jihadist groups Ahrar ash-Sham, Jabhat al-Nusra, and "Islamic State,"[3] a number of political prisoners of the parties belonging to the NCC were also released. Among these were also hundreds of political prisoners of the PYD.

On 16 December 2011, the PYD announced the founding of a People's Council of West Kurdistan (Meclisa Gel a Rojavayê Kurdistanê), which was supposed to be an alliance, but, apart from the PYD itself, de facto only comprised PYD front organizations, such as its women's organization Yekîtiya Star, or its civil society umbrella association Tevgera Civaka Demokratîk (TEV-DEM). In actual fact, the People's Council of West Kurdistan thus became an umbrella organization of the PYD and its own mass and front organizations.

While the Kurdish parties conducted their respective alliance policies, many younger Kurds remained active on a local level and organized protests against the regime. These were supported by some of the parties of the KNC, but as in other parts of Syria they were spearheaded by young people not bound by any party politics, who began to organize themselves in local committees and youth associations. In Rojava, one needs to mention in this respect the Movement of the Kurdish Youth TCK that had already emerged in the course of the protests of 2004, and the new Coordinating Committees of the Kurdish Youth (Yekîtiya Hevrêzên Ciwanên Kurd, YHCK). The demonstrations by these youth groups were directed, in an all-Syrian context, against the regime and additionally raised specifically Kurdish demands. Thus, on 30 December 2011, there were demonstrations in almost all important Kurdish towns of Cizîrê (Qamişlo, Amûdê, Dirbêsiyê, Tirbesipî Dêrik, Serê Kaniyê) as well as in Kobanê; they were part of a Syria-wide day of protest under the slogan "March to the squares of freedom."

The old parties were not the driving forces of these dynamic developments, but rather jumped on the bandwagon. Generally, all these demonstrations took place after the Friday prayer. But this does not mean that the demonstrations had any religious character or were attended only by Muslims. On the contrary, particularly in mixed towns such as Qamişlo and Dêrik, one could see symbols of Aramaic-Assyrian groups at the demonstrations right from the start. However, as in all of Syria, the Friday prayer made it possible for a large crowd that had already assembled to jointly begin their march. For the Syrian security forces it was harder to prevent such demonstrations than ones in which the participants first had to find an independent mechanism by which to assemble.

In the course of the autumn of 2011, the town of Amûdê, which, unlike Qamişlo, is inhabited almost exclusively by Kurds, turned into a stronghold of the protests. At the same time, it served as an early example of the political differentiation of the Kurdish opposition. After November 2011, three separate and competing regular demonstrations took place in the town that were all directed against the regime, but at the same time also served as a testing ground for the intra-Kurdish majority relations. During the autumn of 2011, the following three demonstration alliances formed in Amûdê and were then able to sustain themselves in a similar arrangement until 2013:

1. A demonstration organized by the Tansiqiya Amûdê. Since the election of the Amûdê resident Abdulbaset Sieda as the successor of Burhan Ghalioun to the office of the President of the Syrian National Council (SNC) on 10 June, this demonstration increasingly included the Kurds who supported the SNC and the Free Syrian Army.[4]
2. A demonstration supported by the parties of the Kurdish National Council (KNC), particularly by the Yekîtî and Azadî parties that were very strong in Amûdê, but also joined by the adherents of the other member parties of the KNC.
3. A demonstration of the PYD and its front organizations represented in the People's Council of West Kurdistan.

When I joined the demonstrations in Amûdê on a Friday in January 2013, this picture, which had been well-practised since the autumn of 2011, was still present. The demonstrations of the KNC parties and the PYD were attended by 2,000 demonstrators each, while that of the Tansiqiya Amûdê and the SNC supporters was attended by approximately half that number.

In the first half of 2012, the protests continued in some parts of Rojava. Unlike other parts of Syria, in the Kurdish regions there was no armed fighting, just individual deaths due to the actions of the military and the Syrian security forces against demonstrators.

On a diplomatic level, the Kurdistan Regional Government in Iraq tried to mediate between the various Kurdish factions in Syria. After protracted negotiations, a six-point agreement between the PYD and the KNC was signed in Erbil on 11 June 2012. On 1 July, the parties agreed on a seventh point, namely, the founding of a Supreme Kurdish Committee that was to function as an umbrella organization and, in case of the liberation of Rojava, as a transitional administration of West Kurdistan jointly supported by the KNC and the People's Council.

In the course of the first half of 2012, the regime's war with the Free Syrian Army in Homs, Aleppo, and the south of Syria increasingly escalated, and it thus needed military resources to fight the oppositionists in the Syrian heartlands. Apparently, in this situation there was a point when there were secret talks between the PYD and the Syrian regime about a withdrawal of the latter from Rojava.

The backgrounds of this withdrawal have remained unknown to his day. While PYD functionaries claim to have issued an ultimatum to the government to withdraw and to have threatened to open a new front against the regime in the north should it reject this, functionaries of the parties organized in the Kurdish National Council accuse the PYD of having collaborated with the regime and having entered into secret agreements with it. The accusation against the PYD is that the latter allegedly agreed to a division of labour with the regime in exchange for the latter's withdrawal and that it obliged itself to ensure calm in Rojava and guarantee the security of important military installations.

Which of the two versions is closer to the truth will hopefully one day be realistically assessed by historians. At the moment, there is no accessible evidence for either one version or the other. As a matter of fact, between 19 and 25 July the regime left most parts of Rojava – that is, Cizîrê, Efrîn, and Kobanê – to the PYD-founded People's Protection Units (Yekîneyên Parastina Gel, YPG) with barely a fight and with the Syrian army withdrawing from the region while leaving large parts of its equipment and ammunition behind. Even so, it still controls strategically important points in the town of Qamişlo, such as the airport, the train station, and some official buildings, a military camp south of the town, and the Arab district. The regime and the Syrian military also retained their presence in the ethnically mixed provincial capital of al-Hasaka.

Since that time, the YPG and the Women's Protection Units (Yekîneyên Parastina Jin, YPJ), which are conceived of as an autonomous women's army, jointly control the areas of Syria with a Kurdish majority population. Until the introduction of the draft for men in the cantons of Cizîrê and Kobanê, both the YPG and the YPJ were voluntary armies among whose soldiers the YPJ, according to the PYD, represented approximately one third of the fighters, making it also of military relevance. Since the introduction of the draft for the YPG, which took longer in Efrîn than in the other cantons (interview with Hevi Ibrahim Mustefa, 2 February 2015; interview with Ebdo Ibrahim, 3 February 2015), this relation has of course changed in favour of the men, because the YPJ, as opposed to the YPG, still remains an army of volunteers.

It is difficult to imagine that such a largely peaceful handover and the continued presence of the Syrian military at strategically important points were possible without any previous accords. At the very least, there had to have been agreements between the PYD and the regime on the details of the handover. For the time being, however, whether the PYD promised the regime any rewards and if so, which ones, or whether it was simply in the interest of the regime to free military capacities for the politically and militarily more important regions in central Syria must remain in the realm of speculation.

Whatever talks and agreements may have occurred in the background, the result was that since the end of July, the largest part of Cizîrê, Efrîn and Kobanê, as well as the Kurdish districts of Ashrafiyah and Sheikh Maqsoud (Kurdish: Şêxmeqsûd) in Aleppo were no longer controlled by the regime, but were in the hands of Kurdish forces.

In Aleppo, this situation had developed because of the military escalation between the regime's Syrian Arab Army and the FSA, which led to the establishment of a front line right through the centre of the city. In order to prevent fighting within the Kurdish neighbourhoods, the Kurds declared themselves to be neutral and saw to it that neither government soldiers nor FSA fighters were able to intrude into the two directly adjacent districts. In the course of 2014, the Kurdish fighters step by step retreated from Ashrafiyah, de facto stealthily handing the neighbourhood over to the Syrian government army. Yet in the neighbourhood of Sheikh Maqsoud, the YPG was able to hold its ground even after the end of the battle of Aleppo in December 2016. Even though Sheikh Maqsoud has since been surrounded by government troops, until 22 February 2018 it was able to hold its ground as an autonomous quarter (interview with Rêdûr Xelîl, 14 February 2017).

Apart from the Syrian areas controlled by either the regime or the opposition, there was now a third entity, which, however, was split into three regions and one city district in Aleppo and which, furthermore, had to struggle with massive intra-Kurdish conflicts.

1 Qamishli under Hafez al-Assad: Under the strict control of the regime Assyrian and Armenian Christians, Arab and Kurdish Muslims and Jews offered their products in the Bazar of the largest town of Rojava. (1999)

2 After the death of the last Jew of Qamishli in 2013 the Synagogue is the only relic of the once vibrant Jewish community. (2014)

3 From 2011 to 2013 in every town different Kurdish political movements protested against the regime: Demonstration of the Kurdish National Council (E.N.K.S.) in Amûdê in January 2013.

4 Demonstration of the PYD in Amûdê in January 2013.

5 With the unilateral establishment of autonomous cantons by the PYD the Kurdish National Council lost much of its influence: Demonstration of the E.N.K.S. in Qamishli in February 2014

6 Women´s gathering of the ruling PYD in Qamishli in February 2014.

7 The Cizîrê canton has a very mixed population and a lot of old Christian villages. One of the oldest churches in the region is Bara Baita church in the village of Khan Yunis/Birabê near Dêrik. (2014)

8 Mart Shmone Syriac Orthodox church in Dêrik with a poster for the Syrian Orthodox Archbishop of Aleppo Gregorios Johanna Ibrahim and the Greek Orthodox Archbishop of Aleppo Boulos Yazigi who were abducted by militants in April 2013. (2014)

9 From 2012 until 2013 the frontline between Arab rebels, jihadist militias and the YPG/YPJ went through Ra's al-'Ain/Serê Kaniyê. Since then the town has been in the hands of the YPG/YPJ. (2016)

10 The towns of Rojava are full of small shops and workshops: Car mechanic in Dirbêsiyê. (2016).

11 Since August 2014 Êzîdî refugees from Sinjar/Şingal live in Newroz-Camp near Dêrik. (2016).

12 Internally displaced persons from Aleppo wait to get a job as day labourers in downtown Efrîn. (2015)

13 Hevi Ibrahim Mustefa, prime minister of Efrîn in her office. (2015)

14 Funeral of a YPJ-fighter in Efrîn. (2015)

14

Military Developments since 2012

Compared to Syria's other theatres of war, the areas under Kurdish control didn't change much after the summer of 2012, at least at first. What did change, however, were the neighbours of the three enclaves. While in the summer of 2012, for the most part they bordered areas that were either held by the regime or by units of the Free Syrian Army, in 2013 this situation changed. The military gains of jihadist parties in the civil war, particularly of the Jabhat al-Nusra and the so-called "Islamic State" (IS), which had referred to itself as "Islamic State in Iraq and Greater Syria" until the conquest of Mosul and the declaration of a Caliphate on 29 June 2014, led to a situation where, in the course 2013, the two eastern regions of Cizîrê and Kobanê were increasingly encircled by jihadists and, within Syria, were completely locked in by IS. Responsible for the security of the Kurdish areas were the People's Protection Units (YPG), which were mostly founded by the PYD and were massively influenced by it. Outside the core zone of Rojava, the PYD-associated fighters did not operate as YPG, however, but as the "Kurdish Brigade" (Arabic: Jabhat al-Akrad, Kurdish: Enîya Kurdan), which had originally acted as part of the FSA, but had been expelled in August 2013 because of conflicts between the PYD on the one and the FSA and the SNC on the other hand. This militia, which consists of several thousand fighters, still operates today in the Kurdish quarters of Aleppo and in the regions outside the core zone of Rojava. In addition, since January 2013 Syro-Aramaic Christians, who had united in the Syriac Military Council and had joined the YPG one year later, also fought alongside the YPG and the Jabhat al-Akrad. The same was true for militia of the Arab tribe of the Shammar and the Sharabiyya.

The YPG had their first harsh military clashes as early as 19 November 2012, when fighting between the FSA and the YPG erupted in Serê

Kaniyê, a town that had been partitioned between the opposing parties since the beginning of that month. In these battles, the jihadist groups Jabhat al-Nusra and Ghuraba ash-Sham fought on the side of the FSA. After a few days, a fragile ceasefire was brokered, followed by renewed fighting in January, which the YPG finally won after suffering heavy losses. In July 2013, the YPG succeeded in driving the jihadist fighters out of Serê Kaniyê for good and in pushing the border of the territory under Kurdish control further to the west and beyond the city limits. In the process, the Kurdish fighters of the Jabhat al-Akrad advanced to Tal Abyad (Kurdish: Girê Sipî), a town inhabited by Arabs, Armenians, and Kurds. On 20 July the Kurds even succeeded in capturing the regional commander of ISIS.

In the other parts of the canton of Cizîrê, the YPG was also able to register military successes against the jihadist groups and to moderately expand the territory under Kurdish control. At the end of October 2013, the YPG was able to capture the strategically important border checkpoint of Tal Koçer (Yarubiyah). On 25 October the YPG spokesperson Rêdûr Xelîl tweeted:

> The Border gate of Tal -koçer City (AL-Yarobyah) Now liberated and under our units control, ongoing battles in the city centre.[1]

In the following days, the YPG succeeded in completely driving the ISIS fighters out of the city. Thus Rojava now had a direct connection to the areas in Iraq controlled by the government in Baghdad. For the PYD, this conquest also represented an important trump card in the intra-Kurdish conflict because the latter regularly led to closures of the "intra-Kurdish" border further north near Semalka between the regions of Kurdistan in Iraq and Rojava. The new development introduced a potential alternative to the Kurdistan Regional Government in Iraq. On 28 October, the YPG succeeded in capturing the important oil-producing region of Çil Axa with its villages of Girhok, Yusufiyê, Sefa, Cinêdiyê, Girê Fatê, Ebû Hecer, and Mezraa Kelem. The fighters of ISIS then retreated into the mostly Arab region around Tal Brak and Tal Hamis, which now remained the last jihadist stronghold in Cizîrê. In November 2013, the YPG succeeded in pushing ISIS further back from the surroundings of Serê Kaniyê and in capturing a series of Kurdish and particularly Aramaic-Assyrian villages and small towns in the vicinity of al-Hasaka.

In 2014, there was also heavy fighting for control of Tal Brak and Tal Hamis. However, announcements by the YPG that Tal Hamis had been captured on 1 January turned out to be premature. In fact, the Kurdish fighters had to retreat after a few days and suffered heavy losses. In February, the YPG started a new offensive jointly with the fighters of the Arab Shammar tribe allied to them. However, the Sharabia tribe dominating in Tal Hamis belongs to the old rivals of the Shammar in Cizîrê and was therefore probably loyal to ISIS. While the local Arabs – mostly Shammar – had supported the expulsion of ISIS during the conquest of Tal Koçer (Yarubiyah), in Tal Hamis most members of the Sharabia took a hostile stance towards the Kurdish attackers. Unlike the Shammar, the Sharabia have arrived in Cizîrê only relatively recently. Whereas the Shammar have been living together with the Kurds and Assyrians of the region for centuries, the Sharabia were settled there only in the 1970s by the Ba'ath regime. These Arabs, who were resettled in the regions only as a result of the Ba'athist Arabization policy, are regarded as overwhelmingly anti-Kurdish and are either still Ba'athists, or jihadists. This is probably an important reason for the losses of the YPG and the Shammar during these battles for Tal Brak and Tal Hamir. On 23 February, Tal Brak was at least taken by the YPG, but it proved impossible to expel IS from Tal Hamis.

In March, fighting erupted around Tal Abyad, a town between the two Kurdish cantons of Cizîrê and Kobanê that at the time was held by IS, but in whose surroundings some Kurdish villages were under the control of the YPG. In Kobanê itself, however, the military situation turned out to be considerably more difficult. The region is much smaller and had been, with the exception of the sealed border with Turkey, totally encircled by ISIS since the beginning of 2014. In the nearby city of Jarābulus, which had been inhabited by Kurds, Arabs, and Turks as early as Ottoman times, oppositionists of the Free Syrian Army had taken power on 20 July 2012. In the summer of 2013, ISIS conquered the town for the first time, only to be replaced later on by Jabhat al-Nusra. On 18 January 2014, ISIS again captured power in the city and thereby secured for itself the strategically important border crossing to Turkey. Two days later, the new rulers shut off the water and power supply for the approximately 300,000 inhabitants of the Kurdish canton of Kobanê. Both the town and the region have been living under a de facto state of siege since January 2014. On 30 May 2014, 186 students who were travelling from Kobanê to Aleppo for their examinations were abducted by ISIS.[2] On 2 July 2014, the group, which by then had taken to calling itself "Islamic State," started a major offensive against Kobanê, during which it captured several villages and murdered many civilians who didn't manage to flee in time. In the process, the jihadists came to within 15 kilometres of the city. By mid-July, the situation for the Kurds looked so threatening that a military draft for all men between 18 and 30 years of age was introduced, a step that was later also taken by the other two cantons. With the help of volunteers from Turkey and with the support of the FSA, it proved possible to push back the attacks and to save the canton at least for the time being. Even so, the situation in the besieged canton remains precarious. There is hardly any clean drinking water, there is no power, and the health care system has partially collapsed.

To describe all the battles in detail would lead us too far afield. Yet even this rough overview of the military situation shows that in Cizîrê, the Kurds, with the support of Arab and Christian-Assyrian allies, have proved themselves able to hold their ground very successfully. Though they could not prevent various military pinpricks and terrorist assaults by IS reaching even right into Qamişlo, killing both civilians and fighters of the YPG or the Asayîş (the Kurdish police forces), the YPG and their allies largely succeeded in defending their area militarily. In August 2014, the YPG even had military capabilities left that enabled it to come to the help of the Êzîdî at the Jebel Sinjar (Kurdish: Çiyayê Şingal)[3] who were under attack from "Islamic State" and had largely been abandoned by the Iraqi Peshmerga, and to establish corridors for them through which they could flee from Iraq to Syria.

Yet the protection that the Syrian-Kurdish YPG gave to the endangered Êzîdî at the Jebel Sinjar in August 2014 led to a situation where the PKK party bloc, in its rivalry with the Kurdistan Regional Government in Iraq, could also, for the first time, gain sympathies among the Iraqi Kurds. The PUK had already been slowly moving closer to the PKK/PYD in the preceding months. By then, the common enemy even seemed to pave the way to some sort of dialogue between the respective party blocs of Barzani and the PKK. But whether this dialogue will endure is quite doubtful. Even now, in the Iraqi Sinjar there are clear lines of conflict both between the Peshmerga and the YPG and between the two Êzîdî units, the Resistance Units of Singal (Yekîneyên Berxwedana Şingal, YBŞ) which are close to the PKK, and the Defence Force of Singal (Hêza Parastina Şingal, HPŞ) under its commander Haydar Şeşo, which, since 2015, has called itself the Defence Force of Êzîdxan (Hêza Parastina

Êzîdxan, HPÊ) (Schmidinger 2016b: 42). In March 2017, attempts by Barzani's PDK to oust the allies of the PKK from the region finally led to armed battles between the Rojava Peshmerga of the Kurdish National Council in Syria deployed in the region by Barzani and the YBŞ, which in turn led to retaliatory actions in Rojava against members of the Kurdish National Council in Syria.

At exactly the time when the YPG made an important contribution to the salvation of the Êzîdî of Şingal, there were already signs of an increasing threat from IS further in the west of Syria. The situation in Kobanê already looked very dangerous in the summer of 2014. Although a first offensive in summer could be beaten back, this was only the beginning of a humanitarian catastrophe.

On 16 September 2014, IS started a further major offensive against Kobanê during which it succeeded in capturing all villages of the canton and a large part of the city of Kobanê itself. In full view of the international public that had mounted its cameras on a hill on the Turkish side of the border, the town was destroyed, while the desperate fighters of the YPG and the YPJ tried to defend themselves against the jihadists. In the town itself, there was bitter fighting over each row of houses. It was only massive international pressure that forced Turkey on 20 October 2014 to allow Kurdish Peshmerga from Iraq and secular units of the FSA to come to the aid of the completely encircled Kurdish fighters. On 29 October these forces reached the trapped fighters of the YPG and the YPJ after having crossed Turkish national territory. Apart from 160 fighters of the Iraqi-Kurdish Peshmerga, more than 300 fighters from brigades of the Free Syrian Army also fought alongside the Kurds of the town. Members of the Raqqa Revolutionaries' Brigades, the al-Qassas Army hailing from Deir az-Zor, and the Jarābulus Brigade, all three of which belong to the spectrum of the FSA in Northern Syria, struggled jointly with the Peshmerga, the YPG, and the YPJ against the onslaught of IS on Kobanê. Among the jihadist attackers, there were also a number of international jihadists, among them a certain Firas Houdi from Austria, who had already gained a certain amount of fame among Austro-jihadists and who died in January 2015 during the battle of Kobanê. But international fighters did not fight exclusively on the side of the jihadists. Provoked by international attention on the fighting, a number of European and American volunteers also joined the *defenders* of Kobanê.

Yet militarily, probably neither the Peshmerga, the FSA, nor the international volunteers played a decisive role. Most likely, that was a prerogative of the airstrikes by the United States, which, at the last moment, prevented an IS victory. After initial coordination problems, after November 2014, the US Airforce and the YPG managed to arrange for very well targeted airstrikes against IS positions and to maintain very good cooperation between the YPG forces on the ground and the US forces in the air. The Kurdish fighters were able to relate the precise coordinates of IS positions, the latter of which were then attacked by planes of the US Airforce. Additionally, supplies dropped from the air were able to reduce the impact of the scarcity in ammunition and arms suffered by the defenders. In January and February 2015, the fighters of the YPG and the YPJ were thus able to bring about a reconquest of the whole canton. However, the price for this was terribly high: The town was destroyed, and since Turkey continues to keep the border to Kobanê closed, its reconstruction proceeds only very slowly. Thus one of the most important demands of the canton administration continues to be that Turkey opens its border to Kobanê. Even after the reconquest of the town, the president of the parliament of Kobanê, Aisha Afandi,[4] accused Turkey of still using the sealing of the border to pursue the goal of isolating the canton and obstructing both humanitarian supplies and visits by journalists or commercial contacts (interview with Aisha Afandi, 4 February 2015).

While the Kurdish YPG and YPJ desperately tried to defend the city, most civilians fled into Turkey. According to Kurdish sources, in February 2015 about 180,000 people from Kobanê lived as refugees in Turkey. At the beginning of 2015, more than 67,000 refugees lived in Suruç alone, which is a small town of less than 55,000 inhabitants. At the time, the centre of the town was full of men from Kobanê who were trying to get information about their villages or were looking for jobs as day labourers.

Most of the refugees in Turkey were accommodated in camps set up by organizations of the Kurdish movement. A big camp organized by the Turkish government was from the start virtually empty. Those who lived there had in part simply been forced to go there. The government camp was surrounded by a double row of concertina wire and was located far away from any other settlements. The camps run by the Kurdish movement were located in the city or at least close by. Those who were hosted in these camps were not isolated but part of the Kurdish population of the region.

Kurdish NGOs and some municipalities governed by the pro-Kurdish HDP in the border region played an important role in coordinating aid

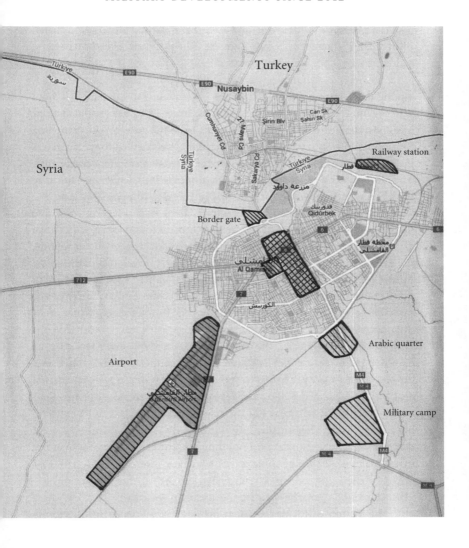

The situation in Qamishli/Qamişlo since summer 2012

Under Kurdish control (PYD/YPG)
Under government control (Syrian Army)
City centre (contested)

deliveries both to the refugees and to Kobanê itself. The HDP-governed municipality (belediye) Suruç and the Kurdish Red Crescent became central actors in the coordination of the aid for Kobanê (McGee 2016: 64).

In February 2015, 3,000 refugees still lived in the camp of Arîn Mirxan, among them 1,706 children and adolescents under 17. A makeshift school was organized in a tent, where teachers from Kobanê continued their lessons in the Kurdish language. The refugees in the government camp had to learn Turkish, and there, a big Turkish flag clearly demonstrated who was in command. In the Arîn Mirxan camp, the Kurdish movement dominated. The refugees housed here were often highly politicized, which explains why the larger part of the refugees there have returned to Kobanê since 2015.

However, their return was accompanied by massive problems. The houses and infrastructure of the town had been totally destroyed. Since Turkey continues to keep the border closed for any traffic of goods, the reconstruction of the city is still faced with severe difficulties. The military successes of the YPG, which was even able to advance further in the direction of Tal Abyad after the liberation of the canton, can thus not directly contribute to the improvement of the humanitarian situation of the population of Kobanê.

In Kobanê itself, it took the canton administration only a few months to reopen two emergency hospitals, a mill, and a bakery. There are, however, still severe problems with the supply of water, power, medicine, and building materials. To this day, there has been no decision as to whether the town will be rebuilt in its original form. In the PYD, there have been voices that suggest leaving the city in its condition of total destruction as a memorial and building a completely new town nearby instead. However, many inhabitants who had held out in the city and a part of the returnees are strenuously opposed to these plans and are instead trying to remake their houses as well as possible.

In the canton of Efrîn, the situation was more stable, but there, the main opponent was not "Islamic State," as this Kurdish canton mainly bordered areas of the FSA, the Islamic Front, and the Shia enclave of Nubl and al-Zahraa,[5] which was always under the control of the regime. Here, the Kurds, with their contacts to both the opposition and the government, have been able to mediate between the two factions of the civil war to end the mutual kidnappings of Sunni and Shiite citizens and to achieve an exchange of prisoners.

In Efrîn, however, there have long been worries concerning the increasing dominance of Jabhat al-Nusra in northwestern Syria. The old FSA has almost ceased to exist in the region and even the political Islamist militias that make up the Islamic Front and that range from groups from the Muslim Brotherhood to jihadist groups have continually lost ground since the beginning of 2015. Since the spring of 2015, the al-Qaida-affiliated group Jabhat al-Nusra has dominated the region. The jihadist militiamen of Jabhat al-Nusra were stationed at the southern border of the canton as early as 2013, but from 2015, they also took over the part of Aleppo held by the opposition as well as large parts of the province of Aleppo. From March 2015 on, Jabhat al-Nusra succeeded in exerting total control over Iblib, a provincial capital, and in increasingly building in their territories their own para-state structures, including Sharia courts. Only civil resistance in the areas under the control of Jabhat al-Nusra led to a containment of the jihadists. In the end, the latter formally separated from al-Qaida and renamed themselves Jabhat Fatah al-Sham. Yet for Efrîn, the most important security guarantee was the military defeat of the rebels in Aleppo, who had come to be dominated by the jihadists, in autumn 2016 and the focus of the battles on the country's second largest city. In the course of the rebel's defeat, the YPG and their allies finally succeeded in expanding their territory to the east at the beginning of 2016.

When the regime, on 3 February 2016, succeeded in breaking the circumvallation around the Shiite enclave of Nubl and al-Zahraa, thus connecting it with the part of Aleppo held by the regime and, at the same time, cutting the connection between the rebel area of Azaz and that in Aleppo, a competition began as to who would exert future control over the areas previously held by the rebels and IS and that were inhabited by Arabs, Turkmens, and Kurds. The offensive of the YPG/YPJ against the rebels in Azaz was probably primarily inspired by the conjecture that should the government army break through all the way to Azaz this would make a future connection between the Kurdish cantons impossible and thus any further advance of the government had to be prevented.

On 15 February 2016, the YPG/YPJ took over the town Tel Rif'at south of Azaz with its 20,000 inhabitants and also captured the southern part of the remaining rebel enclave around Azaz. In the process, the YPG, supported by the Russian Airforce, also conquered the Jabhat al-Nusra airbase Menagh, an event of probably enormous importance for the supply of the isolated enclave. However, the town of Azaz itself was not taken by the YPG.

The Kurdish advance against the Turkish allies then led to the intervention of the Turkish army. On 19 February 2016, Turkish artillery started to pound the city centre of Efrîn from Kilis and Sucuköy west of the town, killing two civilians. In addition, the villages of Deir Ballout, Hamam, Kafr Janneh, Meşalê Hêgicê, Senarê, Anqelê, Firîrê, Hec Hesnê, and Avraz were fired at, killing three members of a family. The Turkish army went 300 metres into Syrian territory and destroyed around 500 olive trees in order to close the whole in a concrete wall at the Syrian border.

In Syria itself, the SDF's US allies exerted pressure on the Kurds not to advance any further to the east in order not to provoke Turkey. After this, the small town of Mari' represented the most southwestern point of the area of Azaz held by the groups of the Islamic Front.

Yet the YPG/YPJ's far more spectacular military successes since 2015 have occurred in the east of the Kurdish areas. To an important degree, they are thanks to military support from the US, but also from France and Germany. The reconquest of Kobanê at the beginning of 2015 marked the turning point in the war. From Kobanê, the YPG/YPJ and their allies then advanced further to the east in the direction of the border town of Tal Abyad, still held by IS. This region has an Arab majority population, but there is also a Kurdish minority, and until the conquest of Tal Abyad by IS it had also been host to an Armenian community. It represented one of the most important supply lines of IS from Turkey. Officially, the border in the city of Akçakale/Tal Abyad, which had been divided since the Treaty of Lausanne in 1923, was closed, but in fact there was a state of peaceful coexistence between Turkey and IS that made it possible for the latter to get an ample supply of fighters, weapons, ammunition, and so on. A large number of the jihadists from Europe also came to IS first from Urfa and then via Akçakale and Tal Abyad.

Here, on 15 June 2015 the YPG/YPJ and the FSA succeeded in establishing a connection between the two cantons of Cizîrê and Kobanê and in expelling IS from the border with Turkey. How precarious the security situation in the region continued to be, however, is shown by the fact that between 25 and 28 June 2015, an IS commando succeeded in advancing into the city of Kobanê and in murdering more than 200 civilians in the town itself and in one of the neighbouring villages. At the same time, the YPG/YPJ and their allies finally succeeded in totally expelling IS from the territory of the canton of Kobanê in the battle of Sarin between 18 and 27 June 2015.

However, NATO member Turkey's insistence that the YPG/YPJ is a sub-group of the "terror organization PKK" made military support from the US for the YPG/YPJ increasingly problematic. For that reason, US military officers and diplomats had been working in the background for some time to bring about a broader alliance that included the YPG/YPJ but that could be viewed as a regional ally whose support by the US would not be seen as direct support of the YPG/YPJ.

The founding of the Syrian Democratic Forces (SDF, Quwat Suriya ad-dimuqratiya, Hêzên Sûriya Demokratîk) on 10 October 2015 was an important precondition for further military and political cooperation with the US against "Islamic State." Apart from the Kurdish units YPG, YPJ, and Jabhat al-Akrad (Enîya Kurdan), the SDF also comprises the Turkmen "Battalion of the Northern Sun" (Kata'ib Shams ash-Shimāl), the Arab "Army of Revolutionaries" (Jaish ath-thuwar) and "Brigade of the Revolutionaries of Raqqa" (Liwa thuwwur ar-Raqqa), the militia "Quwat as-Sanadid" organized by the Arab tribe of the Shammar, the Syriac Military Council that had been allied with the YPG since 2014, and several additional smaller secular units from the former Free Syrian Army. Despite the continuing military and political dominance of the YPG and YPJ, the SDF thus represented the "ecumenical" alliance that the US had again and again mentioned as a precondition for its military support. The alliance also enabled the US government to argue to its NATO ally Turkey that it was merely lending its support to a broader military alliance and not directly to the YPG/YPJ.

Thus, the way was paved for the open military support of the United States, which, since the end of 2015, had acted more and more as an airforce for the SDF and had sent military advisors to the battlegrounds. Already on 12 October 2015, that is, two days after the founding of the SDF, the Pentagon confirmed that US transport aircraft had dropped 100 pallets with 45 tons of arms and ammunition for "Arab groups" in northern Syria, "Arab groups" being a reference to the newly founded alliance. This delivery of ammunition and arms happened a few days after the US had admitted the failure of its "Train and Equip Programme" for the arming of "moderate rebels."

From the al-Shaddadah offensive in February 2016 on, during which the SDF advanced in an area south of al-Hasaka and conquered the small town of al-Shaddadah, the US Airforce acted as the de facto airforce of the SDF. On-site special units seem to have been in direct communication with the airforce and to have coordinated the latter's strikes against IS.

In the process, the frontline against IS could be relocated considerably to the south, wresting Syria's most important oil production areas from IS control. Since the fall of the town of al-Shaddadah on 19 February 2016, almost the whole province of al-Hasaka has been under the control of the Kurds and their allies in the SDF.

The successes of the military alliance led to further gains by secular and tribal militias that slowly reduced the dominance of the YPG and the YPJ, which had been extreme at the start. The new Arab allies were also urgently needed to permanently secure the areas not inhabited by Kurds, but Arabs. After the conquest of Tal Abyad (Girê Spî) in June 2015, the YPG and the YPJ needed Arab allies to prevent a situation in which they were rejected as occupiers by the Arabs of the towns and villages that they had recently captured. The massive expansion of the territory to the south made the integration of Arab units into the alliance of the SDF all the more important.

Until the summer of 2016, the SDF were able to liberate almost the whole province of al-Hasaka as well as neighbouring northwestern parts of the province of Der az-Zor. Until early 2018, when the SDF had to stop their operations against IS due to the Turkish attack against Efrîn, IS could only defend a small strip of the northern side of the Euphrat valley from Hajin to the border of Iraq and some isolated Arab villages in the Markada subdistrict of al-Hasaka province.

In January 2016, the SDF finally advanced to the area west of Kobanê and across the Euphrates (which Turkey had always designated as the "red line" for the advance of the YPG) and established its permanent control of the Tishrin dam. Based on this bridgehead, Kurdish and Arab units of the SDF advanced further to the west and on 10 July besieged the town of Manbij. In a long and costly battle, the SDF finally succeeded in entering this IS stronghold and in completely expelling IS by 13 August. In order to avoid provoking Turkey, the SDF appointed a "Manbij Military Council" (MMC) dominated by Arab units that was supposed to be in charge of the area. Yet this step did not prevent Turkey from military attempts to forestall the establishment of a corridor between the Kurdish cantons of Kobanê and Efrîn.

In the early hours of 24 August 2016, Turkish troops and allied Syrian rebels advanced on Syrian national territory near Jarābulus and conquered the town, which had hitherto been under the control of IS, within a single day. This event is also remarkable in that there was hardly any fighting. While the SDF had to fight over Manbij further in the south for more than a month and had to take heavy losses, IS handed Jarābulus over to Turkey practically without a fight. Kurdish observers regarded this as an indication that this was actually not a conquest, but rather, a handover of the city that Turkey and IS had agreed upon. In the course of just a few days, Turkish troops advanced still further to the south and west, connected the area of Jarābulus with the area near Azaz that was still held by pro-Turkish rebels, and began to advance in the direction of Manbij. The first battles between Turkish soldiers and their rebel allies with units of the SDF were able to be stopped by the mediation of the US, even though the Turkish government denied having agreed to a ceasefire "with the terrorists" – a term by which they mean not just the PKK itself, but also the Syrian-Kurdish PYD and the YPG/YPJ.

That the US was able to mediate so successfully was based on its increasing military importance for the SDF since the battle of Kobanê. In 2016, the most important contact partner for the SDF was Brett McGurk, the "Presidential Envoy for the Global Coalition to Counter ISIL (IS/ISIS)" appointed by President Obama. Since 2016, US special units and military advisors have also played an increasingly important role on the ground. In April 2016, 150 US special troops officially arrived in Rojava.[6]

At the beginning of March 2017, the *Washington Post* reported the arrival of several additional hundred US marines in Syria who were supposed to promote the capture of the IS capital of ar-Raqqa jointly with the SDF.[7]

How many additional foreign military troops are in the region is not entirely clear. What is certain, however, is the presence of French special units, which have established a military basis in the proximity of Kobanê. Kurdish eyewitnesses have also reported German special units in Rojava, but the German government denies this. After the regime declared that the presence of German and French troops was an "unjustified aggression," the German Ministry of Defence again officially disclaimed the presence of German soldiers in Rojava.[8]

Quite independently of the question whether German participation in the support of the SDF can be proven, the presence of French and US soldiers and military advisors is definitely of enormous strategic significance and has had an increasing influence on the military-strategic decisions of the SDF. Diplomatic disagreements with Turkey were impossible to avoid in the process. Photographs of US soldiers in YPG/YPJ uniforms angered the Turkish government, which led to an order in May 2016 that US troops were no longer allowed to wear YPG insignia.[9] Since the end of 2015, the military airport of Rumelan southeast of Qamişlo was again used by the US airforce. In 2016, an additional US airforce base was established near the village of Sabit about 35km south of Kobanê. In November 2016, McGurk announced on Twitter that the first US soldier had been killed in Rojava.[10]

The political price for the military support of the US has been high: Instead of focusing on the corridor between Efrîn and Kobanê as originally planned, the troops of the SDF had to turn to the south against the de facto capital of IS. At the beginning of the spring of 2017, SDF troops stood at the gates of the city of al-Raqqa and had already advanced to the Euphrates east of the town. The latter was then to be attacked from the west, north, and east. At the same time, the race for the corridor between Efrîn and Kobanê played out to the detriment of the Kurds because of the conquest of al-Bab by pro-Turkish units on February 2017 and the conquest of Tadef by the government army on 26 February 2017. According to YPG spokesperson Rêdûr Xelîl, the fact that this corridor was not conquered in the end was due to political and not military reasons (interview with Rêdûr Xelîl, 14 February 2017).

In order to avoid an escalation with the Turkish troops, in mid-March 2017 the SDF handed a part of the area they had conquered east of Manbij over to the Syrian government army. For the time being, the villages in this 5km wide and 20km long strip remained politically a part of the Federation Northern Syria – Rojava, but the SDF hoped to prevent Turkey from further attacks by having Syrian government troops stationed between themselves and the pro-Turkish militia. After all, such attacks could now lead to a confrontation between the two government armies.

That the SDF have by no means simply become an extension of the US and Western Europe, but still try, despite all consideration for the interests of the allies, to hedge their bets with regard to all sides is shown not just by their handing over of this corridor to the Syrian government army, but also by their 19 March 2017 agreement with Russia that will enable this strongest ally of the regime to establish a presence in Efrîn. While the Kurdish side talked about the creation of an airbase,[11] the Russian Ministry of Defence merely confirmed the establishment of an outpost of its "Reconciliation Center"[12] right at the fault line between the SDF and the pro-Turkish rebels.[13] In the end only a small outpost of the "Reconciliation Center" was established.

Among the Kurdish population, the decision to subordinate oneself to the wishes of the US and the French allies between Efrîn and Kobanê in order to avoid a confrontation with Turkey and thus to relinquish the conquest of the corridor between the Kurdish areas was just as controversial as the conquest of the Arab-speaking areas earlier held by IS. While the motivation to defend the Kurds' own settlement areas was high, and far beyond the party basis of the PYD, many Kurds do not appreciate the need to fight and die for "the Arabs."

Yet the SDF and the YPG/YPJ still form a military alliance with the US, an alliance that so far has also continued under the presidency of Donald Trump. With all this, the United States find themselves in a delicate political and military situation. On the one hand, the NATO member state Turkey shows itself increasingly angered by US support for troops that Ankara regards as part of a "terror group." On the other hand, since 2017 the US has also increasingly been caught between the Kurdish factions.

The long-simmering conflict between Barzani's PDK in Iraq and its Syrian allies on the one hand and the PYD/PKK and their Iraqi allies, particularly the Êzîdî Resistance Units of Şingal (Yekîneyên Berxwedana Şingal, YBŞ), on the other escalated during the night of 2 to 3 March in the Iraqi village of Khanasor. In this small place on the northern side of the Şingal mountains, units of the Rojava Peshmerga, that is, troops of the Kurdish National Council in Syria equipped and trained by Barzani's PDK, tried to expel the YBŞ. During the fighting that ensued between Rojava Peshmerga and the YBŞ, there were casualties – dead or wounded – on both sides before the US managed to broker a ceasefire. Later on, the intra-Kurdish party conflict between the PKK party bloc and the PDK supporters once more escalated, but this time in Rojava. In the first two weeks after the confrontation in Şingal, more than 40 functionaries and activists of the parties of the Kurdish National Council were arrested. Between 14 and 16 March, more than 44 party offices of opposition parties in various towns of Rojava were closed, among them not just offices of member parties of the Kurdish National Council, but also of Abdulhamid Hadji Darwish's Kurdish Democratic Progressive Party, which had quit the KNC in 2015, and of Gabriel Moushe Gawrieh's Assyrian Democratic Organization, an Assyrian party founded as long ago as 1957.

The United States, which has long supported the PDK-led Kurdistan Regional Government and is thus now supporting both parties to the conflict, therefore now has an increasingly important mediating role in the intra-Kurdish conflict.

However, the support of the US turned out to be no security guarantee at all, especially not for the western part of Rojava. In the second half of

2017 it turned out that Russia and the US did find some kind of (secret) agreement that the US would be allowed to act with the SDF northeast of the Euphrates, while Russia's sphere of influence would be to the southwest of the Euphrates. That meant that the SDF had to cooperate with Russia in the region of Efrîn, while cooperating with the US in the regions northeast of the Euphrates. While US troops were present in a growing number in the east of the Kurdish region, Russians used the Menagh military airbase under control of the SDF in Efrîn.

Thus it was a deal between Russia and Turkey that enabled the Turkish government to start a ground offensive against the Kurds of Efrîn in January 2018.

After months of threats and minor attacks against villages in the Efrîn region, the Turkish military was finally allowed by Russia to attack Efrîn in January 2018. Together with their Arab-Syrian allies Turkey started started Operation Olive Branch (Turkish: Zeytin Dalı Harekâtı) in the night of 19 to 20 January 2018. The ground offensive in Efrîn was accompanied by artillery attacks against several towns in the Cizîrê region, including Qamişlo, Serê Kaniyê, and Amûdê in the days after the start of the operation. While France and the US publicly denounced the Turkish attacks nobody prevented the Turkish Army and their jihadist allies from conquering Efrîn in March 2018.

However, this big strategic picture does not reflect the local relations of forces everywhere. Regionally, the situation often looks much more complex. In many cases, the precarious calm depends on local agreements between tribes and families. Underneath the official policies of parties and militias, there is an interplay of shadow diplomacy and shadow economy that even led to a situation in 2014 where the fuel needed by the enclave of Kobanê when it was beleaguered by IS was bought from that very same IS, and where certain similar forms of trade between multiple parties in the civil war have been in operation to this day. Many of these forms of local exchange and local ceasefire agreements are arranged on an informal level. In the final analysis, however, even in the two largest cities of the region, al-Hasaka and Qamişlo, there is a continuously changing, precarious equilibrium between different regional actors.

Since 2012, the provincial capital al-Hasaka was de facto divided in three parts. The Kurdish-dominated city parts were managed by the Kurds and controlled by the YPG and Asayîs. The Christian-Aramaic- and Armenian-dominated parts of the town and the city centre were in part under the control of the regime and in part controlled by the Kurds, while the Arab parts were administered in part by the regime and in part by the FSA and Jabhat al-Nusra, and since 2014 IS. In the summer of 2014, the province capital was still divided into these three parts. The regime by then had only the city centre and a few military installations left under its control. In January 2015, fighting broke out between the YPG and the government army, but by July 2015 the YPG and the government had already resumed their joint battle against IS. August 2016 then saw the most violent fighting between the regime and the YPG in al-Hasaka, which ended with the almost complete withdrawal of the government troops from the provincial capital on 23 August. The ceasefire brokered with Russian mediation provided only for a symbolic presence of the regime in the town with lightly armed police units, but no military.

In Qamişlo, the largest part of the town is ruled by the Kurds, but militarily important installations such as the airport, the train station, and a military camp south of the town are still under the control of the regime, just as the gateway to Turkey, some administrative facilities in the centre of the city, and the Arab district in the south of the town are. The latter is predominantly inhabited by the Arab tribe of the Tai who had shown themselves to be loyal to the regime. In the strict sense, no one has total control over the actual historical city centre. There is rather a precarious, unspoken agreement between the parties not to attack each other. Downtown, the symbols of the regime are still on public display. The Armenian community centre is decorated by a widely visible figure of Hafez al-Assad. The synagogue is also adorned with a portrait of the late president, and the widely visible statue of Bashar al-Assad's brother Bassel al-Assad, who died in 1994, still stands at a very busy intersection. A Syrian flag in the form used by the regime continues to fly over his father's original favourite successor, who is sitting high on horseback.

Both the regime and the YPG and Asayîş try to give each other a wide berth in the city centre and to avoid any potential showdown. Yet a mere visit to the old town demonstrates that the Kurdish actors are not really sure whether the mutual sufferance can be trusted. When I visited Qamişlo in 2014 in the company of the PYD and expressed my wish to conduct an interview with the Armenian community and to visit the synagogue in the centre of the city, both of these visits in the city centre were characterized by visible nervousness on the part of my attendants. They insistently emphasized that we should not leave the car and pointed to the example of a US journalist who the Syrian secret service had arrested in the city centre just a couple of weeks ago but who could be liberated by the Kurdish Asayîş before being carted off by the officers. Yet it was not just western journalists in Qamişlo who had to be afraid of being arrested by the forces of the regime. In November 2013, the Military Intelligence Service had arrested the well-known Kurdish hip hop singer Sharif Omari. On 18 December, a taxi driver and his five passengers were arrested in Qamişlo by security forces of the regime, followed by two activists of the TCK on 29 December and by a Syrian journalist of the Iraqi-Kurdish TV station Rûdaw. Even high-ranking PYD politicians concede in interviews that they do not have control over all of Qamişlo and that the Syrian regime continues to be present.

The situation in Qamişlo is further complicated by the fact that in the town there is a splinter group of Christian-Aramaic militia that, on the whole, cooperates with the YPG, but whose faction in Qamişlo works with the regime. In the town of Dêrik, the Christian-Aramaic police unit Sutoro is subordinated to the Syriac Unity Party (SUP) and cooperates with the Kurds, but in Qamişlo its units have split away and have allied themselves with the regime. Even though both are spelt the same way in Arabic and Aramaic, in Latin transcription the pro-regime militia in Qamişlo spells its name "Sootoro." Both identically named militia now use different insignia and symbols and to this day stand on different sides in the conflict between the Kurds and the regime.

In January 2016, there were armed altercations between Sootoro and the YPG after a jihadist attack on a Christian-Assyrian restaurant at the end of December 2016. Before, the Assyrians had accused the Kurds of failing to protect the Assyrian parts of the city.

On 20 April 2016, there followed altercations between government soldiers on the one and Asayîş and YPG fighters on the other side. On the same day, the Sootoro also intervened in the fighting, taking the side of the government. Both sides were supported by a number of fighters of various Arab tribal militias that were partly allied with the regime and partly allied with the YPG. The fighting finally ended in a draw after the death of more than 50 people, a dozen civilians among them, and the destruction of a city block; on 22 April a ceasefire went into effect that led to a return to the status quo.

Renewed armed fighting on 23 November 2016, during which two people were killed in Qamişlo showed the precarious character of this armistice.[14]

The continuing presence of the regime is probably one of the reasons why the small Armenian minority is still ostentatiously loyal to the regime. The pictures of Assad, the Assad cardboard character on the wall of the community centre and the use of Syrian flags during the commemorations for the victims of the 1915 genocide all show that the Armenians do not want to alienate the regime. Just as everywhere else, the Armenians of Qamişlo observe their commemoration day on 24 April. As before, in 2014 they carried a big Syrian flag in the form also used by the regime, alongside an Armenian flag, through the streets of the city. The particularly large commemoration of 2015 that memorialized the 100th anniversary of the genocide was accompanied by similar demonstrations of loyalty to the regime.

Yet the regime continues to be present not just in the form of the military and the secret service, but also as an employer, and not just in Qamişlo, but in all of Rojava. All schools and all civil servants are still paid by Damascus. The relevant professional groups are thus personally dependent on the regime and therefore vulnerable to pressure. Teachers who organize demonstrations against the Ba'ath regime are still being fired. In 2015, school certificates in Rojava still carried the picture of the president. School lessons are based on the schoolbooks of the regime. At the beginning of the school year 2015 this was changed for Kurdish children, who since then have had their own Kurdish schools, where the Kurdish alphabet is used. Only from the fourth grade on are lessons also given in Arabic and English. However, the schools for Arab students are still operated by the regime and accordingly use the regime's curriculum.

Apart from the regime, adherents of the "Islamic State" are also present in Rojava. Even though they are too weak to occupy areas inhabited by Kurds, in the Arab villages of the region there are not only "followers" of IS and other jihadist groups, but also active fighters who carry out terrorist acts against Kurdish facilities. Thus, there have been repeated suicide attacks on Asayîş checkpoints. In January 2014, jihadists in Arab villages south of Qamişlo fired surface-to-surface missiles at the airport of Qamişlo (which was, however, held by the regime), with several missiles hitting Kurdish residential quarters. One of the most devastating attacks occurred in Qamişlo on 11 March 2014, when eight civilians were killed and five more were wounded during an attack on provisional Kurdish administrative offices. Among the dead was the freshly married daughter of the poet Taha Xelîl, who was seven months pregnant and who the poet had named Helepçe[15] in memory of the poison gas attacks on Halabja.

15

Political Economy in the Civil War

Compared to other parts of Syria, the PYD-founded YPG and the Asayîş are quite successful in keeping the civil war away from the Kurdish civilians, a fact that is also recognized by many Kurds who are not members or sympathisers of the PYD. But the safety established thereby is very precarious and does not mean at all that the civil war does not affect Rojava.

The proximity of the war also has massive consequences for the economy of Rojava. All three cantons had previously been important producers of agrarian products. Cizîrê is regarded as Syria's breadbasket; apart from grain, it also produces a lot of vegetables. Efrîn is one of Syria's most important areas for the production of olives. However, the war makes it all but impossible to export the foodstuffs that are produced or to import other important products. Agriculture in Cizîrê, which is in part highly industrialized, is dependent on the use of chemicals and fertilisers that are now no longer in supply. On the other hand, parts of the harvest rot away because the products can no longer be exported. Most of the oil fields of the region have also ceased to produce. The little that is produced is refined in an improvised manner, with severe accompanying health risks for the workers. The canton administrations under the control of the PYD have centralized the supply of the most important goods such as flour or fuel, a fact that is viewed with a lot of mistrust by the other parties.

The PYD and their Western supporters often point to the "creation of an alternative economy in Rojava" (see Flach, Ayboğa, and Knapp 2015: 245ff.). The cooperatives for women founded in 2012 are particularly frequently cited as examples for this "alternative economy." Yet neither the Kurdish self-administration nor independent economists are able to give any reliable facts and figures in that regard. Indeed, since 2012 a number of cooperatives have been founded, particularly for women, that follow the feminist ideology of the PYD and the PKK. The women have thus gained, often for the first time, the opportunity to earn an income independently from their husbands. In terms of gender politics, this development should certainly not be underestimated.

Yet viewed from the economy at large, these cooperatives, founded with the support and under the influence of the new authorities, play a relatively unimportant role. Even the cooperatives presented in the literature close to the party as models for this new organizational form are only small enterprises, such as the cheese cooperative Dêrîk with five women, the women's bakery Serêkaniyê, where six women bake "about 600 flatbreads per day" (Knapp, Flach, and Ayboğa 2016: 212), or a women's cooperative in Amûdê where the "movement trained 21 women as dressmakers" (Knapp, Flach, and Ayboğa 2016: 213). Strategically important areas of production such as electricity or the fuel supply were taken over by the new state authorities. Private enterprises and large-scale landholdings still remained the property of the previous owners. Important as they are for the women employed in them, the new cooperatives hardly represent an "alternative economy." Rojava's economy is based on a mixture of war economy, small capitalism, and subsistence production of food within which the cooperatives lead a niche existence instead of representing a new economic system.

In more than five years of civil war, war-related economic branches have developed in all of Syria, and they are also represented in Rojava. Smuggling and intra-Syrian trade are both important economic factors. Particularly the closure of the border to Turkey and, for most of the time, also to Iraq have turned the smuggling of all sorts of goods into an attractive business in which both family clans and party and military structures are involved.

Despite all the fighting, there is also an intense intra-Syrian trade that, in the case of Rojava, even crosses the areas held by IS. Even while the SDF and IS were fighting each other further to the west, the area between Tal Abyad and Serê Kaniyê experienced the development of a veritable "border station" near the small town Mabrouka, where dozens of trucks were waiting to be processed by Kurdish fighters each day. Many of these trucks came from areas under the control of the regime, such as Damascus and Aleppo, and they then crossed IS territory to arrive at their final destinations in the Kurdish area. The goods were of various sorts, and even alcohol was transported through the areas held by IS.[1] To this day, tour coaches travel to and from Damascus and are able, after being appropriately "taxed" by IS, to drive through the latter's territory.

Informal financial business has also developed into an important branch. It is based both on the desire of refugees to deposit their money safely in Europe and on money transfers from Europe that go to the families the refugees left behind. These form an increasingly important part of the income of the region.

Because there are no longer any functioning banks in Rojava capable of carrying out international transactions, people now resort to the traditional hawala system that is widespread in many parts of the Islamic world. In this system, somebody in, say, Europe, pays a trusted person a sum of money, which will then be paid out in, say, Syria by another trusted person. For the most part, the "hawaladars," the "trusted persons" in this system, are family members located in various parts of the world and functioning in the manner of a family network. In most cases, the money is never physically transferred to Syria. A telephone call to the hawaladar in Rojava is sufficient to prompt the latter to pay out the required sum on the same day. Conversely, money transferred to Europe is used to disburse to the refugees the money they once deposited in Syria. Difficulties only arise with larger sums, for example if the trusted person in Syria doesn't dispose of enough cash. In such cases, an individual transfer can require up to two weeks. Yet on the whole, the system works reliably even without any written documents. After all, the whole setup is based on the good reputation of the hawaladars and the trust in them, which it would be silly to destroy. Should the money fail to arrive even once, in a tribal society such as the Kurdish one this would destroy the offender's opportunities to do business again in this branch forever.

In its basics, this system is operative in very many parts of the Islamic world and is used, for example, by the Somalian diaspora in the US to transfer money to their families in Somalia in just the same way as it is used by Pakistani traders in the United Kingdom. In the case of Rojava, however, the commission fees demanded by the trusted persons are substantially higher than is usual in most other cases. For a transfer to Rojava, the hawaladar today demand about 4 to 5 per cent of the transferred sum, depending on the total amount involved. Given the large sums that are transferred and the small investments necessary – there are no bank buildings or employees, since all is done on the side in some shop in the market – since 2012 some families in Rojava have been able to accumulate substantial funds, which are mostly invested in real estate.

This same hawala system is actually fairly widespread in all of Syria, and it serves the financial needs not only of private persons, but also of the most diverse militias (see Phillips 2016: 141).

Together with the traders and smugglers, the hawaladars are part of the new upper class, but they hardly reinvest any part of their profits into productive businesses. In a country besieged by civil war such as Syria, investments in productive activities run a high risk. Moreover, legal security for investments simply doesn't exist. Confiscations by the YPG – as in the case of a hospital in Kobanê described further below – do not encourage long-term investments in Rojava. Thus, in the end a part of the profits from these operations flows out of the region and into the exile countries, into Turkey, Lebanon, or Europe.

Despite the new areas of business based on war, no evaluation of the economic situation can overlook the fact that many items have become luxury goods in the course of recent years. Even though most goods are available, many of them have become increasingly unaffordable for an increasing number of Rojavans. Meat and some import goods have become much more expensive since 2016. While tens of thousands of sheep and cattle were exported to Iraqi Kurdistan, particularly during the Islamic sacrificial feast Id ul-Adha, most inhabitants of Rojava can at best afford to eat chicken meat. This is accompanied by supply crunches in the realm of medicine (see Schmidinger 2016a: 28).

The war-related shortages are made worse by the presence in Rojava of more than a half million internally displaced persons (IDPs) from other parts of Syria. Between 2015 and 2017, tens of thousands of Kurds from Aleppo, Homs, or Damascus fled to their relatives in their places of origin. Those who do not have relatives with whom they can live are provisionally housed in schools, mosques, or other public facilities. A large number of these IDPs are of Kurdish origin, but in the course of my research in 2013 and 2014, I also often encountered Arab and Christian IDPs. Particularly after the conquest of Raqqa and other bigger cities by IS, more and more Arab refugees came to Rojava in order to be safe from the terror group. Large international NGOs are virtually non-existent. From Austria, the only organizations which are present, in the form of smaller projects, are Caritas and the League for Emancipatory Development Cooperation (Liga für emanzipatorische Entwicklungszusammenarbeit; LeEZA).[2] Together with the Women's

World Day of Prayer, LeEZA supports a women's centre in the town Amûdê. Yet such small-scale NGOs lack the means for effective refugee emergency aid. From Germany, Medico International also supports some projects.[3] Moreover, Doctors without Borders is present in some places. Since mid-August 2014, UNHCR has also been active in the Newroz refugee camp for Êzîdî refugees from the Iraqi Sinjar. Apart from the tens of thousands of refugees in this camp near Dêrik, UNHCR also supports a number of the internally displaced persons.

In addition, a number of Kurds in Europe have become active with private aid initiatives. These are in part donation campaigns for the self-administration structures in Rojava and in part private initiatives. However, the latter have repeatedly met with difficulties. Thus, the Vienna-based surgeon Ezzat Afandi invested his private funds to establish a "Vienna Hospital" in his home town of Kobanê, which started to operate in May 2014. Yet in October 2014, he had to leave the encircled town. His hospital was largely destroyed during the battles in Kobanê. In 2015, a commander of the YPG requisitioned his hospital. Unfortunately, mediation attempts supported by the Austrian MEP Josef Weidenholzer couldn't broker a solution. The hospital was de facto expropriated and was reopened at the end of September by the Kurdish Red Crescent in the presence of a delegation of US soldiers.

Kurds in all of Europe became active particularly for the refugees in Kobanê and sent private aid deliveries to the region. Missing, however, are the big international aid organizations, which are focusing on the refugee camps in the neighbouring states. The IDPs in Rojava thus have to be largely fed by the local population.

Many of these refugees actually wanted to move on to Europe. However, since entry into Europe is no longer legally possible, smugglers have to be paid who now pocket $10,000 per person. In return, the lucky ones among the refugees get a reliable smuggler who does his best to bring his clients safely to Europe. Those less lucky are deserted halfway or find themselves on an unseaworthy tub that sinks between Turkey and Greece. In Amûdê, a local association has created a memorial for 39 citizens of the city who drowned on such a vessel during an attempted escape to Europe on 6 September 2012. Whole families including their children were killed. Here, far from the gates of Europe, people memorialize the victims of fortress Europe.

16

The Kurdish Districts of Aleppo

Nevertheless, the security situation in the traditional Kurdish districts of Ashrafiyah and Sheikh Maqsoud (Kurdish: Şêxmeqsûd) in Aleppo that were now also under Kurdish control was far more dramatic than that in the three cantons. Today Aleppo, which until the civil war used to be one of the most important travel destinations because of its world-famous historical old city and its extensive tiled bazaar, is among the Syrian cities to have suffered the most from the destruction by the civil war. Even though the Kurds managed to keep a neutral district between the part of the city held by the regime and the part conquered by the opposition from July 2012 to the end of 2016, and to administer this neighbourhood through a "People's Council" installed by the PYD, both the supply situation and the security situation remained precarious. In Aleppo, all parties to the civil war were active. Apart from the battles between the government and the opposition, there was repeated fighting between opposition groups and the "Islamic State" as well as between the Kurds and all other parties to the war. As early as 6 September 2012, there was a bombardment by the Syrian airforce during which, according to the PYD, 21 civilians were killed. In October 2012, there was heavy fighting with an Islamist brigade of the FSA. At the beginning of 2013, thousands of inhabitants of Sheikh Maqsoud finally fled after fighting between the government army and the FSA erupted in the district.

In November 2013, the government army advanced to Ashrafiyah and conquered parts of the neighbourhood. However, reports by sources close to the regime that the Syrian army had reconquered Sheikh Maqsoud in December 2013 turned out to be false. Yet since 2014, Ashrafiyah slowly fell back to the regime. A large part of the Kurdish population fled into the Kurdish cantons or even further, to Europe.

While the government had been on the defensive until mid-2013, from November 2013 at the latest it went on the offensive, and on 17 July 2014 it conquered the most important supply routes of the parts of the town held by the FSA and the Islamic Front. In mid-August, the so-called "Islamic State," which had been successfully expelled at the beginning of 2014, started an offensive against the FSA and the Islamic Front in Aleppo. While IS had already retreated from Aleppo at the beginning of 2015, the importance of Jabhat al-Nusra, which belongs to the network of al-Qaida, continued to grow over the course of February and March 2015. From 2015 on, the eastern part of the city was almost exclusively under the control of militia belonging to very strict ideological currents of political Islam. The most moderate groups among these were the Liwa al-Tawhid, founded by members of the Muslim Brotherhood, and the Harakat Nur ad-Din az-Zanki, which became known in July 2016 for its beheading of a 12-year old prisoner of war. Apart from Jabhat al-Nusra, other Jihadist groups such as Ahrar ash-Sham also dominated the part of Aleppo held by the rebels. Secular rebel groups had already been expelled from Aleppo in 2013, and by now, within the Islamist militia, it was increasingly jihadist forces that dominated the eastern part of the town.

With the conquest of the provincial capital Idlib to the west of Aleppo, Jabhat al-Nusra succeeded in further strengthening its power in northwestern Syria at the end of March 2015. Now it exerted control over an increasingly cohesive territory and was approaching both the canton of Efrîn and the Kurdish quarter of Aleppo.

On 26 April 2015, most of the rebel groups remaining in Aleppo merged into an alliance under the name "Fatah Halab."

The dominance of jihadi forces in East Aleppo led to a deterioration of the relationship between the YPG and the rebels. On 2 May 2015, a broad alliance of rebel organizations under the leadership of Jabhat al-Nusra and Fatah Halab declared war on the YPG in Aleppo.[1] Even though that declaration of war was rescinded only one day later and a ceasefire was negotiated, for the Kurds in Aleppo the threat from Jabhat al-Nusra remained.

On the part of the YPG, the attacks on East Aleppo led to a slow rapprochement between the remaining Kurdish district, Sheikh Maqsoud, and the Syrian government army and its allies and, in autumn 2016, to its de facto cooperation with the allies of the regime against the rebels in East Aleppo. Even though some of the refugees from East Aleppo were accommodated by the Kurds, the repeated massive attacks of rebel groups on Sheikh Maqsoud in the end probably contributed

Aleppo: the situation in September 2014

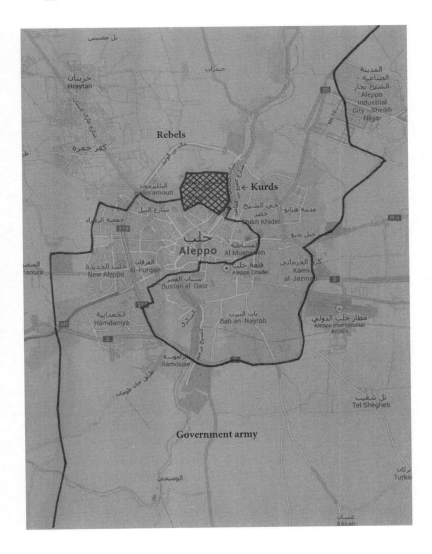

indirectly to the YPG/YPJ's participation in the strangulation of the rebels in Aleppo by the end of July 2016. The Kurdish enclave became a part of the closure of the supply lines for the part of the city held by the rebels. Even the renewed breakthrough of the rebels from the south could not change the fact that Sheikh Maqsoud was now de facto surrounded by the government army and its allies.

In autumn 2016, Sheikh Maqsoud was increasingly faced with acts of revenge from jihadist rebels. At the end of November 2016, Kurdish media even reported a poison gas attack on Sheikh Maqsoud by rebels. They claimed that Ahrar ash-Sham and Jabhat al-Nusra, which by now had renamed itself Jabhat Fatah ash-Sham, had fired rockets into the quarter that were equipped with mustard gas.[2] At the beginning of December, the neighbourhood was still being pounded with missiles fired by Ahrar ash-Sham and Jabhat Fatah ash-Sham.[3]

Yet interestingly, after the final defeat of the rebels in Aleppo in the week between 15 and 22 December 2016, the Kurdish neighbourhood still managed to retain its status as an autonomous district. Only the war in Efrîn forced the YPG to leave Aleppo in February 2018.

17

The Kurdish Para-State in Rojava

Even though the YPG has up to now been largely victorious on the military front and is the only military force that has successfully confronted "Islamic State," the political record of the de facto autonomy of Rojava is much more ambivalent. Thus far, the political split between the PYD and the parties of the KNC has proven impossible to overcome. Instead, opposition forces accuse the PYD of having erected a new dictatorship.

The official proclamation of the three cantons in January 2014 has been unable to change this. The proclamation of the canton of Cizîrê on 21 January, the canton of Kobanê on 27 January, and the canton of Efrîn on 29 January were the work of the PYD alone and were not coordinated with the KNC. Apart from a few individual persons and the small Kurdish Left Democratic Party in Syria and the even smaller Kurdish Left Party in Syria, none of the parties of the KNC – not even the "system-immanent" opposition – has so far participated in the new administration. On 2 February 2014 the Kurdish Left Democratic Party in Syria, the Kurdish Left Party in Syria, and the independent KNC member Akram Kamal Hasu were all excluded from the KNC. Akram Kamal Hasu, who is one of the wealthiest entrepreneurs of Syria, later became the prime minister of the canton of Cizîrê as an independent. In the canton of Kobanê, the PYD follower Enwer Muslim was appointed prime minister, whereas in the canton of Efrîn a woman, Hevi Ibrahim Mustefa, who is also a member of the small Alevi minority, now holds the same post.

As some sort of constitution for all of Rojava, a so-called social contract was put into force. There are, however, no political structures of a joint administration of Rojava in place.

Moreover, the power of all three prime ministers is based on the power of the PYD. The KNC and the Future Movement do not recognize the newly created structures and accuse the PYD of having acted unilaterally and in an authoritarian way in setting them up. So far, the autonomous cantons have been recognized neither by the opposition nor the regime, which deprives them not just of the recognition of parts of their own population, but also of recognition on the level of the whole state.

This lack of a general legitimacy in the Kurdish population in Syria is in part offset by the incorporation of the minorities into the new administrative structures. Thus, religious and ethnic minorities are represented in all three cantons.

The "social contract" declares straight out in its preamble that Rojava is not just a purely Kurdish autonomous area, and that it regards itself as a part of Syria:

> We, the people of the Democratic Autonomous Regions of Afrin, Jazira and Kobane, a confederation of Kurds, Arabs, Assyrians, Chaldeans, Arameans, Turkmen, Armenians and Chechens, freely and solemnly declare and establish this Charter, which has been drafted according to the principles of Democratic Autonomy.

In pursuit of freedom, justice, dignity, and democracy and led by principles of equality and environmental sustainability, the Charter proclaims a new social contract, based upon mutual and peaceful coexistence and understanding between all strands of society. It protects fundamental human rights and liberties and reaffirms the peoples' right to self-determination.

> Under the Charter, we, the people of the Autonomous Regions, unite in the spirit of reconciliation, pluralism and democratic participation so that all may express themselves freely in public life. In building a society free from authoritarianism, militarism, centralism and the intervention of religious authority in public affairs, the Charter recognizes Syria's territorial integrity and aspires to maintain domestic and international peace.[1]

The question of the minorities, in particular of how to deal with the Arabs who were settled in the region in the course of the Arabization policy of the regime,[2] is another controversial topic among the Kurdish parties. While the PYD tries to integrate all minorities, some of the member parties of the KNC demand that the Arabs settled in Kurdistan in the course of the Arabization policies are sent back to their original homes.

Be that as it may, in the cantons founded by the PYD, the minorities are represented.

In the canton of Cizîrê, apart from the Kurds it is particularly the Syrian-Orthodox Christians and the members of the Assyrian Church of the East who support the new administration and take an active part in the work of the canton.

Yet the religious dignities of the churches united with the Catholic churches remained just as loyal to the regime as those of the Armenian-Apostolic church. Thus, on 6 March 2014 the Vatican disseminated a statement of the Syrian-Catholic Arch Bishop of al-Hasaka and Nisbis (Nusaybin), Jacques Behnan Hindo, in which he clearly positioned himself against the proclamation of the autonomous cantons and said that "every choice regarding the arrangement of the region" had "to be equally agreed upon by the three components of the local population: Kurds, Christians and Muslim Arabs." To him, the intention of the Syrian Kurds to co-opt three Christians into their cabinet of 20 ministers was no more than "a mere concession to seek consensus." According to a Radio Vatican broadcast that contained the statement, the three Christians did not represent their community, but rather "only represent themselves." Additionally, Hindo was quoted to the effect that the autonomy in question benefitted only the PKK and "that the moves carried out by the Kurds are only temporarily tolerated by the government in Damascus."[3] Even before this, Arch Bishop Hindo had repeatedly taken a stance against a Kurdish autonomy in Syria.

Another area that proved problematic was the human rights record of the new rulers. After research carried out in February 2014, a report by Human Rights Watch (HRW) came to the conclusion that since 2012, there had been at least nine cases of unsolved murders and disappearances of opponents of the PYD in areas under the latter's control (HRW 2014: 3). The report also sharply criticized both the judicial system, which it said failed to establish due process, and the violent abuse of prisoners. On the other hand, the housing of prisoners in the two prisons visited by HRW was evaluated as adequate. Human Rights Watch faulted the use of children as fighters in the YPG and in the ranks of the Asayîş, but, on the positive side, noted that there had been an announcement that the practice would be stopped in the future and that minors would be demobilized (HRW 2014: 45 f.). How credible these announcements are remains, however, to be seen. Currently, YPG commanders claim not to recruit minors anymore, but this doesn't correspond to at least local reality. When I visited a women's unit of the YPJ, all fighters present claimed to be at least 18. But at least half of the present young girls rather looked like they were between 14 and 16. Even though the YPG had been a purely voluntary army until the introduction of the draft for men in July 2014, this doesn't change anything regarding the relevance of HRW's demand to end the practice.

HRW also investigated cases of torture by the YPG or the Asayîş. Because of the high number of people involved, the case of Amûdê in July 2013 is particularly interesting. During the night of 26 to 27 June 2013 and under circumstances that are still not really clear, several sympathizers of the Kurdish Democratic Unity (Yekîtî) Party in Syria were shot and killed by a unit of the YPG during a demonstration in Amûdê. After the ensuing protests, the party office of the Yekîtî was stormed and requisitioned and 50 members or sympathizers of the party were kidnapped and, in part, severely maltreated. During my second visit to Amûdê, some of the abduction victims showed me their knocked-out teeth as well as singes on their arms allegedly caused by the cigarettes of YPG fighters. They claimed that the torture only came to an end after they had been handed over to the Asayîş. Apparently, the HRW delegation came to similar conclusions after its visit.

The human rights problem is directly related to the intra-Kurdish political rivalry and the transitional administration's lack of political legitimacy. Whenever the conflict between the PKK party bloc and the PDK party bloc intensifies, the Asayîş's line of action against the Kurdish opposition parties correspondingly hardens. For that reason, the violence of the transitional administration primarily hits members of the PDKS and the Yekîtî Party that is allied with it in the Kurdish National Council.

Many of these human rights violations may have been favoured by wartime events and the intra-Kurdish power struggles. Yet even so, it needs to be said that so far, the PYD, the YPG, and the Asayîş have not paid sufficient practical attention to their official affirmation of human rights and have apparently also adopted some of the practices of the previous regime.

Furthermore, so far the transitional administration of the three cantons has lacked democratic legitimacy. The elections originally announced for May 2014 have never taken place. On 11 May the executive council of the canton of Cizîrê announced the postponement of the election to September 2014. But this election date also did not come to pass. To this day, in none of the three cantons have there been elections giving all parties the opportunity to participate. It was only in March 2015 that municipal elections in the canton of Cizîrê took place, which were, however, boycotted by the parties of the Kurdish National Council and have therefore only limited legitimacy.

On 22 September 2017, at long last communal elections took place. Although they were still boycotted by the Kurdish National Council, a high number of at least formally independent members of communal councils were elected.

Elections for the regional councils were finally were finally held on 1 December 2017. Still boycotted by the remaining parties of the Kurdish National Council, three party alliances ran for these elections. The overwhelming majority was won by the Democratic Nation List (Lîsta Netewa Demokratîk, LND). This list was led by the ruling PYD and included over a dozen extremely small Kurdish, Assyrian, and Arab parties. Besides the leading PYD, only the two Christian parties, the Assyrian Democratic Party led by Ninos Isho and the Syriac Unity Party led by Ishow Gowrieye, play a significant role inside the LND. Finally, more than 4,600 seats in the regional councils were won by this list of the PYD and its closest allies.

A list called Kurdish National Alliance in Syria (Hevbedniya Niştimanî a Kurdî li Sûriyê) was supported by former members of the Kurdish National Council who had decided to participate in the administration. It was composed of Muhammad Salih Gedo's Kurdish Left Party in Syria (Partiya Çep Demokratîk Kurdî li Sûriyeyê), Muhiyuddin Sheikh Ali's Kurdish Democratic Unity Party in Syria (Partiya Yekîtîya Demokrat li Sûriyê) and the Syrian-Kurdish Democratic Reconciliation (Rêkeftin), the latter a splinter group of the PYD, and won only 152 seats.

The third list, the predominantly Arab Syrian National Democratic Alliance, only won eight seats out of more than 5,600. In Cizîrê, the LND won more than 93 per cent of the votes, in the Euphrates Region (including the canton of Kobanê) over 88 per cent, and in Efrîn over 89 per cent. Thus the dominance of the PYD and its allies was confirmed by these elections, while the conflict with the major rivals of the PYD in the Kurdish National Council could not be resolved.

The current system in Rojava derives its political legitimacy exclusively from a council system in which, however, only the supporters of the PYD participate and which is, on these grounds, denied any legitimacy by its intra-Kurdish rivals.

The council system practised in Rojava is based on four levels: At the base, there is the commune, consisting of a village or 30 to 150 households in an urban neighbourhood. These communes consist of commissions from five to ten persons each that are formed around certain topics such as defence, women, and economy. Delegates of 7 to 30 communes then form a council of a village community or a city district, which, in turn, by analogy to the communes, consists of various commissions. Several of these councils of city districts or village communities then elect city or regional councils, which, again, consist of several commissions. And finally, the city and regional councils elect the People's Council of West Kurdistan (Meclîsa Gel a Rojavayê Kurdistanê, MGRK).

All these levels follow the principle of co-chairmanship, that is, all councils are always jointly led by a male and a female. Moreover, in addition there are also autonomous women's councils, which reflects the importance of feminism in the ideology of the PYD and the PKK.

In theory, this creates a council system based on direct democracy, but which is, however, in fact dominated by the supporters of the PYD and the latter's front organizations. Moreover, just like other historic council systems such as in the former Soviet Union, the question is who is really in the possession of political power: Is it, in the end, really "all power to the councils," or is it, after all, still "all power to the party," or even to the army, that is, in this case, the YPG?

How significant the council system actually is to the real power structures in Rojava is controversial. While activists close to the PKK/PYD idealize the system as a direct democratic council system and understand it as the realization of the political theory of the US eco-anarchist Murray Bookchin and the "attempt at a unification of the [...] concepts of Democratic Autonomy, Confederalism, and a Democratic Republic on a small scale" (Flach, Ayboğa, and Knapp 2015: 110), less enthusiastic observers such as the political scientist Michael M. Gunter opine that the councils created by the PYD only act as if they actually represented the local population, but, in reality, do not have the power to make important decisions. According to these observers, the leadership of the PKK in the Qandil mountains and Abdullah Öcalan are the ones who exercise real control, through various PKK/PYD commanders for different regions (see Gunter 2014: 128).

My own field research in the region allows me to suggest a somewhat more differentiated intermediary picture that contradicts both the enthusiasm of the PKK adherents and the thesis of an authoritarian rule of the PKK leadership. There are, indeed, indications that the YPG, and, via the YPG, the headquarters of the PKK in Qandil, has the final say in decisive questions. But Öcalan, who is isolated on his prison island of Imrali, hardly plays any significant role in all of this anymore. For years, Öcalan has primarily been a provider of ideas as well as the identification figure for an excessive personality cult, but not the strategic head of the party. Much more important today are Öcalan's old companions in Qandil, most of all Murat Karayılan, the supreme commander of the People's Defence Forces (Hêzên Parastina Gel, HPG), the guerrilla army of the PKK. The long-lasting civil war has certainly contributed to a strengthening of the role of the military, that is, the YPG. The members of the competing militia in the Syrian civil war have always regarded the commanders of the YPG as their serious contact partners, not the representatives of the political structures. At the same time, the council system does play an important role in the small daily administrative decisions and the supply of the population. However, this role of the councils seems to cut into both directions. The councils are important as feedback loops and local organizers, but also provide propaganda for and the dissemination of the social model the PYD is striving for. Particularly with regard to the role of the women in Kurdish society, the councils play an important role in reforming an extremely patriarchal society.

One of the biggest problems for the new system remains the lack of support of a large number of the Kurdish parties. An agreement between the PYD and the Kurdish National Council, reached on 21 October 2014 and since called the Dohuk Agreement, was never realized. It envisioned a new partition of power in Rojava. A 30-person council composed of 12 representatives of the PYD and 12 representatives of the parties with a close relation to the Kurdistan Regional Government in Iraq as well as six representatives of other parties was supposed to take over the supreme power of government in Rojava. Another point was the creation of joint military forces. Yet at the outset, even the KNC members were unable to agree among themselves on the distribution of the seats assigned to them. The realization of the agreement subsequently faltered because the KNC and the PYD could not reach a consensus.

Therefore, the three cantons that were declared in January 2014 did not really form a joint political structure of Kurdish political forces, but rather a political structure under the leadership of the PYD. To this day, most of the other Kurdish parties refuse to recognize this structure, first and foremost among them the rivalling Kurdish Nation Council in Syria.

Yet since the establishment of the self-administration in Rojava opposition to the PYD has also eroded. With the founding of a big sister party of the PDK through the fusion of four parties in March 2014, many of the other parties felt increasingly marginalized. Several miniscule parties went over to the new self-administration structure of the PYD. The biggest bloodletting, however, was certainly the resignation of Abdulhamid Hadji Darwish's Kurdish Democratic Progressive Party in Syria, which, though it didn't join the self-administration structures, had now also ceased to cooperate with the Kurdish National Council.

In July 2016, the Kurdish National Council finally withdrew from the Syrian National Council, since the latter had appointed a transitional government without appointing even a single Kurdish minister.[4] In September 2016, the Council of the Syrian Êzîdî (Encûmena Êzîdiyên Sûrî) under Serhan Îsa withdrew both from the Kurdish and the Syrian National Councils.[5] This relatively small organization had been the only Êzîdî group that was represented both in the Kurdish and the Syrian National Council while, particularly since the events of Şingal in 2014, the majority of the Syrian Êzîdî sympathized with the PYD, and therefore, also with the Êzîdî association close to the PYD. At the end of February 2017, the group, which was mostly based in German exile, finally applied for readmission to the KNC.

In 2016, the intra-Kurdish political rivalry between the PYD and the Kurdish National Council in Syria, where the latter was supported by the Kurdistan Regional Government in Iraq, also sharply intensified. On 13 August, Ibrahîm Biro, the president of the KNC, was arrested in Qamişlo and deported to Iraq within just a few hours. On the same day, the office of the PDKS in Qamişlo was attacked and partly demolished by adherents of the PYD. At the sidelines of the funeral of a Rojava Peshmerga who had fought against IS in Iraq, and related to protests against the deportation of Biro, over the course of the following days a couple of dozen activists and functionaries of various parties of the KNC were arrested. On 16 August 2016, the National Council organized demonstrations against the PYD in the towns of Qamişlo, Dêrik, Girkê Legê, Tirbesipî, Amûdê, Dirbêsiyê, and Girê Xurma. Even in the diaspora – inter alia, in Vienna – there were demonstrations against the PYD by supporters of the Kurdish National Council.

A further escalation of this intra-Kurdish conflict was triggered in March 2017 by the deployment of KNC Rojava Peshmerga in Şingal in Iraq, near the small town of Khanasor. In the course of fighting on

3 March 2017 between the Rojava Peshmerga – the troops of the KNC trained by the Iraqi PDK Peshmerga – and the Resistance Units of Şingal (Yekîneyên Berxwedana Şingal, YBŞ) allied with the PKK, both sides suffered fatal casualties. This escalation on Iraqi territory was followed by another one on the Syrian side of the border. In the days after the fighting near Khanasor, more than 40 supporters of the PDKS and the Yekîtî Party were arrested in Rojava. Furthermore, an office of the Kurdish National Council in Amûdê was burnt down, an act that the KNC attributed to the PYD.[6]

The confrontation further intensified and on 9 May 2017, the headquarters of the Kurdish National Council was stormed and shut down, with the arrests of 13 leading cadres of the KNC who were present.

Even so, today the opposition to the PYD is more fragmented than at the beginning of Rojavan autonomy. Currently, the role of the Kurdish National Council has been reduced to an extension of Barzani and his PDK. With the resignation of Abdulhamid Hadji Darwish's Kurdish Democratic Progressive Party from the Kurdish National Council, the latter was crucially weakened, just as it was by the deportation of Ibrahîm Biro. Most importantly, however, many activists and sympathizers of the Kurdish National Council have left the country in recent years. Among the more than 100,000 Kurdish refugees among the 233,000 Syrian refugees in Iraq, there is a particularly large number of supporters of the KNC. And the number of Kurdish exiles from Syria in Europe who oppose the PYD is also significantly higher than that of its supporters. Since the introduction of the draft for the YPG in 2014, it has been particularly young men associated with the PDKS and the Yekîtî who have attempted to flee from Rojava.

But the PYD itself is also not as monolithic a bloc as it may appear at first sight. In part, one can already sense the inner-party conflicts that are typical for many liberation movements once they are successful and control a territory. With the effective takeover of Rojava by the PYD, many opportunists have affiliated themselves with the party who, before 2012, had nothing to do with it or with the Kurdish movement but had made their peace with the Ba'ath regime up until that time. Many of these freshly baked PYD members quickly managed to grab positions of responsibility because they had often already been in high positions under the Ba'ath regime and their knowledge was needed now. Many old activists of the party who had a record of political work over many years but had never had the opportunity to gain a higher education or had been in jail for many years now felt disadvantaged vis-à-vis these new opportunists. That big businessmen who had never had anything to do with the party, such as Akram Kamal Hasu, were now rising to positions such as that of prime minister appears hard to comprehend for many of the old leftists in the party.

The integration of an old elite into a new system follows a certain logic in the exercise of power and always confronts societies in political turmoil with massive challenges. No new system can simply replace all policemen, teachers, or state officials from one day to the next. However, with the cooptation of the old elites, the new rulers also always inevitably change. This is all the more problematic as a situation of civil war makes it imperative to try to get as much support as possible. In this, one's own party basis is taken for granted anyway: One must work to win over those who might otherwise be proselytized by one's respective enemies.

Among the ordinary population, a clear change of mood has been observable since 2013. During my field research in Amûdê in January 2013, a revolutionary atmosphere was prevalent. The people suffered from supply bottlenecks and uncertainty, but still took to the streets every week and bristled with hope and dynamism. Almost everyone wanted to tell their stories. By and large, at that time an optimistic mood prevailed and the assumption was that the commitment of each individual in such a challenging situation was worth the effort, because at the end of the road there would probably be a democracy in Syria and autonomy in Kurdistan. Yet in February 2014, not much of this revolutionary atmosphere was still palpable among the ordinary population. Even though official declarations were still talking about a revolution, what one sensed now was the mood typical of a civil war. The former optimism was gone. Now people were grateful to the YPG for the fact that it had managed, at least, to shield the population from the worst and that Qamişlo and Amûdê had not turned into battlefields like Aleppo and Homs. Even though there were still occasional demonstrations against the regime in February 2014, these were as rare as they were small. In an anti-regime demonstration of the KNC in a town like Qamişlo, the number of demonstrators who took to the street barely reached 100. At the same time, the supporters of the Ba'ath regime again started to demonstrate in Qamişlo. On the anniversary of the founding of the party or on other occasions, Ba'athists or state employees who do not dare to resist the call again march through the inner city of Qamişlo, carrying the portrait of their president, Bashar al-Assad.

Despite this continuing presence of the regime, the influence of Damascus is dwindling. The conversion of the school system for the Kurdish population in 2015 and the long-term establishment of para-state structures have to a certain degree normalized a new system of government. With the proclamation of the Federation of Northern Syria – Rojava (Federasyona Bakurê Sûriyê – Rojava) on 17 March 2016, and the establishment of a joint government under the co-chairmanship of the female Kurd Hediye Yusuf and the male Arab Mansur Selum, a basis was finally laid for a joint administrative unit in Northern Syria that comprises not only the Kurdish settlement area, but also includes Arab and Assyrian settlement regions and thus also integrates representatives of these population groups.

With the expansion of this area into regions inhabited by Arabs, the political and military structure of the region also changed. Even though the core of the SDF still consists of the Kurdish People's Protection Units (YPG) and Women's Protection Units (YPJ), since 2016 the number of Arab fighters has significantly increased. Up until November 2017, with Talal Ali Silo from the Slejuk Brigade, the SDF was even externally represented by a Turkmen, though Silo then defected to Turkey. (Following the event, the PYD and the SDF claimed that Silo had been blackmailed and pressurized either by Turkish agents or by members of his own family, but it is also quite possible that the Syrian Turkmen had been a Turkish agent right from the outset.)

In the course of 2016 and 2017, the front of the SDF moved to the south and "Islamic State" was pushed back, and, in autumn 2017, largely smashed in collaboration with the Syrian government army. On the other hand, the military developments in the summer of 2016 prevented the SDF's desire to create a connection between the two largest Kurdish areas from being realized. The decisive factor in this was the military intervention of Turkey at the end of August 2016. Since then, the military support of the SDF by the US has continued to expand.

In January 2017, SDF troops captured the Turkish enclave of Qal'at Ğa'bar (Turkish: Caber Kalesi), where Turkish soldiers had guarded the alleged tomb of the grandfather of the first Turkish ruler Osman I, Suleiman Shah, from the time of the Treaty of Ankara until February 2015.

With the capture of al-Bab on 23 February, the Turkish troops and the militias allied with it finally won the race for the corridor between Efrîn and Kobanê. After the capture of Tadef on 26 February by the government army – at which the government troops stood practically face to face with the troops of the pro-Turkish rebels – the SDF would have had to challenge either the government army or the Turkish military and its allies had it fought for the corridor. Although the exact backgrounds to these decisions for now remain speculative, it seems very likely that the US, as the SDF's most important ally, vetoed any further advance of the Kurdish forces to prevent any further provocation of its NATO ally Turkey.

In the meantime, the military forces of the SDF continued to be armed by the United States. Heavy armaments continued to be delivered in the months afterwards, while the frontline moved, in several phases, closer and closer to the de facto capital of IS. On 22 March, SDF units crossed the Euphrates west of at-Tabqa and thus managed capture a bridgehead. From there, the SDF advanced further to the east, capturing the airbase of Tabqa on 26 March. On 6 April, they encircled the town and the dam. The battles for the dam lasted until 10 May, on which date the SDF were finally able to announce the capture of at-Tabqa. Moreover, until mid-May hundreds of villages north of ar-Raqqa were conquered. Notably, the supreme commander of the attack on ar-Raqqa was Rodja Felat, a female officer of the YPJ born in 1980 in al-Hasaka.

On 6 June 2017, the SDF, with US air support and the support of several hundred members of US special units, began its attack on the town. On 12 June 2017 the attackers for the first time reached the walls of the old city. On the same day, however, the Syrian government army also began an offensive against IS south of the areas held by the SDF and advanced relatively quickly towards the east and up to Resafa. Moreover, on 18 June, the Syrian airforce began to bomb positions of the SDF. As a result, a Syrian SU-22 was shot down by a US F-18, but even so, any further escalation could be avoided. In mid-July the US carried out huge arms deliveries to Raqqa that included armed bulldozers and mine-proof vehicles. By the end of July, the SDF was able to capture about half of the area of the city, and by August of the same year, around two-thirds of the city was in the hands of the SDF. Parts of the town, however, were still held by IS, which managed to inflict tangible losses on the SDF.

The alliance of the SDF with the US notwithstanding, Rojava remained an interesting area for volunteers from all over the world. Although the International Freedom Battalion (Tabûra Azadî ya Înternasyonal) – founded in June 2015 and primarily composed of members of Turkish Marxist-Leninist groups, but also with Spanish, Greek, German, French, British, and US groups in its ranks – is less important in military terms than the units sent by the US government, its international volunteers repeatedly played a significant role in connecting Rojava to the global solidarity movement. Also part of the International Freedom Battalion were the more or less anarchist International Revolutionary People's Guerrilla Forces (IRPGF) founded in March 2017, which at the end of July 2017 announced the founding of a "Queer Insurrection and Liberation Army" (TQILA) supposed to organize LGBTQ fighters in the ranks of the IRPGF. The SDF, however, immediately declared that there was no such thing as TQILA within the SDF itself.

In June 2017, there were increasing attacks by the Turkish army on the canton of Efrîn, which escalated in the course of July and were primarily directed against villages in the northeast of the region. Although secret negotiations between Turkey and Russia very probably deferred an invasion by Turkey already planned for the beginning of July, behind the scenes there are suspicions that Russia is pressuring the YPG and the PYD to hand the enclave back to the regime. At the end of July 2017, the supreme commander of the YPG, Sipan Hemo, declared in an interview with a news agency close to the PKK that the Raqqa operation could not "be carried forward if the attacks on Efrîn continue."

Similarly connected to an impending attack on Efrîn is the dissolution of the pro-Turkish militia called the "Brigade of the Descendants of Salahuddin" (Liwa aḥfād Ṣalāḥ ad-Dīn) led by Mahmūd Khalo, who in July 2017 refused to participate in a pro-Turkish attack on Efrîn. As a result, Turkey disbanded the brigade, which had been founded in 2015, and its approximately 600 Kurdish fighters. Its commander was arrested by pro-Turkish Arab militias and was, according to his own account, tortured.

It would be another six months before Turkey started its Operation Olive Branch (Turkish: Zeytin Dalı Harekâtı) against Efrîn in January 2018.

Also at the end of July, there was a decision to repartition the administration of the area under the control of the SDF into three regions and six cantons. Thus, in the future Cizîrê is to be divided into two cantons around Qamişlo and al-Hasaka, respectively. The central Euphrates region is supposed to include, apart from the canton of Kobanê, the newly created canton of Tal Abyad, and the region of Efrîn is to comprise, apart from the canton of Efrîn, another newly created canton called "The Martyrs" that is to include the areas south of Azaz newly conquered at the beginning of 2017.

While the Kurds in the regions captured by the SDF are largely safe, the picture of the area occupied by the pro-Turkish rebels between the cantons of Efrîn and Kobanê is quite different. On 12 June 2017 in this area traditionally inhabited by Arabs, Turkmens, and Kurds, the Êzîdî inhabitants of the small village Elî Qîno northwest of the town of Azaz were expelled. This very small village is located west of the separation wall that the YPG/YPJ had erected at the border of the region under its control and was thus de facto controlled by pro-Turkish rebels. On that Monday, the Êzîdî population of the village was given one hour to leave their houses, which were afterwards confiscated by pro-Turkish rebels.

At the 7th Regular Party Congress of the ruling PYD, two new co-chairs of the party were elected on 28 September 2017. Salih Muslim and Asya Abdullah were replaced in their positions by the hitherto somewhat unknown Şahoz Hesen and Ayşe Hiso. Salih Muslim, who had presided over the party since 2010, and Asya Abdullah, who had acted as co-chair since 2012, presented themselves at the party congress together with the new chairpersons and thereby tried to demonstrate publicly that the change in the top positions had been voluntary. However, before the congress, it had been rumoured for months that Salih Muslim would be replaced because he had become too popular and influential for the taste of the PKK's centre of power. According to these rumours, Salih Muslim had tried to put a greater distance between the PYD and the PKK. There were, however, not the slightest hints, let alone public statements, from Muslim himself that pointed in any such direction. What speaks against these rumours is the fact that Salih Muslim is still regarded as some sort of elder statesman within the PYD. The precise party-internal backgrounds for this change thus remain as of yet uncertain.

On 17 October 2017, the Syrian Democratic Forces, that is, the military alliance around the YPG, announced the conquest of Raqqa after four months of fighting within the town, up to that point the "capital" of the so-called "Islamic State". In the course of the months-long fighting and around 4,500 air attacks by the US Airforce allied with the SDF, large parts of the town were destroyed. The losses on the part of the SDF were probably very high and would presumably been higher still had it not been for an agreement with the remaining IS fighters concluded towards the end. Thus before 17 October, a total of around 4,000 persons (IS fighters together with their families) were allowed to evacuate the town on trucks and to move into the remaining IS area on the Iraqi-Syrian border. On the one hand, this enabled a peaceful handover of the remaining parts of the town and prevented further destruction, but on the other, the move allowed both high-ranking IS functionaries and fighters and international fighters to escape, a fact that was subsequently made into a scandal by the western media, particularly the BBC.

In parallel with the defeat of IS in Raqqa, east of that area there was a race between the Syrian regime and the SDF for the remaining region of IS in eastern Syria. While the government army displaced IS from Deir az-Zor on 5 September 2017, and also captured the region south of the Euphrates, the SDF succeeded in conquering the larger part of the northern bank of the Euphrates by November 2017. During these events in autumn of that year, there were repeatedly smaller clashes between the government army and the SDF. Yet by and large both mainly fought against IS. Whereas the SDF was able to bring additional areas south of the Euphrates around Raqqa under its control, the government army conquered the eastern bank of the Euphrates near Deir az-Zor. Otherwise, the Euphrates now formed the demarcation line between the government and the SDF. On 14 October, the government army succeeded in invading the town of Mayadin with its airbase and 44,000 inhabitants, followed by al-Quriyah on 22 October. Simultaneously, the SDF advanced, to a similar degree, on the northern side of the Euphrates. On 3 November 2017, the Iraqi army finally succeeded in capturing the border between Iraq and Syria near Qaim, which meant that IS was now reduced to the control of a mere 50km long section of the Euphrates valley stretching in a northwesterly direction from the Syrian-Iraqi border near Abu Kamal.

While the government army and the SDF advanced eastwards against IS, Turkey tried to establish a kind of circumvallation around the Kurdish region of Efrîn. The eastern border of the canton had already been under the control of the Turkish army and its militia allies since the summer of 2016 ("Protective Shield Euphrates"), but on 12 and 13 October 2017, the Turkish army and its allies finally advanced on Syrian national territory south of Efrîn near Atmeh and occupied a strip about 15km long and 5km wide south of the border of the area of Efrîn under the control of the SDF. One striking feature of this operation was that the takeover of this area did not lead to any fighting with the jihadist Hai'at Taḥrīr asch-Schām, the successor group of the al-Qaida organization Jabhat al-Nus'ra, which had previously controlled this area. The takeover therefore had to have been negotiated and agreed upon with the jihadists.

On 15 November 2017, it transpired that Rêdûr Xelîl, who had been removed from his post as speaker of the YPG in May 2017, had replaced the Turkmen Talal Silo as spokesperson for the SDF. According to Turkish media reports, Talal Silo had defected to the pro-Turkish units in Jarābulus and had passed information on the structure of the PYD to the Turkish secret services. But Kurdish sources talked about a kidnapping or blackmail of Talal Silo by the Turkish secret service MİT. The SDF thus did not condemn Silo as a traitor; on the contrary, in a statement published one day after the event, they wrote very respectfully about him and his merits as a spokesperson for the SDF. This statement of 16 November claimed that he had become the victim of a plot hatched by Turkey and members of his own family, and, moreover, that he had been repeatedly threatened in the past and that he had asked to be allowed to resign from his post as SDF spokesperson.

At the end of 2017, the para-state of IS had finally been smashed in both Syria and Iraq. This does not mean that the organization has ceased to exist, nor that there are no jihadist militias anymore in the Syrian civil war, however. These militias are now primarily active in the province of Idlib and the regions adjacent to it in the northwest of Syria. Apart from the remaining areas of the Arab opposition and the pro-Turkish militias in northwestern Syria, a few smaller opposition areas in the south, and of course the areas occupied by the regime, currently the only remaining area is actually the one under the control of the Syrian Democratic Forces, which is now more than twice as large as the core Kurdish settlement areas and comprises more than a fifth of the Syrian national territory.

With Russian and Iranian support, the Syrian regime has largely succeeded in deciding the war in its favour. It will thus also depend on these supporters of the regime whether or not a negotiated peace with the remaining Arab opposition and the Syrian Democratic Forces can be accomplished in 2018. Such a negotiated peace would have to include a decentralization of at least some regions of Syria as well as autonomy for the Kurds. In any case, 2018 will show whether such a solution is possible or whether the regime in reality also wants to reconquer the regions held by the Syrian Democratic Forces.

Six years after the withdrawal of the Syrian troops from Rojava, we can still do no more than sketch an intermediate record of the short history of a precarious autonomy in Rojava. In the following chapter, I want to give the floor to some of the actors in the region, who are thus given the opportunity to elaborate their views and perspectives themselves.

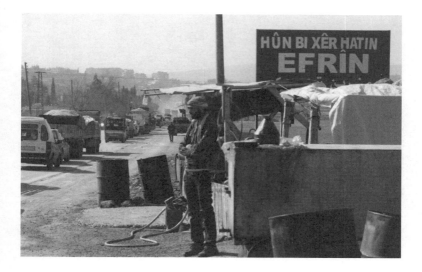

15 Entrance to the town of Efrîn. (2015)

16 Young middle class people in Efrîn would like to have international coffee chains in town. Meanwhile they imitate them. (2015)

17 YPJ-training in a training camp near Efrîn. (2015)

18 Cemetery and village of Gundê Faqîra, one of the Êzîdî villages of Efrîn. (2015)

19 The centre of Kobanê after the war with the so-called "Islamic State". (2015)

20 What is left over from downtown Kobanê. (2015)

21 The oldest mosque of Kobanê survived the war with the so-called "Islamic State". (2016)

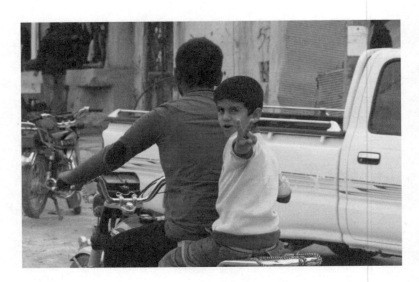

22 Life comes back to Kobanê. Many inhabitants returned after the liberation of the city. (2015)

23 The reconstruction of Kobanê included new licence plates of the Kurdish self-administration saying Kobanê instead of the Arabic 'Ayn al-'Arab. (2016)

24 Elder women of some Kurdish tribes in Rojava are still tattooed with symbols of their extended family and tribe. Halime, a woman from the village Qarah Halinj (Ghassaniye) carries the symbols of the Mîr-Clan of the Eşiret Berazî, a large tribal confederation in Rojava and Bakur (Kurdistan of Turkey). (2016)

25 In some of the villages between Kobanê and Tal Abyad traditional mud architecture can still be seen. (2016)

26 The so-called "Islamic State" erected this cage in the centre of Tal Abyad/Girê Sipî as a pillory for smokers. Since the YPG and YPJ conquered the predominantly Arab town in June 2015 their flags have been waving over it. (2016)

27 "Border station" at Mabrouka, where lorries from the territory of the "Islamic State" enter Rojava. Where the road from Raqqa joins the main road of Rojava, fighters of the YPG check the cars before they are allowed to enter. (2016)

28 Since 2012 the Syrian-Iraqi border at Semalka became the first Kurdish-Kurdish border with antagonistic parties on both sides: the PKK ally PYD in Syria and Barzani's PDK in Iraq. (2016)

18

Voices from Rojava

In the following, I present, in the form of interviews, different voices from Rojava, which are rendered here as verbatim as possible. I conducted these interviews in Europe, Turkey, and Syria between 2006 and 2018 and then translated them for this book. They reflect both different phases of the political development and extremely different perspectives. Particularly in the light of the intensified intra-Kurdish conflicts since 2011, it seemed important to me to make the different voices accessible in their original form in order to give the reader the opportunity to develop their own picture of the latest development and the different positions. Since this book quite consciously does not adopt, and does not want to adopt, the position of any one political party, the various opinions and explanatory attempts are presented side by side without comment. The order of the interviews that follow is chronological. The interviewees include not just political actors of different parties and movements, but also representatives of religious groups and artists. Even though the interviews together cannot give a comprehensive picture, they should enable a multi-faceted perspective of the current developments in Rojava.

The interviews with the various party leaders convey a direct impression of the situation pertinent at the respective time and highlight the intra-Kurdish faultlines between the political parties. The disunity between the Kurdish actors represents a part of the local political reality that cannot be simply fantasized away even by a solidary perspective on the conditions.

KHEREDIN MURAD

Secretary General of the Kurdish Freedom Party (Partiya Azadî ya Kurd li Sûriyê), 22 January 2006

The Syrian regime has recently come under pressure both domestically and internationally. How do you see the current situation in Syria after the murder of the Lebanese Prime Minister Hariri and the flight of the former vice president al-Khaddam?

When we look at the current situation in Syria, three parallel developments stick out. First, the internal pressure exerted on the regime by the Syrian population has clearly increased in the course of the past months. Both the Kurds, who have again and again taken to the streets after the uprising in Qamişlo in 2004, and the Arabs no longer want to live under these conditions. The demands for democratization, for freedom of speech, of the press and of movement and for the liberation of political prisoners have become much louder recently.

Second, the pressure by the international community, particularly the UN, has also markedly increased. Since the murder of Rafik al-Hariri, the demand has been raised that the regime must cooperate with the investigators in a transparent manner and must account for its involvement in the murder of the Lebanese prime minister.

Third, the flight of the former vice president al-Khaddam, who has held important positions in the Syrian government in the course of the past 40 years, has left a great impression in the Arab world. In an interview with the Arab paper *al-'Arabiya*, he had accused the Syrian president, Bashar al-Assad, of having been the mastermind of the murder of the former Lebanese prime minister, Rafik al-Hariri, sharply criticizing the regime of which he had been a part for so many years. Now he criticizes the fact that there is no freedom and democracy in Syria and wants to contribute to the unification of the opposition.

These three developments have put the Syrian government in a very difficult situation. It finds itself under domestic and international pressure and will have to change quite a few things if it wants to stay in power.

But the Syrian opposition is by no means as well-organized as one might expect from al-Khaddam's proclamations about a broad oppositional alliance. How do you see the relation between the Kurdish and the Arab opposition and the relation between the secular and the Islamist opposition? Are alliances between the various forces even possible?

You are certainly right in pointing out that the Syrian opposition, after decades of Ba'ath Party rule, is very weak and splintered. The regime itself has also successfully worked for many years to split the opposition. But there are also a number of questions with regards to which there are genuine disputes within the Syrian opposition. You have just mentioned two of the central questions. For one thing, there is the question about the relation between state and religion, and for another, there is the one about the rights of the Kurds and other non-Arab population groups in Syria. We as Kurds demand of the opposition to at long last recognize our rights, something that is far from being taken for granted on the part of many Arab opposition parties.

Which kind of solution is the Azadî Party striving for? Do you seek an independent Kurdish state or a democratic Syria? Would you be content with a certain autonomy within the Syrian state?

As Kurds, we are a minority in Syria, but even so, we represent 15 per cent of the population and want to be recognized as a nation with the same rights within Syria. For one thing, this includes the recognition of our language as an official language and a language of education, and for another, the revocation of the expulsions of Syrian Kurds in the course of the project of an "Arab Belt" at the Turkish border, and the recognition of Syrian citizenship for all Syrian Kurds. After the retraction of Syrian citizenship for hundreds of thousands of Syrian Kurds in 1962, these Kurds as well as all their offspring are still regarded as "stateless." One of our minimal demands is to restore their Syrian citizenship and give them full rights.

Bashar al-Assad has promised already months ago to solve the problem of citizenship and to give Syrian citizenship back to the "stateless" Kurds. But to this day, he has not kept that promise.

In a Syria that recognized rights like that and that conceded us a certain amount of cultural and political autonomy, we could certainly live as Kurdish citizens of the country.

But pressure on the Syrian Ba'ath regime is not the only thing coming from Europe. In Austria, for example, there are two lobby organizations that closely cooperate with the Syrian regime: the Society for Austrian-Arab Relations (Gesellschaft für Österreichisch-Arabische Beziehungen, GÖAB) with its secretary general, Fritz Edlinger, and the Austrian-Syrian Society, (Österreichisch-Syrische Gesellschaft), which was founded by the former minister of defence, Herbert Scheibner (FPÖ). What significance do such groups have for the Ba'ath regime?

In principle, we are not against contacts between Austria and Syria, but if there are such contacts, we think they should also be used to demand that the regime at long last permits a process of democratization. Unfortunately, this is not what these organizations do. If business interests are stronger than political principles, we probably can't hope for any support. But still, we would certainly hope for a stronger commitment to the democratization of our country.

Is it really realistic to hope for a democratization of the existing regime from within? After all, the policy of the Ba'ath Party, with its ideological borrowings from European Fascism and German National Socialism, is based on an aggressive Arab nationalism, which is in turn based on an authoritarian leader state.

This is entirely correct. The Ba'ath Party is a Fascist organization and as such is scarcely capable of any democratization. But the regime has hardly any other option. Either it creates openings and allows for a democratization or it will sooner or later be overthrown. It is quite possible that the regime does not have left much time anymore for that decision.

ABDULBASET SIEDA

Former Chairman and highest Kurdish functionary of the Syrian National Council (SNC), 10 January 2013

Why does cooperation between the Kurdish parties and the Arab opposition not work? After all, you seem to be the only Kurd who participates in the Syrian National Council, and for that, you have been sharply criticized and scolded as a traitor by other Kurdish parties.

Yes, many Kurds have stridently attacked me for this commitment. But nevertheless, at the moment I think it is important for the whole Syrian opposition to cooperate. What irks me about the Kurdish parties is the fact that they have no all-Syrian perspective and do not want to do anything for their country, but only focus on the interests of the Kurds. But the time has come for all of us to ask ourselves what we can do for our country.

One reason for the aloofness of the Kurdish parties has certainly been that the Arab opposition has so far never been ready to make substantive concessions to the Kurds. As of yet, the Syrian National Council has also refrained from promising the Kurds any autonomy or a federalization of Syria, which is why many Kurds are afraid not to gain anything by an overthrow of the regime. Does the SNC by now have a position with regard to the Kurdish question in Syria?

Yes. Meanwhile there is a document of the Syrian National Council on the question of the Kurds in Syria. In it, we state that we have to accept the Kurdish identity in our constitution. We have to give the Kurds all their rights and must abolish all discrimination against the Kurds. We have to institute measures for the improvement of the situation in the Kurdish regions and we have to pay reparations to those who were expropriated or have suffered other massive disadvantages in the course of the last decades.

And what about the demands for autonomy?

Here, we have opted for a decentralization of all of Syria, not just for the Kurdish areas.

But no special autonomy for the Kurds?

No, no special solution for the Kurds. But that way, the local administrations will acquire more power, and, therefore, the Kurds will also be able to exercise their rights.

Many Kurdish parties, that is, both the PYD and the parties in the Kurdish National Council, regard this rejection of a special autonomy as a reason not to join the Syrian National Council and to keep their distance from the Arab opposition. What would your response to those critics be?

I seem to remember that before the revolution not a single Kurdish party raised any demands for autonomy or federalism. These demands came to the fore only in the course of the revolution. But we are now in the midst of a revolutionary process. This is not a normal situation. At the moment, one can't discuss these questions in a meaningful way. After the revolution, once we have successfully overthrown the regime, we can also have a discussion about autonomy or a federal system. Right now, the goal is the overthrow of the regime, and all forces must cooperate in that goal. Therefore, the question of autonomy can be posed only later. But as I mentioned, we now have our document which guarantees the

Kurds all rights as true citizens. This is a good base for the discussion of the pertinent questions after the revolution. At that point, one will also have to define what exactly is meant by that, how such an autonomy is supposed to look, how far it should go, etc. Right at the moment, we can't discuss such details.

But we've been having a discussion with the Kurdish National Council about this for a long time. And the KNC has assured us that our declaration will solve 90 per cent of the problems. We are really having a positive dialogue with the KNC, which in the end will lead to a cooperation. But with the PYD, the situation is different. The PYD collaborates with the regime and it promotes slogans that don't make clear what they actually want.

That is, you are cooperating with the Kurdish National Council, but not with the PYD?

Yes, we have formed joint working groups and tried to solve the problems still existing between us. Things became more difficult with the formation of the Supreme Kurdish Council, because the parties in the Kurdish National Council now also cooperate with the PYD, which in turn reduces the possibilities for a cooperation with us. We want the KNC to become a part of the opposition coalition – but not the PYD.

Why not? Why this strict rejection of the PYD?

We don't reject the PYD as a matter of principle. But they must reconstitute themselves as a purely Kurdish party purely in Syria and renounce their connections to the PKK and to the regime. This is a condition for the cooperation with the PYD.

But they will hardly discontinue their connection to the PKK. After all, they emerged as a sister party of the PKK and were founded by Syrian members of the PKK.

For us the issue is that we only work with Syrian political parties and not with groups that are directed by foreign political forces.

But since the PYD levels the very same charge against the Syrian National Council – namely, that it is directed by Turkey – there is probably no good base for any rapprochement here.

No, there don't seem to be any prospects of an accommodation between the PYD and us.

HASSAN SALIH

Member of the Political Bureau of the Kurdish Union Party in Syria
(Partiya Yekitîya Kurdî li Sûriyê), 11 January 2013

*For outsiders, the present intra-Kurdish power struggles are very difficult
to understand. What is the relation of your party to the other Kurdish
parties? Which role does your party play in the Kurdish movement?*

When we founded our party, we took the decision to confront the
regime with concrete and clear demands and to formulate clearly
which kind of future we wanted for the Kurds in Syria. After we saw
the repression by the regime against the Muslim Brotherhood or against
the Worker Communists, we realized that we could not go on like this
anymore. At our first party congress in the year 2000, we decided that
we had to protest against the regime more actively and that we had to
strengthen our presence in Syrian society. On the International Day of
Human Rights in 2002, we organized, for the first time, a demonstration
in front of the Syrian parliament. This was the first manifestation of its
kind in Damascus. Before we took the decision to organize this rally, we
invited all the other parties to participate. But unfortunately, none of the
other parties wanted to take part. At the time, some 200 Syrian women
and men demonstrated in front of the Syrian parliament.

On the occasion, we suggested five solutions for the problems in Syria:
First, the recognition of the Kurdish language in all of Syria; second, the
same rights for all Syrians; third, the restitution to the stateless Kurds of
their citizenship; fourth, the return of the Arabs settled in Kurdistan to
their homes; fifth, the reintroduction of Kurdish place names that had
been Arabized by the regime.

Even though we were afraid of getting arrested or murdered, we
went forward with this action on that day. The rally in Damascus has
given the Kurds of the capital a great amount of hope. Five days after
this demonstration, the Ministry of the Interior invited us to a talk.
We thought this might perhaps turn out to be a kind of negotiation or
discussion, and so we went. But instead, we were arrested.

At that time, very many Kurds in Syria were very enthusiastic about
our demonstration, even though it had actually been pretty small. Even
though we were sentenced to jail time, we still continued with our
demonstrations. The people there now simply demonstrated for our
release.

In 2004, we were released and tens of thousands of people celebrated our liberation jointly with us and demanded a peaceful solution to the Kurdish problem.

Actually, the soccer riots in Qamişlo also occurred in 2004.

At the time, the regime tried to stir up a civil war between Kurds and Arabs in order to stop the opposition. But during the riots of 2004, we always stated very clearly that our struggle was directed against the regime and not against the Arab people. We are no enemies of the Arabs, but enemies of the regime. At that time, 12 parties cooperated with each other, including even the PYD. Back then, the Kurds spoke with one voice.

But the regime proceeded to smash that uprising.

The Ba'ath Party reacted in an extremely repressive way; many Kurds were arrested and tortured, and some even died in prison. But we wanted to continue with our actions and organized demonstrations against political persecution in front of the courts. Frequently, other parties also participated in these actions, particularly the Azadî Party. In 2005, Sheikh Mashuq al-Khasnawi was murdered by the regime because he was on the side of the people. After the death of Sheikh Mashuq al-Khasnawi, we organized a demonstration in Qamişlo jointly with the Azadî Party and Mishal at-Tammu's Future Movement; 50,000 to 60,000 people participated. But the regime again reacted with brutality. At the same time, it also understood that things couldn't go on like that, and it tried to destroy the basis for our protest with a few small improvements, for example, the release of even more political prisoners. During my time as the secretary general of the party, we also continued our demonstrations and actions, and we began to meet with the ambassadors of European states in Damascus in order to describe the situation to them.

How did these ambassadors react?

They showed a lot of interest and always thanked us for the information. But they also clearly stated that they could do no more than pass on our information. Two ambassadors took particular interest in us. The ambassadors of Sweden and Norway even accompanied us all the way to Qamişlo to listen to what we and our people had to say. In 2006, we again organized manifestations jointly with the Azadî Party and the Future Movement, and once again two leading members of our party were arrested.

There is thus a longer tradition of cooperation with the Azadî Party and the Future Movement. But how do things stand at present? I'm particularly interested in your relationship to the PYD.

Up until 2008, we always tried to include the PYD whenever we organized a demonstration. We always invited them, but they never participated. Since the extradition of Öcalan in 1999, the relationship between the PKK (and then the PYD) and the regime worsened. From then on, the PYD was persecuted, and from 2008 on, they have always claimed not to be able to participate in these demonstrations because of the repression.

Since the founding of the PYD in 2003, we have always tried to include the PYD and to negotiate with it. But the main problem was that it was actually impossible to agree on anything with the PYD. The PYD always explained that it couldn't take autonomous decisions because it had to wait for the green light from the PKK. The PYD is dependent on the PKK, and therefore, it is not really possible to conclude agreements with them. We have tried that time and again, but so far, no agreement has ever survived.

After 2004, the regime tried to exert pressure on the Kurdish parties in order to force them back into their former passivity. But we, the Azadî Party and the Future Movement, have always carried on and have therefore become stronger and stronger.

On Newroz 2008, the Kurds lit candles as a sign of protest, and the regime again responded by killing Kurds. Moreover, the regime tried to starve Kurdistan economically. In 2008, eight political parties again organized a big political demonstration in Damascus, in which the PYD also participated. In 2009, we decided as a party to demand autonomy for Syrian Kurdistan. After that, the regime again persecuted our cadres, including myself.

Why is this demand for autonomy so dangerous for the regime?

The Ba'ath Party has always regarded autonomy as a mere prelude to secession. I, for one, was kept in solitary detention for three months at the time. In court, I again insisted that we want to liberate our people, telling them that they could do with us what they wanted, but we would stick to it. The regime then charged us with separatism. In actual fact, we do everything in our power to prevent a split-up of Syria. But in 2011, the Arab Spring showed that prolonged opposition work can finally bear fruit.

When the protests began in 2011 and many of us were still in prison, all of a sudden there were rumours that the regime would yield to our demands and would, for example, return citizenship to the Kurds who had been deprived of it.

But these steps were apparently no longer able to pacify the situation.

The regime could have negotiated and could have accepted a transitional administration. Instead, it has chosen the military road, the path of repression. Actually, the regime wanted to annihilate the revolution. But that was impossible. Had the regime strived for real reforms, we would not be where we are at now. But nobody is ready to simply be annihilated.

How did your party react to this repression?

Most Kurdish parties came together and founded the Kurdish National Council (KNC) on 26 November 2011. The PYD was the only relevant force that didn't want to participate. Instead, it founded its own national council, the People's Council of West Kurdistan, and didn't want to cooperate with us.

Thereafter, several Kurdish activists such as Mishal at-Tammu were murdered. The regime simply wanted to silence these defiant parties. However, these groups have not fallen silent, but have continued with their work.

But what exactly is your problem with the PYD?

The problem is that the PYD wants to dominate everything and actually creates its own structures wherever it can. By acting this way, it really puts itself outside of the traditional party spectrum because no cooperation can work like that. Even so, through the mediation of President Masud Barzani, with the Supreme Kurdish Committee we have now found a form that still allows us to cooperate with it. This was a very positive signal vis-à-vis the Syrian regime. The demand for some form of federalism was formulated in a very clear way by this. But at a more concrete level, the cooperation works very sluggishly; moreover, by now we are also increasingly threatened by Islamist groups that represent the exact opposite of what the democratic protest movement stands for.

Why have these jihadist groups become so strong recently?

For one thing, we know that Turkey supports these groups. In part, they also operate under the name of the "Free Syrian Army." Even though we know that the latter actually has nothing to do with them, at the moment there are very many freeloaders who do lasting damage to the revolution and represent a threat to us Kurds.

How do you see the social situation in Rojava?

After the recent battles in Serê Kaniyê, the situation here has worsened very much. There is a lack of fuel, power, and food. The threats by the regime are another unsettling factor. The fact that President Assad recently described the opposition as "bacteria" and "parasites" gives reason to fear the worst. We need to anticipate the worst and are thus forced to arm ourselves to defend our civilians.

How do you evaluate the European positions with regard to Syria? What does your party actually want from Europe?

Europe should give the Syrian opposition political and humanitarian support. But unfortunately, so far we have seen little of it.

But you don't demand a military intervention, do you?

No, we don't think that that is necessary. But Europe should exert political pressure on Assad, rather than evade its own responsibility.

HISHAM SHEIKHO

Kurdish Youth Coordinating Committee (Yekîtiya Hevrêzên Ciwanên Kurd, YHCK), 11 January 2013

When was your organization founded?

We founded it in 2011 during the Syrian revolution because we wanted to support the revolution in our country. We wanted to work jointly with the Arab youth for the overthrow of the regime.

What kind of activities do you undertake?

We have organized demonstrations right from the beginning and have spread information about them. Moreover, we have tried to do as much public relations work as possible.

What is your relationship like not only to the Kurdish parties, but also to the Arab opposition groups, for example armed organizations such as the Free Syrian Army?

Because we understand ourselves as part of the Syrian revolution, of course we also cooperate with the Kurdish parties and the other revolutionary forces. We are a part of the revolution.

Is this still a revolution? Is there no danger that this is degenerating into a civil war?

These are worries I share. Unfortunately, in some towns, a development towards a civil war has already begun. But here in Syrian Kurdistan, there is no such danger. But in Aleppo or in other towns, there certainly is.

How do you see the policy of the US and Europe vis-à-vis development in Syria? What would you expect from Europe and the international community?

We are glad about everyone who supports our revolution, and we need such support from Europe and the US.

Yes, but what kind of support do you want? Are you for a military intervention or do you reject it, asking for more diplomatic or humanitarian support instead?

We expressly want military support. We have taken a decision to support military attacks against the regime from the outside.

How does your movement see the actions of the regional powers, for example Saudi Arabia, Turkey, or Iran?

At the moment, they all pursue their own interests, and unfortunately, this leads to undesirable side-effects. All those who support the revolution actually pursue their own interests in this, just as those do who support the regime.

If Turkey now supports the revolution, doesn't that also represent a danger for the Kurds, because Turkey will then try to prevent any Kurdish autonomy in the future? Is such a support then not actually counterproductive?

Turkey is of course afraid of Kurdish autonomy and is primarily concerned with trying to look for its own interests. Here, we also have conflicts of interests with Turkey.

How does your movement see the future of the Kurds in Syria?

We want a democratic and federalist state. The Kurds should then get autonomy within Syria, similar to the situation in Iraq.

MANAL HUSSEINI

Chairwoman of the Association of Kurdish Women in Amûdê (Komela Jinên Kurd li Amûdê; now Women's Centre Kolîşîna), 11 January 2013

When and why did you found an independent women's association in Amûdê?

Our association was formed in the context of the revolution. At first, we participated in the demonstrations; we really wanted to contribute and to also have a say. In the beginning, we were just a few women. We were very fearful and kept our cover because the security situation was so bad. But with time, the situation improved, more women joined us and gradually, we developed into a women's association here in Amûdê. It is now called "Komela Jinen li Amûdê," the Association of Kurdish Women in Amûdê.

What are the focal points of your work?

We have been carrying out various projects for quite a while; for example, we offer seminars on the role of women in our society. Now it is possible to talk about this openly, because we now have this free space. Free space means no police, no security forces – before, everything was secret, it was forbidden by the Syrian regime.

What are your demands at the demonstrations?

One of our main demands is to put the principle of equal rights for men and women into the Syrian constitution. That is, we raise political demands and at the same time, we do enlightenment- and consciousness-raising work for women in the form of seminars.

What kind of topics do these seminars cover?

We work on different questions concerning the status of women. We have already carried out seminars on the oppression of women, but we also deal with legal aspects such as equal rights in the Syrian constitution. We also illuminate the political side: In the Kurdish political parties, only 5 per cent of the members are women, and the rest are men. We also only have chairmen and no chairwomen. What role does the woman then play in politics? Only in the PYD is the situation a bit better.

Why is this so in all parties, with the lone exception of the PYD?

Our society is a male-dominated society. As of yet, our politicians, the men, have still not accepted that the woman is able – and entitled – to participate. It is a closed society. The PYD is a little better in this regard, because they have supported the participation of women. Therefore, women were less afraid of the security forces. Whenever we dared to do something, this could immediately lead to persecution by the regime.

And this has nothing to do with the feminist positions of the PYD?

Of course this plays a big role. The PYD knows how important the role of the woman in society is, and therefore, it is more interested in achieving the participation of women and not just men.

Do other Kurdish parties now also realize the importance of gender? Do other Kurdish parties have women's programmes?

The reason why women don't play any role in the parties is that the parties themselves deny them the opportunity. Therefore, women used to back away from participating. Once we had founded our association, many women immediately flocked to it. Women have to defend and to fight for their rights themselves.

The Kurdish associations in Syria are very often mere front organizations for political parties. How independent is your association?

We are an independent association. But if individual members support a particular party, that doesn't mean that *we* work for that party. If a party takes a stronger stand for the Kurdish people, we will of course support it. We are, after all, Kurds and part of the Kurdish people – that is a natural connection. But that still doesn't mean that we belong to any one party. We have founded our association because we want to fight for our rights. We have women on our board who are members of different parties.

Which are the most important problems that women face here?

The first problem is that this is still a male-dominated society. A ten-year-old boy is still able to boss around his 20-year-old sister. And as a wife, too, you have to follow the instructions of your husband. The second point is that women are financially dependent on the husband because they don't work. The woman is therefore not able to fulfil her own wishes and aspirations, because she can't get along without the money of her husband. Religion and culture also play a role. A woman is not allowed to say "No." If someone wants to marry her and her father or brother agree, the engagement is valid even without her consent.

Do you have supporters for your concerns?

Our society is still not ready to accept women as equals. In addition, many women stand in the way of others. When we demand our rights, others say: "No, this is not possible. We are women. We must stay the way we are." So women are even oppressed by other women! But of course it is also important that *the men* acknowledge the role of the woman. Lack of support from men is one of the reasons why women cannot make greater strides. The woman must be regarded as a human being; she has rights and she is indeed capable of achieving something. Therefore, we also have to have seminars for men. The man has to refine himself and must learn to support the woman.

The Ba'ath regime was a secular dictatorship. In the other Arab countries, the Islamists are in power. Are you not afraid that after Assad, a regime might come to power that oppresses the women even more?

We have three concrete demands: First, we want the overthrow of the regime. Second, we demand a federalist state since this is the best solution for the Kurdish question. Third, we demand women's rights, rights that must be written into the constitution. Of course, it would be a catastrophe if the Islamists came to power. But these groups are not very strongly represented among the Kurds.

We know from other parts of Kurdistan that there are still forced marriages. Is that also still a problem here?

It depends on the families, but the problem is not as bad as it used to be. A girl who is forced into a marriage can go to one of our lawyers and get legal advice. In our association, we have different working groups, and one of them occupies itself with children and women. There, our psychologists and pedagogues take care of children and women who have problems at home. It is our task to talk with the children about their traumas, about their experiences, and to then jointly find a solution or a way out. Up to now, we've had many children from Hama or Homs, but recently, our own children, the children of Amûdê, have also started to come. We are striving to give better care to these children. But to do this, we need the support of other children's rights organizations, because our own means are not sufficient.

That means that you have two working groups in your association, each of which has a different focus point?

In our association here, we have different competencies. Thus, apart from legal and psychological care we also offer health counselling. Young women who are reaching sexual maturity are sometimes counselled about diseases transmitted by sexual intercourse. But we also give women a course in first aid for their further education. Moreover, we try to supply financial support with small sums. Once, a pregnant woman came to us who couldn't afford to go to a doctor. We then accompanied her to the doctor and covered part of the costs.

Is the use of contraceptives also a topic in this connection?

Yes, it is even one of our focal points. Many women do not want to have additional children, and we educate them about their possibilities. But our problem is that we don't have our own centre where we can meet without being disturbed and where other women can come to us.

One of your biggest wishes is to have a space of your own for your activities?

Yes, and access to the media. We are so limited with regards to means and personnel that we can't bring our work to all places where it is needed. But we would like to offer our work to as many people as possible.

I, for one, will try to organize support for your important activities via our Austrian NGO LeEZA.

That would make our work much more easy. At the moment, we really depend exclusively on the unpaid work of our activists and the kindness of people who supply us with a room once a week. The men here have public spaces at their disposal the whole day long; they go to the bazaar, to the coffee houses or they sit together in the street. For us women, there is no public space anywhere in Amûdê where we can meet. And it is similar in all towns here in Rojava. We really need a lot of change in this regard.

ZERDAŞT MUHAMMED

Member of the Political Bureau of the Kurdish Democratic Union Party (Partiya Yekîtî ya Demokrat a Kurdî li Sûriyê), 12 January 2013

From your perspective, how does the cooperation between the Kurdish National Council (KNC) and the PYD's People's Council of West Kurdistan in the Supreme Kurdish Committee (SKC) work?

The Supreme Kurdish Committee, which was founded with the Agreement of Hewlêr in summer 2012, doesn't work at all. We, the parties of the Kurdish National Council, will never arrive at an agreement with the PYD. The SKC is just a rotten compromise. Just one example of this is the fact that we had agreed at its founding that external contacts should only take place on a joint basis. But to this day, each party executes its own foreign policy. On the one hand, the Agreement of Hewlêr puts us, the member parties of the KNC, in shackles, because we can't continue to work autonomously, but on the other, the PYD simply ignores the agreement and continues to work as before.

> *But don't you also understand the critique by the PYD that the Kurdish National Council has, through its dependence on the Kurdistan Regional Government in Iraq, given too much influence to the Barzanis and has thus also strengthened the Turkish influence? After all, by now Barzani and Turkey have a pretty good relationship. Some even fear that he wants to use the troops he has trained in Iraq against the PYD.*

Masud Barzani has taken the side of the Syrian revolution right from the outset. The Syrian Peshmerga he trained in Iraq were never conceived as a means to fight other Kurdish actors, but only serve the defence of the population in case of emergency. They serve the purpose of safeguarding the peace once the regime collapses. Barzani has repeatedly declared that they will never be used against other Kurdish parties.

> *What about the contacts with Turkey? Does your party have contacts with Turkey?*

We have never had any contacts with the Turkish government. The mere fact that Turkey supports the Syrian revolution doesn't mean at all that we are cooperating with Turkey. These accusations by the PYD are simply absurd and are designed to obscure the fact that it is the PYD that cooperates – namely, with the regime. Furthermore, it is the PYD that entertains close contacts with a Turkish party, the BDP, which furthermore actively supported the PYD during the battles in Serê Kaniyê. We are also neither part of the Arab opposition nor of the Syrian National Council (which definitely entertains contacts to Turkey). But when people from Homs or Aleppo flee to us, of course we support them to best of our abilities. After all, the Arab population also suffers under this regime.

Is this still a revolution or is it already sliding into a civil war?

The revolution was a self-organized process from below. None of the parties and groups can claim to speak for the revolution. When the protests began in 2011 and then turned into a revolution, this was definitely a genuine revolution. But the regime has strong allies. Malik's government in Iraq, Hezbollah, Iran, and Russia all support the Ba'ath regime politically and militarily. We, the opposition, don't have such allies. The EU and the US largely leave us high and dry, even though the EU of course could intervene, even without a Security Council resolution.

What do you want from the EU? A military intervention?

We want a humanitarian intervention, not a military one. This conference of the "Friends of Syria" was nothing but talk. We are here, right at the Turkish border, and we have neither gas nor electricity, nor can we cross the border. They talk their way out by pinning the blame on the Security Council. Actually, they are not interested in human rights, but only in their economy.

By now, in Europe many observers fear that an overthrow of the regime could lead to a takeover by the jihadis.

The Syrian people doesn't want the jihadis and has tried for a long time to keep terrorists out of the country. But by now the political situation has led to an invasion by groups such as Jabhat al-Nusra and an increasing strength of these groups. In case anyone has decided that all terrorists come to Syria in order to have them annihilated here, this is costing us very much in terms of human lives.

Do you believe that there is such a master plan, such a plot?

Many Syrians believe it. But we don't know. What we do know is that, the longer the civil war drags on, the more terrorists we will have.

MUHAMMED WELI

Speaker of the Coordination of Revolutionary Students (Hevreza Xwendevanen Şoreşe), 12 January 2013

Since when has your organization existed and what are some of your activities?

We founded it on 10 November 2012, that is, two months ago. As students, we want to make our contribution to the revolution and to the overthrow of the regime. But we also work for our own interests as students who suffer very much under the present situation.

What are the specific problems of students?

By now, several schools have been closed for months because the teachers don't receive their salaries anymore, and even if the schools are open, many teachers have ceased to come to work. There are no coaching lessons. Many students can't afford to go to school anymore because they have to work.

I, for one, have to work as a painter just to be able to go to school at all. That is, I get up very early in the morning, work, and then go to school – or the other way around. Teachers and students do all kinds of work to scrape by somehow, and then school necessarily comes up short.

How do you try to do something against this?

We organize our own learning groups and private lessons for ourselves, and try to support the families of poor students so that their children can continue to attend school.

You call yourself "revolutionary students," indicating a conscious political outlook. What does your political work look like?

We participate in the demonstrations and cooperate with the Kurdish National Council. We understand ourselves explicitly as part of the Syrian revolution. The Kurdish people are a core part of that revolution and we need a recognition of the Kurdish people in the Syrian constitution.

Since you're a student organization, you are all very young. How old are you?

I'm 17 and attend the seventh grade of grammar school.

With that, you're certainly the youngest person who I'm interviewing for my research. How does a young person like you imagine the future of Syria? In what kind of country do you want to grow up?

We want to live in a peaceful land with freedom of speech in which there are modern schools for all. We hope that there will be no civil war, and we work for that goal.

Do you believe that is a realistic hope for the future? At the moment, we see sure signs of a confessionalization of the conflict.

I am convinced that the Syrians are intelligent enough and that they can live together peacefully once this regime has finally been overthrown. At the moment, repression by the regime of course leads to conflicts between the Sunni, Alawi, Shiites, Christians, and so on. But once Assad is finally ousted, we will certainly live together peacefully again. This is my hope and my conviction.

Yet another danger on the horizon are the radical jihadists. Are you not afraid that Syria could fall from one dictatorship to the next?

We all took to the streets for democracy. This revolution is a revolution of democrats and young people who are fed up with having to live under a dictatorship. We will most certainly not overthrow the regime just to wake up under a different dictatorship. That these groups are gaining in strength has to do with the regime's reaction to the revolution. But the Syrian youth will not stand for being oppressed again – neither by the Ba'athists nor by the Islamists.

MUNZUR ESKAN

Co-founder of the Supreme Committee of the Movement of the Kurdish Youth (Tevgera Ciwanên Kurd, TCK), 12 January 2013

When and how was your youth movement founded?

We came together after the events of Qamişlo in 2004 because we were dissatisfied with the reaction of the Kurdish parties and wanted to found a new, more radical youth movement which consistently challenged the regime. At that time, we were all still very young, and some of us even dreamt of an armed uprising and founded a group that prepared for armed struggle. Unfortunately, our group was infiltrated by the secret service and our plans were disclosed. Therefore, in 2006 I and many other members of our group were arrested.

How many of you were arrested at the time?

All in all, more than 40 of our members were arrested. Even though we were all still teenagers, we were all tortured. Torture is actually par for the course in Syrian prisons. We were tortured by means of electricity, beatings, and waterboarding. But the psychic forms of torture were just as terrible as the physical ones. At first, for fifteeen months my family knew nothing of me and my whereabouts. I had simply disappeared. Many of the family members of our activists had the same experience. Personally, I was in prison for altogether four years and three months.

Torture is of course always a traumatic experience, but it must be particularly horrible at such a young age. Is there a place where people who were tortured as adolescents can get support?

There is no professional help. In my case, the torture did not just leave psychic harm, but also physical damage. Since then, I've had to wear strong glasses. We don't have anything like psychotherapy here. But with my friends, I feel that I am in good hands, and the political struggle gives me additional strength. That is my form of therapy.

When did you re-establish your group after your release?

We always continued to exist as an organization. It is just that at the outset, we were all but incapable of acting. As for myself, I restarted my political work immediately after my release, and the same is true of my comrades-in-arms. With the protests of 2011, many new boys and girls joined up with us. I should say right away that, different from other groups, boys and girls have always fought side by side in our group. We have also never had an autonomous women's organization like the PYD, but have always done all our work together. This distinguishes us from all other movements.

How are you organized today? What kind of activities do you carry out?

We are really a movement with different regional groups in which young men and young women are jointly organized. At the moment, we have groups in ten different towns, with Qamişlo, Kobanê, Efrîn, Amûdê, Serê Kaniyê, Darbasiye, Tirbespiye, Dêrik, and Aleppo among them. There is also a "prep" group for teenagers under 18 to prepare them, with others of the same age, for the TCK. We organize demonstrations, seminars, and courses for young people, and we don't offer only political stuff, but also first-aid courses or language lessons.

Your movement is known for its particularly critical stance towards the PYD. Why?

The PYD works with the regime and is, right now, itself establishing an extremely repressive regime. If the PYD rules alone, this is again a dictatorship which we will then have to fight just as we fight the current regime.

The intra-Kurdish conflicts have come to a head in the last months, and many even fear an intra-Kurdish civil war. How does the T.C.K. see this problem?

We would actually be quite glad if there were other armed units not belonging to the PYD. Perhaps, the PYD would then observe the Agreement of Hewlêr. But now they treat the other political parties and movements any way they like. I would welcome it if Barzani would at long last send the people trained by his Peshmerga across the border and would thus create a counterweight against the monopoly of violence held by the PYD. Only then would the PYD see itself forced to make compromises.

How do you see the stance of Europe and the US with regard to the conflict in Syria?

Both Europe and the United States are extremely hesitant and leave us at the mercy of the regime. The regime gets powerful support from Iran and Russia. We are forced to face all the violence empty-handed. On that background, we are very disappointed that the West has left us hanging dry.

But the Syrian opposition – including the Kurdish opposition – is disunited about the question of what, concretely, they want from Europe and the US, and this makes any kind of intervention difficult. What do you, the TCK, concretely expect from Europe and the US?

We have already officially formulated the answer in a written declaration: We are unequivocally for military intervention and the support of the revolution by the EU and the US. Europe and the US should have no problem with sharing the related costs and risks. If we get no military support, this means that we are left high and dry and the regime is allowed to win.

HASSAN DRAIEÎ AND HLA DRAIEÎ

Founders of the Amûdê Committee for Art and Education, 12 January 2013

An old communist who here, in the darkness within a small house above the bazaar, teaches young people how to play the flute, and his young daughter, Hla, who participates in this both as a student and an organizer – are you the core of the cultural life of Amûdê?

Hassan: In the course of the revolution, we have simply become active ourselves and have begun to give lessons in Kurdish and Arab music, to organize readings and poetry evenings, and to arrange small concerts.

Hla: We have two different musical groups here. One consists of experienced artists who play music together, and then we have the teenagers who, of course, have their talents but who also still have a lot to learn and who are taught by my father.

To sit in the darkness in a town in which there is no power supply anymore and to play music is fascinating. But are these good conditions in which to learn to play an instrument?

Hassan: Perhaps they are not the best conditions. But the most important thing is motivation, and it is very strong! Over many years, we could live our Kurdish music and culture only secretly, privately or at weddings. Now we can do this in the open. Culture is an important part of a revolution!

Hla: I am not as interested in politics as my father, and I am certainly not a communist.

Here in the darkness, the picture of Khalid Bakdash is invisible anyway.

Hla: [laughs] I am interested in culture. As humans, we have to play music or recite poems even in a difficult situation. To do this, you don't need money or electricity, and now we have the freedom to do that publicly without being molested. In that regard, we really have already liberated ourselves here in Amûdê.

But doesn't that show that culture is also political?

Hla: Perhaps, but it doesn't have anything to do with any one political party.

How are you organized?

Hla: Apart from the music groups, we have five further sub-committees. The first occupies itself with translations and research, the second with theatre and poetry, the third with the media, the fourth with finances, and the fifth with PR. These sub-committees do their work all unsalaried and of course cooperate with each other. Therefore, since our founding we have managed to organize theatre and poetry evenings that were attended by very many people. The people here, the young people in particular, are really hungry for culture! Many of us up to now haven't had the opportunity to develop, or have read our poems only to our best friends. Now we can all do so in front of a large audience!

Hassan: And we, as musicians, do not merely pass on the Kurdish culture, but we also play Arab and international music (begins to sing a Kurdish version of "Bella Ciao").

MUFID AL-KHAZNAWI

Son of Sheikh Muhammad Mashuq al-Khaznawi, Naqshibandi-Sheikh, 21 November 2013

After the death of your father, you went into exile and now you live in Norway, but you are still active in the spirit of your father.

Yes, I am the director of a Kurdish Islamic centre in Norway near Oslo and I am still active in the spirit of my father, in inter-religious dialogue. I am a religious person. But because the current situation doesn't permit to just be active only religiously, I am now also politically active. In such an international situation, but especially in the situation in which Syria finds itself, the religious communities must commit themselves to peace.

Since when have you been in exile?

In a certain sense, today is my birthday. I arrived in Norway exactly seven years ago. On 10 May 2005, my father was kidnapped and a year later, I went into exile. After the death of my father, the situation in Syria became too dangerous for me.

Do you now have a clearer picture of what happened to your father, whose murder was never really solved?

Up to about 70 per cent, I know what happened. I have worked very hard to find the truth and have talked to witnesses. You know that the regime is suspected to have masterminded the murder. My father represented a danger to the regime because he played an important role as a mediator between the Kurds. My father had a centre for inter-religious dialogue in Qamişlo in which he promoted a very modern and democratic Islam and worked with Christians, Jews, and Êzîdî. But it was primarily his intra-Kurdish mediating role that made him very popular. This great popularity turned him into a real threat to the regime. But I don't want to go into any more detail at this point in time.

Which role does Islam play for the Kurdish society in Syria?

The problem of us Kurds is that we have repeatedly regarded religion as the enemy. We are one of the few families who are both religious and Kurdish. Most other religious families have become alienated from the Kurdish people at some point in time.

But the Naqshibandi and Qadiri Sheikhs have always played an important social and political role among the Kurds.

The Naqshibandi have played a more important role. Almost all important personalities of Kurdish history such as, for example, Mulla Mustafa Barzani, have been Naqshibandi. But since Mulla Mustafa Barzani, many Sheikhs have played a negative role. For that reason, many Kurds now regard religion as an enemy.

Your father also had an important mediating function between the parties. Since 2013, the intra-Kurdish conflict has intensified quite a bit. Could people like you here in Europe play a role as mediators between the PYD and the parties of the Kurdish National Council?

The intra-Kurdish conflict is very detrimental to us. Unfortunately, we as Kurds are prone to being ready to bring sacrifices for others, but also to constantly quarrelling among ourselves. To me, it is important to keep the communicative channels to all sides open. But by now, I've been in exile for seven years. So far, our mediation attempts have all been unsuccessful. In a situation like this, people listen only to the strong. But we continue to work to de-escalate this conflict lest we finally end up with an intra-Kurdish civil war.

SALIH MUSLIM

Co-chair, together with Asya Abdullah, of the Democratic Union Party (Partiya Yekitîya Demokrat, PYD), 30 December 2013

Your son Şerwan was recently killed in battle at the age of 17. May I first express my condolences.

Thank you. When we fight for freedom, we have to pay a price. This was the price I had to pay.

For what political project did your son die? What is the goal of your party for the Kurds in Syria?

We want a democratic self-administration, which represents a certain form of autonomy. We want democratic rights and a constitutional recognition of the Kurds within Syria. But we don't strive for independence or a Kurdish national state. We have also submitted this concept to the National Coordinating Committee for Democratic Change, and the Arab parties have agreed to this. How exactly this autonomy will look like is a matter for future negotiations. After all, every state has its own form of federalism. Germany, Switzerland, or the United States also differ from each other in this regard. We can check out later which of these models is the best for Syria. The decisive point is that we want to administer ourselves, on the basis of human rights and democracy. What we certainly don't want is new borders! We are no separatists. We don't want a new Kurdish national state independent of Syria. Everything else can be negotiated.

It is understandable that, one and a half years after the withdrawal of the regime from Syrian-Kurdistan, there are still problems with this self-administration. There are, however, also grave conflicts between your party and the other Kurdish parties, and there are still no democratically legitimized structures. When will there be free elections?

We have only made a *proposal* for the self-administration. We certainly don't want to govern alone and are preparing elections in the areas under our control. We definitely don't want to rule alone, but we want the other parties to participate. Actually, both of the Kurdish councils, the Kurdish National Council and the People's Council of West Kurdistan, have in principle already agreed on this way to proceed. We now have a committee preparing the elections, which has decided that there will be three cantons – one in the Jezira, one around Kobanê, and a third one around Afrîn – in which the elections are to take place. That is, we are right in the midst of the preparations and hope that the elections can soon be carried out.

But for a few months, there have been massive conflicts between the PYD and some of the parties of the Kurdish National Council, particularly those close to Barzani's PDK. Are these parties now also involved in the preparations for the elections and will they run in these elections or not?

The KNC is actually not a united bloc with regard to this, and by now most parties cooperate with us. But there are some forces that would really like to destroy everything and that would also like to sabotage the Agreement of Hewlêr of summer 2012.[1]

Who do you mean by that?

The parties that are connected to Masud Barzani. They also always claim that the Asayîş are the security forces of the PYD, and then they accuse them of doing this, that, and the other thing. But that is not true, they are Kurdish security forces.

But you will certainly not deny that it was the PYD that founded these security forces and the People's Protection Units (YPG)?

No, I don't deny that. We founded the YPG and the Asayîş because we saw that this was becoming a necessity. But they are not our party militia. We want unified security forces and a unified army, as opposed to each party entertaining their own militias. But we are constantly confronted with the charge that these are *our* armed forces, and we, in turn, are equated with the PKK.

But even though perhaps you are not identical with the PKK, you certainly are a sister party of the PKK.

Yes, nobody denies that. But the permanent equation between the two is simply false.

Let us come back to the elections. Which parties have, so far, signalled their willingness to participate in these elections? And even more concretely, will the parties that, up to now, have distanced themselves the most from the PYD, that is, the Azadî Party and the el-Partî, the sister party of Barzani's PDK in Iraq, also participate?

A whole number of parties of the Kurdish National Council have signalled their readiness to participate. At the moment, there are three Kurdish parties with which we cooperate. But unfortunately, there are also parties which don't participate. The only two parties who refuse any cooperation at all are the Azadî Party and the el-Partî.

But they would be welcome to participate in the election?

Yes, of course. If they want to, they can.

In November, the PYD also pronounced the regional self-administration in Syria officially. How did the regime react?

Quite similar to the so-called opposition. Even though there were also other voices on both sides, the majority still accuses us of being separatists, and they refuse to recognize the self-administration. Thus, we have to win it against the resistance from both sides.

In recent months, the secular opposition groups in Syria have been weakened considerably. On the other hand, jihadist groups such as Jabhat al-Nusra, the "Islamic State in Iraq and the Levant" and other groups have grown stronger. Even from Europe, more and more young Salafists travel to Syria to join the jihad. What does that mean for the Kurds?

We had cooperated with the genuine oppositionists in Syria right from the start. But then groups such as the Syrian National Council emerged that were not based on any local groups and were actually created in the West. Even the Muslim Brotherhood, which had been very strong here before its persecution in the 1980s, did not have any local organization anymore. Here, the West has tried to create a new opposition that did not have a domestic basis. We were against a militarization of the conflict right from the outset. As soon as one starts to procure weapons, one becomes dependent on those who deliver them and has to follow their policy. For that reason, the jihadists are actually not autonomous actors, but instruments. They have no independent strategy, no own goals, they are just instruments.

Instruments of whom?

Of the United States, or rather, of imperialism or financial capital. They want to do the same to Syria that they did to many other states in the region. For that, they need complacent, armed groups that do their work for them in Syria. They did the same thing in the Kosovo, and now they are doing it here.

But what is their goal? Do they want to install a pro-Western regime?

No, it is more complicated than that. Today, it has become impossible to simply maintain the old authoritarian regimes, because, given the new reality of globalization, the internet, and many other possibilities, the desire for freedom is much more pronounced than before. But just as the revolution in Tunisia was stolen, the plan is to steal it here, too. We are in contact with several leftist oppositionists in Tunisia, and they all say that we have to be on the watch to prevent our revolution from being stolen, which is what happened to them. But an Islamist regime such as, say, in Turkey could be an alternative for imperialism that would allow it to stay in power.

You have just said that in a militarized conflict, one becomes dependent on those who supply one's arms. Where, then, does the PYD gets its arms from? Who supplies the Kurdish security forces and the YPG with their equipment?

Most of our arms come from our own sources and were simply bought on the black market, and when we pressed the regime to withdraw its forces from Kurdistan, we did not allow them to take their weapons and ammunition with them. Thus we have captured a fair amount of the arms of the regime.

In Syrian Kurdistan, there are more than 500,000 internally displaced persons from other parts of Syria. Already in the last winter, I could observe on-site that their supply situation is very bad and that no international aid reaches the region. How is their situation today, one year later?

We have at least been able to remedy the lack of diesel. Thus the people will have at least heating in the winter. But the supply situation with regard to food and other consumer goods is pretty bad even for the local people and even worse for the displaced persons from other parts of Syria. There is still no international aid whatsoever. Most of the big aid organizations are not even represented and the International Red Cross cooperates with the Syrian Red Crescent, which is an Arab organization and works with the regime and not with us. Actually, the regime has never completely disappeared from our region and still controls the airport of Qamişlo. If there are aid deliveries, they go to these authorities, not to us.

It's not just the airport that continues to be controlled by the regime. In recent months, there has clearly been a stronger presence of the regime in Qamişlo, the capital of the Kurdish self-administration. On 14 November, adherents of the Ba'ath Party could freely demonstrate in Qamişlo and were not prevented from shouting their usual slogans such as "We will sacrifice our blood and our soul for you, Bashar." Apparently, the security forces of the regime have also resumed their activities in the Kurdish regions. In November, the Military Intelligence Service arrested the well-known singer Sharif Omari. On 18 December, the security forces of the regime in Qamişlo arrested five taxi patrons and a taxi driver, and on 26 December, they arrested two activists of the Kurdish Youth Movement TCK. Who controls the capital of the Kurdish self-administration? The regime or the Kurds?

As I said, the regime has not completely disappeared there. The situation in Qamişlo is very complex. It is not just the airport that is under the control of the regime; the same is true for the neighbourhoods inhabited by the Arabs. There is an Arab tribe called Tai in Qamişlo whose 35,000 members still stand behind the regime. The city districts where these Arab tribe members live are not under our control. The demonstrations of the Ba'ath Party and the arrests took place in these Arab districts. One of our main aims is to avoid an ethnic conflict. We believe in the brotherhood between the peoples and don't want any fighting between the Kurds and the Arabs. And because we also do not want a war with the tribe of the Tai, the local situation is very complicated. Up to now, we could prevent a situation as in Serê Kaniyê, where there was fighting between Kurds and Arabs because of the Islamists. But this is possible only by trying to find some form of coexistence with the Arab tribes. In al-Hasaka, the situation is even more difficult. There, the Kurdish districts are under our control, one part of the Arab districts is under the control of the regime, and another part is controlled by the Islamist opposition. In such a situation, it is our priority to prevent fighting within the towns.

In Qamişlo, there are also very many Syrian-Aramaic and Armenian Christians. Where do they stand and who controls the districts where they live?

The Christians are on our side. Their districts are controlled and protected by the Kurds.

Kurdish critics of the PYD often accuse your party of having established a very authoritarian regime. There have been repeated reports of abductions of members of other Kurdish parties, and on 20 June, there were deadly clashes between demonstrators and fighters of the People's

Protection Units (YPG) in Amûdê after protests against the arrest of activists. How do you justify these repressive measures against competing Kurdish groups?

I want to stress once more that the Asayîş and the YPG are not the armed units of our party, but the security forces of the Kurdish self-administration. Whenever someone is arrested, our opponents always claim that it is the fault of our party. But we have security forces and courts, and they are not identical with our party. If some criminal is arrested, it is immediately claimed that the PYD kidnapped them.

But in Amûdê, the dispute was about political activists, who in fact were released at the beginning of July.

Yes, but these people were actually only questioned about where they got their money from and what connections they had, and then they were released. The whole thing was a staged provocation by Abdulbaset Sieda of the Syrian National Council, who comes from Amûdê, by his Turkish allies and by his supporters in Iraqi Kurdistan. Even before the clashes, ambulances were already parked on the Turkish side of the border, and journalists of Barzani's Rudaw TV were told that they would have to work a longer shift that day. Moreover, even before the clashes erupted someone in the demonstration fired shots at the soldiers of the YPG. It was only then that the fighters of the YPG opened fire on the demonstrators.

But your critics report this differently.

Yes, but they also didn't tell you anything about the connections of these people with Abdulbaset Sieda and Turkey or about the waiting ambulances. But as a politician, I still want to clearly state that the fighters of the YPG overreacted in this case and made a mistake when they fired into the crowd. They should not have done that. But such things can happen if they don't know who they are dealing with here.

But Kurds from other parties or from the Kurdish Youth Movement have told me that by now, people hardly dare anymore to conduct demonstrations without the PYD, let alone against it.

Everyone who registers a demonstration can demonstrate here. We have nothing against peaceful demonstrations, even when they are directed against us. But we also have to guarantee the security of our region, and in a war such as the one in Syria, in which very many foreign actors are also trying to exert their influence, it is far from easy to at least keep the war away. Because we have succeeded in doing this, the population loves us now. The fighters of the YPG are heroes for the Kurds, and it may even happen that the population itself attacks some people who come out against the YPG and the Asayîş. However, we as a party have nothing to do with this, but are doing our best to continue to guarantee the security of the Kurdish self-administration.

Actually, one of these security problems is probably the mounting number of jihadist groups. Even from Central Europe, more and more young men are hitting the trail to Syria to go to what they consider as a jihad. How should we deal with this?

One has to talk to these young people and prevent them from taking this road. I don't know why young men from Germany or Austria come to Syria to fight. That has probably more to do with the situation in their home countries than with the situation in Syria. But I'd really wish for someone to attend to these people and to talk to them before they act so stupidly. One probably needs some prevention programmes for radicalized adolescents.

What else would you hope for from the Austrian government with regard to Syria?

Austria has always been an internationally renowned country and has often proven that even a small state can be of diplomatic importance. Austria has long played an important role particularly in the realm of peace policy, and it is a great pity that today, states such as Austria that don't promote any selfish interests in the region but stand for a peace-oriented foreign policy contribute so little to the international debates. We would want Austria to intensify its commitment to a diplomatic solution to the civil war in Syria.

MUSTAFA KHIDR OSSO

Secretary General of the Kurdish Freedom Party in Syria (Partiya Azadî ya Kurd li Sûriyê), 18 February 2014

In January 2014, the PYD declared the autonomy of three Kurdish cantons in Syria. The Azadî Party and most of the other parties of the

Kurdish National Council didn't recognize this and refuse to cooperate with the PYD in this realm. Why?

The PYD cooperates with Bashar Assad's Ba'ath regime. Therefore, this autonomy won't help the Kurds at all. As long as the PYD doesn't end its collaboration with the regime, such an autonomy is of no value. Only the *population* of Rojava can declare an autonomy, not any particular party alone. My party wanted to cooperate with the PYD in order to jointly work for the autonomy of the Kurdish people. We wanted the PYD to join us in cooperating with the opposition. But the PYD has refused any such cooperation. We wanted to convince the PYD to liberate itself from the embrace of the regime. But these attempts have failed. We work for a federalist system in which all Syrian citizens work together independently of their religious and ethnic origin. We don't fight just for the Kurds, but in the final analysis, for all Syrians. After all, Syria does not consist only of Arabs and Kurds, but is also host to a number of Christian minorities. We can only overthrow this regime together.

But the PYD has now proclaimed these cantons and has also announced that there are to be elections in May. Should these elections really come to pass, would your party participate or would it boycott them?

We will certainly not participate in such elections.

At the time, there are negotiations between the two Azadî parties, the el-Partî and the Yekîtî-Kurdistanî Party concerning the fusion into a new party. How are these talks going and what is the goal of such a merger? After all, the Azadî Party split into two parties with the same name only in 2011. Will such a fusion work?

Yes, this fusion process has been going on for months and we expect the unification of our parties in the course of the next weeks.

One of those behind this is Mustafa Barzani, who has massively promoted this fusion. What role do the Kurdistan Regional Government in Iraq and the PDK-Iraq play for this new PDK-Syria?

President Barzani was the provider of ideas for this fusion. He wanted this unification and supports it. Barzani's support enables us to do the best for our Kurdish people.

But how will the new party work in Syria? De facto, at the moment the PYD rules Rojava. By what means do you want to struggle against this dominance if you don't run in the elections? Do you also think about fighting against the PYD militarily?

You mean, whether we want to lead an armed struggle against the PYD?

Yes, there are, after all, Peshmerga who Barzani recruited among Syrian refugees in Iraq. This raises the question for what purpose these people were trained.

We are a political party and after the unification with the other three parties, we will still remain a political party. We will definitely not use violence against the PYD or create any military units on our own in any form. For us, the most important thing is democracy and we will fight for democracy with civil and democratic means. The PYD and the regime are so closely connected that the regime of the PYD would be easily defeated anyway if the Ba'ath regime collapsed. That is, right now we are fighting against the system of the Ba'ath Party. After that, it will be easy to also get rid of the rule of the PYD.

The accusation against the PYD according to which it collaborates with the regime is commonly countered by the latter with the counter-accusation that the Azadî Party and other Kurdish opposition parties closely cooperate with Turkey. What does your relation to Turkey look like?

Our party does not have any special relation with Turkey. But Turkey supports the Syrian revolution, and that is a good thing. Turkey is our neighbour and Turkey is, after all, a strong regional power. But we have always told the Turkish government that they have to solve their own problem with the Kurds in Turkey.

But the Kurds are not only confronted with the regime, but increasingly also with jihadist groups such as Jabhat al-Nusra and the so-called "Islamic State in Iraq and Greater Syria". How do you want to deal with this danger?

In Rojava, all people have arms anyway and are thus able to defend themselves. These jihadist fighters don't stand a chance here.

Are you not afraid that these groups could come to power after the fall of Assad?

The rest of Syria may perhaps really be faced with the danger that these groups could take control. But we Kurds are not very Islamic, and therefore I see no danger for us in that regard.

We have repeatedly heard the accusation that Turkey supports the jihadist groups in Syria.

About this, we only have the same information from the media as you do, and no insider knowledge whatsoever. Turkey supports the Syrian revolution. Whether it also supports groups such as Jabhat al-Nusra or the "Islamic State in Iraq and Greater Syria," we don't really know. Our party doesn't know anything at all about this. And this kind of news might also simply have been disseminated by the regime.

What goal do you see for Syria and the position of the Kurds in Syria?

We want a united, democratic, and federal Syria in which all minorities can peacefully speak and live their own languages and cultures.

That is, not just an autonomy for the Kurds, but a general federalization?

We would like to have an autonomy for the Kurds on the model of Iraqi Kurdistan. But the other minorities in Syria could also have their own autonomous regions. After this war, it is entirely possible that the Alawi and the Druze will also want their own autonomy.

FADI YAKUB

Commander of the Assyrian police unit Sutoro in Dêrik, 19 February 2014

When and why was the Sutoro founded?

The Sutoro was founded in October 2013 and pursues the goal of protecting the people here.

And why did you found a specifically Christian-Assyrian police unit?

Because we Assyrians simply want to share responsibility and don't want to rely solely on the Kurdish police units.

Sutoro is a New-West-Armenian term and is also written, in your own script and side-by-side with the Latin variety, on all police cars. I can imagine that this also gives a great sense of empowerment. My Syrian friends in Vienna would probably look at something like this quite starry-eyed if they encountered it.

Of course, the fact that we now carry arms and use our own language in public is also a sign of our new self-confidence. Armed Assyrians will not allow themselves to be simply slaughtered.

But how can I picture the local police work, for example, if someone here in Dêrik needs the police. Who will they call: you or the Kurdish Asayî? Who is responsible for what?

We take it as it comes. We work together closely. We are a single unit and it is completely irrelevant whether we or the Asayîş are called.

Are there only Aramaic-speaking Christians in the Sutoro or also Armenians?

We have everything. Even Kurds and Arabs.

Including women?

As of yet, no. But if God wills, soon.

ABJAR MUSA

Chairman of the Syriac Unity Party in Dêrik, 19 February 2014

When was your party founded?

We already founded our party in 2005, in the underground, and in 2011 we went public in the course of the protests against the regime. We are active not just in Cizîrê, but also in Homs and some Christian municipalities in Central Syria. But there, the political work is of course much more dangerous than here in Rojava.

How do things look in Damascus?

We used to have an office in Damascus, but had to close it down because of repression by the regime, which arrested many of our cadres. Now we have offices only in Cizîrê and in Homs.

And your office in Homs is in the area that is still held by the Free Syrian Army?

No, it is in a valley inhabited by Christians.

But who controls the valley, the regime, the FSA, or who?

The last time one of us went there, he was arrested by the regime. We don't know exactly what's the matter with him and our people there. But the important thing is that we regard ourselves as a Pan-Syrian party that is active not just in Rojava, and that sees itself as part of Syria's secular opposition.

Your party cooperates closely with the PYD, has ministers in the government of the canton of Cizîrê and is in charge of the Assyrian police Sutoro and the Military Council of the Suryoye.

We are, together with the PYD and several Arab opposition parties, a member of the National Coordinating Committee for Democratic Change and try to make our contribution to the democratization of Syria in this way. It is also true that we have been very active in building the Sutoro and the Military Council of the Suroye. We can't simply let the Kurds fight for us and we want to make our own contribution. But the Sutoro and the Military Council see themselves as national units of the Suroye and not as a party militia. Now that we are armed, it won't be so easy anymore to butcher us. We are no longer defenceless when confronted with the attacks of the "Islamic State" or other jihadist groups such as Jabhat al-Nusra or Ahrar ash-Sham.

If you work so closely with the PYD, why do you then have your own Christian-Aramaic parallel structures? Why don't the Christians simply join the YPG or the Kurdish Asayîş?

The Military Council of the Suroye joined the YPG in January and has now become part of the YPG. And the Sutoro works very closely with the Kurdish Asayîş. But we are a separate people and we also want to make this visible. We are not just Syrian Christians, but we speak our own language and have a right to our own cultural and national identity. We Suryoye are a people and not just a national minority. You must not forget what we have suffered in the past. Our own police and our own armed units thus also play an important role for our self-confidence and our self-assertion as a people.

In recent years, so many of our young people have fled or migrated to Europe. With our own units, we also make a contribution to stopping this unfortunate trend. This here is our homeland. We are the indigenous population of this region and we refuse to let anyone expel us from it. One of our means of showing this is the fact that we are now armed with our own flag.

At the same time, Aramaic Christians are still seeking asylum in Europe.

Please don't call us that but call us Suryoye or Assyrians, because we are a people and not just a religious community.

OK, then I will say that Suryoye are still seeking asylum in Europe. How do you see the refugee policy of Europe and Europe's approach to the conflict in Syria?

The European policy with regard to Syria is a catastrophe! What is your goal? Do you want to expel us from our homeland? We have lived here for millennia and now you are trying to get us to emigrate to Europe instead of supporting us here.

You have the impression that we are facilitating the emigration to Europe? Actually, it is very difficult to get asylum in Europe!

From our point of view, for Christians it is too easy. If our whole youth migrates to Europe, then our existence in our ancestral homeland will come to an end. We are fighting for a future right here, and you should support us in this and not become the stooges of those who want to expel us from here.

I understand very well that if all the young people emigrate, it is terrible for those who stay behind. But don't you also understand those who say that they don't have any hope anymore?

Take a look at Dêrik. Here, we are really safe. We have our own police, we have our arms; today, we can live our language and culture in complete freedom. We have never had so many rights as we've had since 2012, when the regime withdrew from the region. Of course, the economic situation is difficult and I understand that not all people are able to endure this. But each person who goes away from here weakens our position. If you in Europe push our young people to emigrate, you are contributing to aborting our existence in our traditional homeland after thousands of years. With this, you are destroying a millennia-old culture that will not survive in exile. Therefore, we must fight here for our existence and our rights.

MURAD MURAD

Minister of the Syrian-Orthodox Parish of Dêrik, 19 February 2014

How is the situation of Syrian-Orthodox Christians in Rojava?

It is as good as it is possible to be. In Dêrik, we don't have any problems.

How big is your parish in Dêrik?

Today, we have 550 families.

But aren't many Syrian-Orthodox Christians leaving Syria at the moment? If the situation is so good, why do people leave?

They emigrate for economic reasons because they can't find a job here on account of the economic situation.

Austria has specifically admitted Christians from Syria and has also cooperated with the Syrian-Orthodox church in Austria in this. Were the local parishes involved in the decision as to who was put on the list?

We here were not even asked. These people seem to have been selected entirely by chance.

How do you personally see this policy of privileging Christian refugees?

This is a very ambivalent situation. If you want to admit Christians, this is good for the people concerned. But on the other hand, these young people are also the pillar of our country and our community. Once they are all gone, what will become of us and our existence as Christians in Syria? This emigration had already begun before the war and is continuing now.

How many people have already emigrated?

As I said, today, we are 550 families. Ten years ago, we were 1,200. That is, we have lost more than half of our members in the course of the last decade. But this wave of emigration doesn't affect only Dêrik, but also other cities of the region. These are really very massive losses.

DAJAD AKOBIAN

Minister of the Armenian-Apostolic Parish of Dêrik, 19 February 2014

How long have you been minister of the Armenian-Apostolic church in Dêrik?

Here in Dêrik for 28 years. Before that, I was active in other places, one of them Germany.

How big is your parish?

About 80 families, approximately 400 persons altogether.

How do the Armenians fare here in Rojava since the Kurds have taken over the area? Do you have problems?

No, not at all, we have a good life here. Our situation is normal. We feel safe and have a good relationship with the Kurds and Assyrians. Actually, we don't have any problems.

Where do the forebears of the Armenians in Dêrik come from?

We come primarily from Van, Diyarbakır, and Maraş.

And you came here during the genocide of 1915?

That's true for most, but some only came considerably later. My mother, for example, was born in Diyarbakır, survived the genocide there, and then fled to Syria only at a later date. But my parents have told me only a little about their own history. Most of what I know of the history of the genocide, I know from books.

What does the infrastructure of your parish look like? For example, do you have your own school?

There is an Armenian school that is attended by children up to the sixth grade. We have teachers for Armenian, Arabic, and English here. After that, they have to go to secondary schools in Qamişlo or Aleppo. Thus, one of my sons is still in Aleppo where he is undergoing education in physiotherapy.

Despite the war?

Yes, he is still there despite the war. Another son of mine is in Armenia, and my daughter and my youngest son are here with us.

There are no Kurdish lessons in the Armenian school?

No, no Kurdish. But many students speak it nevertheless because they learn it in the streets.

How do you see the future of your parish? Are you afraid of the jihadists of the "Islamic State" or of Jabhat al-Nusra?

At the moment, we are not afraid. Here, so far everything has remained quiet and the Kurds have succeeded in keeping the civil war away from this region. So far, the People's Protection Units (YPG) protect us from the jihadists. We hope this will remain the case. As I said, our relationship to the Sunnis here is very good. But the Sunnis here are, after all, no fanatics. Of course we know what happens to Christians under the rule of the "Islamic State." But here in Dêrik there is no one who has sympathies for them, and therefore I don't believe that we will ever have to leave from here.

But if so? Would you then flee to Europe?

Why don't you ask my daughter – she is still young.

(Question to the daughter, Talar Akobian, who is about 16 years old): *Where would you go?*

Talar Akobian: Certainly not to Europe. I am not interested in that. My home is here in Syria and my second home is Armenia. Should I really be forced to leave Syria, I would go to Armenia. But the Syrian army is strong and I don't think that the Islamists have a chance in the long run. I will quit my homeland not so easily!

AKRAM KAMAL HASU

Prime Minister of the canton of Cizîrê, 20 February 2014

Why was Amûdê, and not the much larger Qamişlo, made the capital of the canton of Cizîrê?

Our constitution states that Qamişlo is the capital of the canton. But since at the moment there are not enough available buildings there, we have turned Amûdê into the preliminary administrative seat of the canton. In the future, the administration can come back to Qamişlo.

Are there no political reasons for this, for example, that there are still parts of Qamişlo that are still in the hands of the regime?

No, because then I would not even sojourn in Qamişlo.

Which tasks does your canton government have?

We integrate the various tasks and local councils for the administration of the region and are in the process of building a functioning administration of the canton.

Is there any joint administrative structure of all three cantons, or, so to speak, a joint government of a Kurdish autonomous region?

We have a certain amount of coordination and cooperation.

But there is no joint government of Rojava standing above the three cantons?

No, there is no joint administration of Rojava.

Are there any future plans to establish such a joint administration of the three cantons, or will the three cantons continue to be separated?

Our constitution says that every other area, and not just Kurdish areas, can join our canton. But at the moment no such thing is being planned.

So far, none of your institutions is democratically legitimized. There haven't been any elections anywhere. Is there a roadmap for democracy in the canton of Cizîrê?

In the beginning, we agreed with various groups of the population of Cizîrê to build a transitional administration. At that time, the Kurdish National Council was also part of this coordination. In addition, Assyrian and Arab organizations participated. By now, we have established the current government, and we plan to have elections in four months. It is difficult to carry out elections during a war, but we will try, and then there will be a democratically elected government.

So far, the parties in the KNC don't accept this form of self-administration. Will you try to integrate these parties into your government?

I was myself a member of the governing body of the KNC. This project was originally a project of the Kurdish National Council and the People's Council of West Kurdistan. A committee was established that had five members each from both the National Council and the People's Council. In September 2013, we signed an agreement. After the signing, we were supposed to implement the agreement. We had three meetings on this, but in the end, the PDKS no longer approved of the agreement. On 5 December 2013, at a meeting at which I was also present, the Kurdish National Council stated that even though it considered this administration as necessary, it had disagreements with the People's Council of West Kurdistan with regard to the form of the administration. After this, I, as an independent, and four members of the PDKS decided to join the administration. But we kept the door open and have always told all parties that this is an administration for everyone and that they are all welcome to participate. We have also always said that we envisage elections under the supervision of an independent election committee within four to six months. We will accept the results regardless of who wins. We would really want these parties to participate, be it only as a genuine opposition, because we also need an opposition. We don't want an opposition that simply doesn't accept us without us even knowing why, but a constructive opposition. In the current administration, there are also different personalities with different views, but we work together for the good of the population and we hope that the opposition will change its views and participate.

The representatives of these parties have told me that they don't accept your administration because the PYD has created an authoritarian regime and collaborates with the Ba'ath regime.

First of all, I must deny that the PYD collaborates with the Ba'ath regime. The PYD pursues a policy that protects the population. But it doesn't collaborate with Assad. The accusation of authoritarianism is also untrue. Locally, we see that the PYD is very popular and has very many followers. The other parties don't accept this popularity, and seen from there, they are totalitarian themselves.

The other parties are totalitarian in your view?

Yes, if they don't accept the popularity of the PYD, they are totalitarian. They can participate in the elections and defeat the PYD. But simply refusing to accept the party is totalitarian. I was a member of the Kurdish National Council and have asked the parties there to participate. But there, in the KNC, I have really experienced a lot of totalitarianism. I, for one, am not a PYD member and the foreign minister, Salih Gado of the Kurdish Leftist Democratic Party also isn't a member. We would not be part of this administration if the PYD were totalitarian.

But there are serious human rights violations like, for example, the events in Amûdê in June 2013, when the YPG shot and killed civilians during a demonstration. The parties of the Kurdish National Council cite this as evidence of the authoritarianism of the PYD.

We have martyrs from the YPG on a daily basis, but nobody talks about them. But what happened in Amûdê is now also being politically misused. We respect all martyrs, including those who died in Amûdê. We have created a committee that has established contact with the families of the killed. We have apologized to the families and paid compensations. The fighters of the YPG are volunteers and not experts, and volunteers make mistakes. There were dead on both sides. A fighter of the YPG was also killed. Let's not forget that we are in the midst of a war and people are killed here every day.

We got rid of the regime here to 90 per cent. But we don't have any experience with democracy, and at the moment all sides make mistakes. In Europe or in the US, civilians are also killed by the police, but this is not considered a big deal.

In Austria it would create quite a stir if the police killed someone at a demonstrations.

The point is that this tragic case is now being misused for political purposes.

I'm glad that you regard it at least as a mistake.

We have formed a local committee and ensured that the families received apologies and compensation. I know that blood cannot be compensated with money, but at least the suffering of the bereaved can be ameliorated in this way.

This is certainly an important step. But in a constitutional state there would also be a criminal prosecution of the perpetrators. Have there been any trials of the YPG fighters who shot at the demonstrators?

Our committee that investigated the case came to the conclusion that there were mistakes from both sides. But since we wanted to pacify rather than incite the situation, we have, as I mentioned, apologized and given compensation to the relatives.

Apart from the war and the question of democracy, the economy is also one of the biggest problems. Rojava suffers from both a blockade from Turkey and a siege by the "Islamic State." But with Iraq and the Kurdistan Regional Government (KRG), things also do not seem so easy. You are known to be one of Syria's biggest entrepreneurs and have thus certainly thought about the economic development of your canton.

Our foreign minister Salih Gado has established contacts with Turkey, the KRG in Iraq, and the Iraqi government in Baghdad. We have tried to send the clear message that we want to cooperate with them all. Just today, Salih Gado is in Baghdad, and before, he was in Suleymania. Just yesterday, he called me to tell me that there is now an agreement with Baghdad on the opening of the Tal Koçer border crossing into Iraq. We as a government have no preconditions for cooperation with

Iraq or Turkey. Earlier in the day, I had a phone conversation with Hamid Darbandi and assured him that we respect Masud Barzani and really want to solve the border problem with the KRG. The border near Semalka had been opened for humanitarian reasons, and it is inacceptable that it has already been closed again. We have also established contacts with Turkey. Since we do not simply pursue the policy of the PYD alone, but represent all parts of the population here, we have also succeeded in establishing contacts in this case.

Should the negotiations with Turkey ever succeed, you will have another problem. The border post is, after all, still in the hands of the regime. In addition, there are some parts of Qamişlo, such as the airport or the Arab district, that are still under the control of the regime. How does your administration intend to deal with the fact that you have such a strategically important presence of the regime right in the midst of Qamişlo?

At the moment, we have a very special situation. We still have more than 100,000 people here who get their salaries from the regime in Damascus. Many services are still organized by Damascus. Of course, we are against the regime. But if we attack the regime now, first, we will have a war here, and second, all these payments from Damascus will collapse. Therefore, right now we simply can't afford to start an attack on the regime.

TAHA XELÎL

Writer, painter and intellectual and one of the first PKK activists in Syria, 20 February 2014

You are a writer, intellectual, activist, and now, also a TV presenter. What exactly are you doing at the moment right here in Rojava?

I work in two places, one of which is Ronahi TV, where I have a regular programme on the media once a week. Sometimes, I also moderate discussions where I invite certain politicians and intellectuals, who then discuss certain topics relevant to Rojava. I don't know exactly why they gave me this programme, because I would see myself rather as a man of letters than as a political activist. But OK, that's just the way it is.

Simultaneously, I work for a centre called Rojava Centre for Strategic Studies, of which I am one of the three directors. There, we work on various social developments in Rojava, the collection of data etc.

That is, some sort of think tank?

Yes, that's what you could call it. We counsel our government and also publish a magazine by the name of *Darāsāt Kurdīa*.

Which means Kurdish Studies, *but in Arabic. Is the magazine written in Arabic?*

Yes, right now it is in Arabic. We would like to publish it also in Kurdish. But at the moment, we don't have the money or the potential to publish it bilingually, and because of the Ba'athist educational policy all of us can read and write Arabic better than Kurdish. And we want the Arabs to also be able to read the magazine. Very few Arabs know Kurdish. But on the other hand, all of *us* know Arabic. Thus for the time being, we publish it in Arabic. In the future, the magazine will appear every three months, and just now the first issue has come out. The magazine also has a website.

Let's still stick a little bit to language. In Iraq and in Turkey, I have observed that Kurdish intellectuals are pursuing a kind of language purge policy quite similar to what Ataturk once did with Turkish. Widely used words are being replaced only because they come from Arabic, and very quickly a kitab *has turned into a* pirtuk *and no normal person understands the words anymore. How do you see this language purge policy?*

We have problems with our own language. We weren't allowed to study this language for many years. But nevertheless we have very different dialects even in Rojava. Even here in Cizîrê we have two different dialects. We understand each other, but we are still far away from a norm. Now we are trying to achieve such a standardization. Is that sensible? I really don't know.

There were three conferences in Amed and Diyarbakır and I was also there. There were many discussions among the Kurdish intellectuals about which variety we should introduce as the standard language. Some suggested Soranî because it is already the de facto official language in Iraqi Kurdistan and there are many more books and newspapers in Soranî. Therefore, they suggested, everyone should learn their language. The Kurmancî speakers said: "No, we have more speakers than you do, you must learn *our* language!" These are the problems we are having. But I think that all of this is already gradually relaxing. I can already see that due to all the Kurdish TV programmes and the new media, there are more and more words from Kurmancî appearing in Soranî and the other way round. Perhaps this whole problem becomes redundant once our varieties begin to converge in a genuinely natural way. In the course of time, there will perhaps be a common standard language. This may not include the other varieties, but these two might really coalesce.

I think that there is also a psychological factor in this. Formerly, some Kurds would frown upon us when we wrote in Arabic. This is different now, because now, everyone is allowed to write in Kurdish. Due to the long-standing repression, Kurdish has now become a kind of a badge of honour. Personally, I also remember that in secondary school, I repeatedly got into trouble because I spoke Kurdish. I was always punished for that, but I stuck to my guns. However, I also like Arabic. Now, we can finally choose which language we speak. At the time, it was a sign of strength to demonstrate this Kurdish identity. Formerly, I often said, I am a Kurd. But now, I don't say that anymore, because now everyone can do that. This reminds me of the Palestinian poet Mahmoud Darwish,[2] who once wrote a marvellous poem with the title "Write Down, I am Arab!" I will live, write, die, and so on in Arabic. After a few years, when he had to leave Palestine, he came to Beirut and had a reading there. The audience wanted to hear this famous poem, but he refused to read it. The next day, he was asked why he had disappointed his audience and had not read the poem. He responded: "It is ridiculous to stand among 100 million Arabs and say: I am Arab!"

I think we are repeating this right now. In a while, the language will not be so important anymore. It will remain our language, but no longer so ...

Perhaps it will become less political?

Yes, perhaps it will then deal more with love and beauty, not with politics.

These debates are also present in Iraqi and Turkish Kurdistan. In Iraq, the debate is not just about the language, but also about the script. Over here, you almost only have Kurmancî. But do you also have the debate over the script, that is, the choice between the Latin Bedirxan script and Arabic?

Here in Syria, at the time we adopted the Latin alphabet developed by Celadet Alî Bedirxan. This was at the same time when the Turkish changed to the Latin script. Since then, we have written Kurdish in this Bedirxan alphabet, and this is a good thing. Personally, I find the Bedirxan alphabet much more suitable for Kurdish than the Arabic system, because we have so many vowels in Kurdish, which can be much better represented in this way.

Since 2012, teachers have, for the first time, had the opportunity to teach Kurdish in schools. How does that work? As far as I know, the instruction is still mainly in Arabic. But now, Kurdish is also taught.

Now we have two hours of Kurdish lessons per day. Some private schools have even more Kurdish lessons. But in the state schools, it is only two hours.

How do the lessons actually work? I imagine that introducing such a subject in the midst of a war encounters many difficulties.

There are many problems. First of all, we don't have trained teachers for that. Many of the teachers actually have no command of really good literary Kurdish. And then we lack books. We don't have school books or grammar books and so on. In part, the Kurdish instruction is rather more political instruction than genuine language instruction. I think this is a beginning. But the children and the young people are so happy that they are now able to learn Kurdish. By the way, tomorrow is the Day of the Mother Tongue, and the students have been preparing for days for the celebrations and demonstrations on that day.

How do things stand in the realm of teacher training?

We are now creating a kind of "university" in Qamişlo that will also give the opportunity to study Kurdish. We are establishing teacher training classes there. It's not yet a real university, and we don't call it that, but rather, an academy. But this is a beginning, and in a few years from now we will have qualified Kurdish teachers.

The salaries of the teachers in the state schools in Rojava are still paid by Damascus. Does the government also pay for the Kurdish classes?

No, it doesn't pay for them, and here in Rojava we organize them really independently. That has nothing to do with Damascus.

Are they paid by the canton administration?

So far, they haven't been paid at all, but in the future, the Ministry of Education in the canton government will cover the costs.

You just said that there is a lack of books. What about the Kurdish publishing industry? Are there already publishers releasing books here in Rojava?

There are two publishers. But actually, they only copy existing books. And the quality of the books, as far as manufacturing is concerned, also leaves a lot to be desired. Sometimes, the letters are barely decipherable. At the moment, it is impossible to import books from Iraq or Damascus, and here in Rojava, we don't have any modern print shops. It is thus really difficult both to get books and to publish here. The two publishers are actually more like simple print shops or copy shops than real publishers as you know them in Europe.

But what do they publish in terms of content?

Almost everything. If you have the money and pay them, they will do almost anything.

That is, they are purely commercial publishers?

Yes, everyone who can afford to can publish books. And to this you have to add the fact that due to the long-term repression of the language, everyone who has penned a few poems is of the opinion that they must also be published. Once you have written three poems, your neighbours will very quickly consider you a poet.

You mean not everything that is published is really good literature?

No, not at all. Some of these texts are really very simple.

What about schoolbooks? Is there any educational material for the Kurdish classes?

In many subjects, we still work with the old schoolbooks from Damascus. Here in the canton, Kurdish material is available only for the first two grades. In this area, too, we are just at the beginning.

How is the situation with regard to the print media? Are there newspapers in the Kurdish language?

There are two newspapers that appear bilingually in Kurdish and Arabic. *Ronahi* appears once a week, and *Mudam* every two weeks.

And are they close to any political parties?

Ronahi is close to the PYD and *Mudam* to Barzani.

The Kurdish culture has also always very much been about music. Music has also been important for poetry. What is today's situation in Rojava in this regard?

Music has always been very important for the Kurds. Actually, we have "transported" our whole history and literature through our songs, and even though our language was banned, they could never ban our songs. And therefore, many people have told their stories in the form of songs. When you hear such songs, you think that you are actually in the midst of a novel.

For example, the Dengbej.

Yes, the Kurds really have a great tradition of sung history. In the past, the singers moved from village to village and sang whole novels about aspects of Kurdish history or about love or some other important topic. Such a song could easily last for a whole hour. These are really beautiful songs, and I'm saying this not only because I am a Kurd. I believe that Kurdish music really represents one of the most important musical traditions of the Middle East, and the other peoples of the Middle East have always adopted – or as we say: stolen – our songs. In Turkey, about 60 per cent of the songs actually have Kurdish melodies.

OK, but let's move from the basic facts to the situation today. How does the production of music look like in today's Rojava? Are there places where one can study music?

We have a big centre here, the Muhammed Sheikho Centre,[3] which is named after a well-known Kurdish singer who died about 20 years ago. And in this centre, the young people can learn all about theatre, music, and other forms of the performing arts. Meanwhile, there are several music studios in Qamişlo where people can record music, and where in fact enormous amounts of music are produced.

You are also a painter. What is the situation with regard to painting and the visual arts?

There are two things that they can never prevent us Kurds from practising, and these are painting and music. There have always been Kurdish painters. One of our most famous painters, Malwa Omar Hamdi, now lives in Austria. Others live in Germany, France, or in Lebanon. Unfortunately, due to the war many Kurdish painters have again emigrated abroad and are now missing here. Only the crazies have stayed here [laughs].

In my personal case, my poems and my paintings are closely connected. Both deal with feelings and not so much with thoughts. Even as a child, I already compared between Arabs and Kurds – for example, the clothing they wore. As a child, I regarded our clothing as more colourful and beautiful. I always tried to paint these things. It was only later that I heard that there were famous Kurdish painters abroad. And when I went to Damascus later on, I sometimes also attended courses in painting. I think we, the Kurds, actually paint differently from the Arabs. Our colours are different. Our colours are stronger. I don't know what the reason for this might be. But it is true. Moreover, we were able to express our political ideas by way of our colours. It was simply impossible to prohibit us from painting in yellow, green, and red.[4] In this way, we played with the government. We addressed Kurdish topics. Against painters, the secret service simply didn't act as harshly as it did against writers. On the one hand, they didn't always understand the paintings, and on the other, painting was less important to the government because it was somehow less unequivocal.

But what does the understanding of art on the part of the now ruling PYD look like? This question is perhaps a little bit delicate, but I have already gained the impression that the prevailing appreciation of art here is – let me say – pretty much in the vein of "socialist realism." The PKK and the PYD seem to use art primarily as a political vehicle; they seem to think that art has to serve politics, and that's it. How does all this look from your point of view, as an artist who is politically close to this party but who expressly does not merely practise art-as-propaganda? What ramifications does this have for the artists here?

I think this is a problem not just of the PYD or the PKK, but a problem of all communist parties, that is, all groups somehow coming out of the Leninist school. They have an understanding of art that reminds one pretty much of Zhdanov.[5] These parties don't really try to understand art or to think about it. If, for example, some artists here each paint a woman and one of them makes a victory sign, everyone will automatically say that this is the most beautiful picture of all. It hurts me to say this, but actually, there is no appreciation of art here. At the moment, I show my pictures to no one, even though I work with these people. But I know from the beginning that my paintings would not be appreciated and taken seriously. Therefore, I rather paint them for myself.

The same is also true for the poems. For example, I have done readings together with Mahmoud Darwish and he listened to my poems and praised them. I don't think that a Mahmoud Darwish would say such a thing just like that. Among the colleagues among whom I now live, there are some who write poems. They then show these poems on TV two or three times a week. Most of them don't even know that I also write poems, and if they hear them, they say: "For whom do you write this?" or "Who is supposed to understand this?"

I think that an understanding of art necessitates yet another revolution. When I read Apo's[6] books, I always think that he doesn't think like that at all and has an appreciation of art totally different from the one of his followers.

The books he has written in prison seem to indicate that he has refined his thinking very much.

Yes, exactly. He now occupies himself with the most different cultural aspects. But you know, for those who come from the mountains,[7] it's different. They have lived in a different world for a while. They have permanently hovered between life and death. When I look at the autobiographies of the fighters, they write purely political stories and don't dare to talk about their human side. But guerrilla fighters are not stones; they are human beings. They have headaches or diarrhoea, they are afraid, perhaps they long for their mother or for a lover while they are in the mountains in the midst of snow. But nobody will talk about that. I have already said this several times at readings for the guerrillas. In my view, it is a problem if you merely write that you are faced with a Turkish pig who you have to kill to prevent him from killing you. I think it will take a lot of time to leave this kind of narrative behind.

Just to give an example, I once read one of my poems in Diyarbakır, and in it, I wrote about a Turkish soldier who has just cut off the heads of two guerrilla fighters and has a photo made of himself with the heads in his hands. In the poem, I reflected about his hands, which could just as well pluck a flower or caress his girlfriend, but which instead hold these two heads. Afterwards, I was criticized for this poem – how could I write something like that about a murderer, that he has a girlfriend and so on. But I responded that I was sure he had a girlfriend. He is a human being, even though he is a corrupted human being. But all the same, I have to talk to him as a human, so that he becomes ashamed. I could of course say, "Hey you, soldier, I will squash your head!" But why should I do this? I want to address him as a human being.

This understanding of art also has to do with the Palestinians. At the outset of his career, Mahmoud Darwish also once said: "Beware, beware of my hunger and my anger! If I become hungry and angry, the usurper's flesh will be my food!" Later on, I once asked him, in Berlin, whether he was Dracula or what. He looked at me with big eyes and said: "You are right! It is these attitudes that are responsible for the fact that we still don't have freedom." In later years, he revised his attitude and learnt something new. In one of his poems from this time, he talks with a Jew. He says, we sit in the same café, read the same paper, drink the same coffee. Sometimes, he looks up from his paper and briefly looks at me, and sometimes, I look up from my paper and briefly look in his direction. He is afraid of me and I am afraid of him. Unfortunately, these texts were written only towards the end of his life. Maybe the Jewish Israeli is also afraid that the Palestinian will kill him.

I don't want us to wait for 40 years, like Mahmoud Darwish, to recognize that our enemies are also human beings. Yes, the Turks, Arabs, Persians have oppressed us for a long time. But even so, we have to get over it and see our oppressors also as human beings. These people didn't oppress us because they liked it so much, but because they learnt it that way, from their religion or from racism or from some other form of propaganda.

In the Kurdish literature, on the one hand we have a fair number of kitsch poems where somebody writes about a beautiful flower or landscape or about love, and on the other hand, heavily political and ideological "battle poems." There is little room in between for other things. But it is there, and some people try their best to do something different. But this leads to attacks from two sides, namely, from those who believe that they should write this simple propaganda that says the Kurdish woman or the people must rise up and so on, and from those who actually want to write in a modern fashion but who don't want to base this modernity on Kurdish tradition, but on Arabic or Turkish. It is curious when a Kurd tries, in this way, to simulate a Kurdish modernism which is not genuine.

And then we also have the Kurdish political movements, which often see the poet as a horse that is expected to carry their ideological baggage in its saddle. This is true not just of the PKK, it is an all-Kurdish problem. The poet is supposed to make propaganda for them, and conversely, some poets have regarded the political movements as *their* horse, which is expected to carry along their bad poems.

Such things have indeed a long afterlife. We see this in the lack of a serious cultural life in Iraqi Kurdistan where the people are actually free to become active, but where there is no theatre and where the first two movie theatres have opened only very recently. In fact, even in Iran there is more Kurdish cultural life than in Erbil or Suleymania.

This will hopefully be different here. The PKK has a social and economic policy that is totally different from the one of Barzani. The PKK has, right from the start, banked on the ordinary people and the women and not on the old feudal lords. We do already have a cultural revolution here, and when the men see our women fighting with their weapons in their hands, they simultaneously see that things can really change.

SHAHIDA ADALAT

Nom de guerre of the Commander of the unit (Toga) Daria of the Women's Protection Units (Yekîneyên Parastina Jin, YPJ), 21 February 2014

How long has the Toga Daria existed?

For more than a year. We have already fought in several theatres of war, among them Serê Kaniyê, al-Hasaka, and Tal Hamis.

How did the very patriarchal Kurdish society react to the sight of young women fighting?

In the beginning, it was really quite difficult to get social acceptance. But just through the mere fact that we as women fight, we fighters have also changed the society. Today, there is nobody left who doesn't take us seriously.

Your opponents were in large measure fighters of the "Islamic State in Iraq and Greater Syria" (ISIS), that is, the worst jihadists here for far and wide. For them, it had to be a particular surprise to be suddenly faced with armed women.

Yes, and in the beginning they didn't take us seriously at all and made light of us. But then we showed them that we were just as good at shooting as our male fellow combatants. After a few military defeats, they began to take us very seriously. Now they have even founded their own women's units, but these actually pursue more or less propagandistic goals and are hardly ever really used.

Many of your fighters look very, very young. Do you use child soldiers?

No, our fighters are all at least 18 years old. Previously, we also took in younger ones, but now we deploy them only once they are 18, even though they can begin training at the age of 17. We are trying to enforce this consistently now.

Have you, during your battles, also arrested ISIS fighters from Europe, and have there also been people from Austria?

Yes, ISIS has fighters from all over the world, from Libya, Yemen, Iraq, Chechnya, the UK, Germany, France, and Austria. During the battles at Tal Tamer we arrested an Austrian.

What happens with the prisoners of war? Are they brought to a prisoner camp?

No, normally we exchange them for our own prisoners.

Do you have only Kurds in your unit, or do other inhabitants of Rojava also participate?

In our unit, there are also Christians and Arabs, some of whom only start to learn Kurdish once they come to us.

Why don't you have mixed units? Why do you have such a strict separation of the sexes?

That way, we, as women, learn to lead ourselves and to work under our own command. As a women's unit, we also have a specifically feminist political self-conception, and if we had mixed units, it would perhaps again be the men who wielded the command.

THOMAS THOMASIAN

Office for Foreign Relations of the Armenian Apostolic Parish in Qamişlo, 21 February 2014

How has the situation of the Armenians in Qamişlo been changed by the civil war and the Kurdish self-administration?

Previously, everything was perfect for us.

You mean, under the Ba'ath regime it was perfect for the Armenians?

We Armenians worked in the industry, were active as merchants, and didn't have any problems. Since 2012, this has changed. Many Armenians have emigrated, the prices have risen, and there are security problems everywhere in the country. But we still entertain good relations with everyone, with the Arabs, with the Kurds, and with the Assyrians.

How many Armenians have left the city in the last two years?

About 30 per cent have emigrated to Lebanon or to Armenia.

How many Armenians still live here?

In the whole of the Jezira, we have about 1,450 Armenian families. Qamişlo itself at present still has 750 Armenian-Apostolic families. Moreover, there is a smaller Armenian-Catholic parish with about 1,000 members, that is, individual persons.

Both Armenian parishes, the Armenian-Apostolic one and the Armenian-Catholic one, consist of descendants of the survivors of the genocide of 1915.

Yes, when our forebears came here in 1915, this was an extremely underdeveloped area. We Armenians were the first to build an industry here and we have done enormous work for the development of Qamişlo and other cities in the region. Thus, an Armenian, Manuk Hatschatorian, build the first mill here and also did a lot for the development of grain cultivation. Therefore, we actually always had a good relationship with the Kurds and the Arabs of the region.

What about the Armenian school education in Qamişlo?

Here in the town, we have an Armenian school up to the ninth grade. The Armenian-Catholic church has yet another school in which the students are instructed in Arabic and Armenian. After this, our students used to go to Aleppo to the Armenian secondary school. This is no longer possible because we can't send our students through the areas held by the "Islamic State" and Jabhat al-Nusra. This has become a real problem for our young people.

Do the Armenian schools teach only Armenian or Arabic, or do they now also teach Kurdish?

No, Kurdish is not taught. Our students have to speak Arabic and they can communicate with the Kurds in Arabic. Many of them have certainly learnt Kurdish in the streets. But Kurdish has never been a subject of instruction in Syria. Therefore, we, too, have never taught it.

But you could do so now, couldn't you?

Yes, possibly at some point in time we will. But there is also no instruction material and we are still a part of Syria, where Arabic is the official language. We Armenians see ourselves as guests in Syria and have always behaved accordingly. Therefore, we have also always obeyed the law. In 1970, this even went so far that all our schools were nationalized and transformed into Arabic schools. Only a year later, we were again allowed to teach Armenian. But the Kurds are free to teach Kurdish in their schools, just as we teach Armenian in ours.

Next year, we will have the 100th anniversary of the genocide of the Armenians. How will the genocide memorial day be observed here in the Armenian community, and is the ambivalent role of the Kurds in the genocide of 1915 a topic?

We hold annual memorials on every 24 April. Like every Armenian church in the world, each church here has a commemorative stone or a monument for the victims in front of it. But all of this is mainly a topic for us Armenians, not so much for the Kurds. Each group has their own victims to lament and the Kurds actually never participate in our commemorations.

Are you offended by that? Wouldn't it be nicer to work on a common understanding of history in which everyone doesn't just lament one's own victims, but where there is also something like the emergence of a joint memory culture?

Well, of course we are glad whenever a Kurd shows interest in our history as well as sympathy for us. But primarily we want to see to it that our own youth doesn't forget our history. It is OK if everyone respects their own history and their own dead. Today, we no longer have any problems with the Kurds. Perhaps, even, it is better if we don't rehash all of this again.

SHEIKH IBRAHIM

Chairman of the Mala Êzîdîya, an umbrella organization of the Êzîdi in Rojava, 21 February 2014

Since when has your organization existed and what goals do you pursue?

The Ba'ath regime had never allowed us Êzîdî to found religious organizations. Unlike the various Christian churches or the Shiites, the Druze, and other minorities, we were never allowed to do that. But we were also not persecuted. At the same time, our religious identity was simply ignored. We were therefore able to found our own organization only in 2012, after the regime had withdrawn from Rojava and we could create a Kurdish self-administration here. But we as Êzîdî also wanted to have an input into this new self-administration, and that is why we have united in a new separate association.

Your umbrella association is regarded as close to the PYD. But there is also a rival Central Association of the Êzîdî in Syria that reproaches you for this closeness. What do you say to this criticism?

You have to ask yourselves how many people this other association represents. These are just a few exiles in Germany. Here, locally, they are not present. We are grateful to the PYD, and particularly to the People's Protection Units (YPG), because they protect us from the "Islamic State" and other jihadist terror groups, and we cooperate in the structures of the self-administration. But this doesn't automatically mean that we are an organization of the PYD. We are a non-party organization that tries to reflect all positions of the Êzîdî communities.

There are conflicting data about the number of Êzîdî in Rojava, ranging from a few hundred to 50,000. How many Êzîdî would you say are here, and where do they live?

We are about 50,000 Êzîdî in all of Syria.

That is certainly a very generous estimate.

We are really that many. Of course, a number of us have emigrated in the course of the last years. But we hope they will come back again. But many others are still here. The Êzîdî villages are all in the cantons of Efrîn and Cizîrê. In Cizîrê alone, it's 52 villages. And we are also active in the political institutions. Our board member Burhan Barri is the representative of the Êzîdî on the Council of the Religions of Cizîrê, Anwar Jund is a minister in the canton government, Amin Bakhdash is member of the Council for Village Affairs, and so on.

That means I do not even need to ask you whether you have any problems with the Kurdish authorities?

No, there are no problems with the PYD whatsoever. The problems we have are all with the Islamists. Jabhat al-Nusra and the "Islamic State" have repeatedly and deliberately targeted us Êzîdî and have purposefully attacked Êzîdî villages both in the proximity of Serê Kaniyê and in the canton of Efrîn. In the process, the fighters have again and again systematically murdered civilians who were not able to flee in time. This is another reason why we are so grateful to the YPG. They are the only guarantee that prevents us Êzîdî from being annihilated.

How do you judge the European attitude towards the Kurds in general and the Êzîdî in particular? Is there anything that you'd like to tell the Europeans?

I would like to ask the Europeans why you only help your own brothers in the faith and are only interested in the Christians and not in us. And why do you want to push us Êzîdî to emigrate? You make it far too easy for the Êzîdî to get asylum in your countries. Do you want us to disappear from our homeland, from Kurdistan? We want our young people to stay here and to fight together with us for a future in Rojava, instead of going to Germany or Austria. You should rather bother yourself about the situation here and, for example, help us to become able to make our pilgrimage to Lalish. As you know, the Iraqi Kurds have closed the border to Rojava. During the last pilgrimage, 190 Êzîdî had to be smuggled illegally across the border to get to Lalish. At present, to be in contact with the Êzîdî in Iraq has really become difficult. And then, since we are already talking about Austria, we have yet another important concern: In some museum or library in Vienna, there is a very rare old copy of our Black Book.[8] Why don't you give this book back to us? This book belongs to all Êzîdî and not to one private person who has unlawfully bought it from some other private individual.

ASYA ABDULLAH

Together with Salih Muslim Co-chairperson of the Democratic Union Party (Partiya Yekitîya Demokrat, PYD), 21 February 2014

What vision do you have for the future of Rojava? How do you want it to look a few years from now?

Up to now, we have barely had the time to occupy ourselves with such questions. All the same, we have managed to build a stable basis here in Rojava in the last three years, and this is an insurance policy for a good future. Of course we can't say that all problems have been solved, because our problems are part of the Syrian problems. But what we want here is a democracy with strong organizations of the civil society, with a strong society in general. We work to build a democracy and a democratic culture, not just for the people in Rojava.

Does socialism still play a role in the ideology and future perspective of the PYD?

Scientific socialism is still a basis for us because it is a heritage for all of humanity.

What, then, is the political economy of Rojava supposed to look like?

At the moment, we are building our administration really from scratch. The economy plays a huge role in this. We want a self-administered democratic society and we have similar plans for the economy. But the problems are that the infrastructure here is in a terrible shape, and that we can't export our commodities because of the blockade.

Who will own the means of production? The state, the cantons, the capitalists? What about private property? Who is to own the factories and the land?

Fundamentally, we do all we can to protect private property. But the property of the people is exactly that and is protected by the people. Just recently, we founded a Council for Trade and Business, which will work out rules for trade and business relations and establish economic relations with other countries.

But back to the means of production: Are there any forms of cooperatives or other alternative forms of production in Rojava?

We encourage people to try such things. Thus, in Kobanê there is a women's cooperative that employs about one hundred women. They sew clothes and sell them themselves.

It is interesting that you mention a women's cooperative because the PYD and the PKK has always had a strong focus on gender equality and feminism. You are also the only female co-chairperson of a party in

Rojava. How does feminist policy work here? What does the approach of the PYD to gender policy look like in concrete terms?

First of all, we must fight within the party to enable women to formulate their political will at all, and then women will also be able to participate in political decisions. If women don't participate in politics, there will be wars, because men wage wars and do not take decisions for peace. For that reason, feminism isn't just a movement for the protection of women's rights, but much more than that. We protect all that by supporting the identity of the woman.

We have very many feminist movements here, and also a lot of historical research. Women have made a lot of headway since the French Revolution. But a lot still remains to be done and women can again lose the positions they have conquered.

What do the women in the PYD do to prevent the accomplishments they achieved from being lost? It wouldn't be the first time that women have been needed in a situation like that and then disappeared again after the revolution.

In our model of the administration of Rojava, women are present in political positions on all levels. We focus very much on the mobilization and organization of women. The better women are organized, the more power they have.

What about the women in the YPJ? Right now, they are very strong young women waging an armed struggle. But what will happen after the armed struggle? What do you do for the future of these young women?

We live in a war and the women should participate in the military aspect of that war. Women have always been regarded as weak and not involved in politics. Now they are present even as fighters. They protect Rojava. If only the men fought, afterwards they would do what they wanted, because, after all, they alone would have been the ones who fought.

Western feminists often also commit themselves to the rights of lesbians, and by now, in the Kurdish movement in Turkey there are also groups such as Hebûn in Diyarbakır which, for the first time, fight for the rights of lesbians, gays, and bisexual people. I can imagine that here in Syria these topics are even more sensitive than in Turkey, but here, there are certainly also lesbian, gay, and bisexual people, and the only difference is that they are even more invisible and oppressed than in Turkey.

Have these questions ever been topics in the PYD or in the women's organizations close to the PYD? What, then, are the living conditions for lesbians, gays, and bisexuals in Rojava?

We are well aware of the existence of these groups. But in Syria, there is no basis for such an organization. There are very many different feminisms in the world, and they hold very different views. Some of these are so liberal that they address even these topics. But for us, the feminist work is much more basic. At the moment, we are working for the most fundamental rights of women, for an end to the violence against women, for the possibility for women to work. Our goal is the freedom of our nation, not just personal freedom. For us, women are the core of the liberation movement.

What role does the thinking of Abdullah Öcalan play in the PYD's feminism? When talking to female fighters of the PKK, I have repeatedly noted the extent to which Abdullah Öcalan was a point of reference for their feminism. For European feminists, it often looks strange that a man can have such a central role in a feminist conception.

The women here did not used to be strong enough to simply say: "I am a feminist." For us, the liberation of women is a way to liberate the whole society. Feminism should therefore not be placed at the margins of society but in its centre. If feminists isolate themselves, they cannot change society, and then they cannot even solve the problems of women.

But let's get back once more to the role of Abdullah Öcalan.

Almost all of what I just said about how feminism should proceed can also be found in the writings of Abdullah Öcalan.

Now on to yet another question: The PYD has now proclaimed an administration with three autonomous cantons in Rojava. Has there been any reaction to this declaration of autonomy on the part of the regime?

No.

Actually, the regime is still present here in Qamişlo and is in control of the airport, the border gate, and the Arab district. Reportedly, there was also a demonstration in support of Assad not too long ago.

Yes, but these were only 800 demonstrators of whom perhaps 200 were soldiers, and it took place in a part of the city still under the control of the regime. They even brought in soldiers from al-Hasaka for the purpose.

BARZAN ISO

Journalist in Kobanê, 13 July 2014

What does the present situation in Kobanê look like?

As you know, Kobanê has been under siege for more than a year, first by Jabhat al-Nusra and now, after parts of Jabhat al-Nusra west of Kobanê have deserted to the "Islamic State," by the latter. Since we became encircled by IS in January, it has become even worse. You know, all people here are armed and, whenever necessary, they divide into small groups and defend their villages and come to the help of others. We have thus been able to defend the larger part of our area. In the town itself, life is still surprisingly normal. We have always lived from retail trade and growing food. Somehow this form of the economy is still working.

Do you still have enough food?

Yes, the most important foodstuffs are still available. The people here have found their own solutions. Thus, we hadn't had tomatoes for a long time, but the people simply started to grow them themselves. As of a month ago, there have been cheap tomatoes in the market once more. We have also simply grown the corn for our bread ourselves. It is more problematic with things that do not grow here, for example, coffee, and it is similar with medicine. Getting these things is very difficult because they have to be smuggled from Turkey or from other parts of Syria. But somehow, the smuggling works. Arab drivers bring contraband to us even through the area of the "Islamic State." At the moment, even alcoholic beverages are still available in the town.

What about water? ISIS did, after all, cut off the water supply of Kobanê after it conquered the town Jarābulus west of Kobanê in January.

The water supply of Kobanê used to come from a water pump in a village near Jarābulus which was destroyed by IS immediately after the capture of the town. But even before, we repeatedly had similar problems with Jabhat al-Nusra. Now we get our water from groundwater wells. Even though this works, there is a big problem with this, because the sewer system in the town is terrible and, therefore, waste water mixes with the groundwater and we thus have to use contaminated water. For that reason, we've repeatedly had severe illnesses such as cholera in the town over the course of the last few months. But the canton administration is already working on a new solution. In the future, the water is to be pumped from a place 20 kilometres outside of the town. But a still bigger problem is electricity. Until January, we had electricity for about two hours per day. But IS has destroyed all power lines and now there is no longer any power at all, or rather, only power from generators.

But do you still have enough fuel to operate these?

Yes, because IS also wants to sell the oil it produces. We are able to buy fuel from IS through Arab smugglers.

What is the military situation? When I look at the situation on the map and consider the fact that a general mobilization has already been proclaimed, I ask myself whether the YPG has a chance to successfully defend Kobanê.

This is a very difficult question, but I would still want to remain optimistic in this regard. The YPG has only light weapons for the defence and is not as well equipped as IS. But we are highly motivated. And it is not just the YPG that fights. The YPG represents something like the strategic spine of all our fighters. But by now, all of those who are fit for action actually fight. The reason why we are so highly motivated is that we know what would happen to us if Kobanê fell. We also have many refugees in the town who have fled the "Islamic State," Kurds and Arabs, and what the people of the "Islamic State" say leaves no doubt that we must not lose this battle!

What do you fear would happen if Kobanê fell?

That would mean genocide. Actually, they have already captured nine villages. In three of them in particular, there has already been a genocide. Every single civilian who did not flee in time was killed. Only a couple of days ago, they publicly hanged 17 villagers in one of the Kurdish villages that had already been under their control for a while. We know perfectly well that we would not survive if they won.

What does the population in Kobanê expect from Europe?

Already in May, there was a European assessment of the situation saying that the Kurdish areas in Syria were safer than the other parts of the country. At present, IS wants to create a conflict here between Arabs and Kurds. But there are a number of Arabs who have fled to us and some of them fight in our ranks against IS. Europe should primarily exert pressure on Turkey and other states in the region to stop their support for IS! We don't need military support, but we need diplomatic pressure to achieve an end of the military assistance for IS. And we need civil support. The EU still supports civil Syrian opposition groups with educational measures and materials. That's something we also need. Moreover, here in Rojava, we also still have to learn how to build a democratic self-administration, and for that, we would certainly need the assistance of the EU. Here and in the educational realm in general, Europe could really help us.

HEVI IBRAHIM MUSTEFA

Prime Minister of the Canton Efrîn, 30 July 2014

In many parts of Syria, there is civil war. How is the present situation in the canton of Efrîn?

The situation in all of Syria is very difficult. But we are in the fortunate situation that so far, we have been able to keep the war away from the canton Efrîn. While there is an increasing amount of confessional violence in other parts of Syria, here, the most different people continue to live together in peace. We have Sunnis, Shiites, Êzîdî, and Alevi here who live together peacefully. In Efrîn, there are Kurds, Arabs, and other minorities who have no problems with each other. The solidarity works. And this also shows that the same could work in other parts of Syria.

You belong to one of the smallest religious minorities yourself and you are an Alevi. Was this a problem for your role as the prime minister of the canton Efrîn?

No, we are a secular force and there are no problems between the religions here. Of course, the terrorists of the "Islamic State" hate us for that, but for our society in Efrîn, it is not a problem that I am an Alevi. In our canton, Sunnis, Êzîdî, and Alevi have been part of the population for centuries. Part of what we do here is to defend the freedom of religion against the jihadists.

You are also the only woman among the prime ministers of the autonomous cantons in Rojava. Have the women in Rojava profited from the revolution?

The PYD has always fought for the rights of women. This includes the recognition that women are able to occupy politically responsible posts. I am the living proof that things have really changed in the Kurdish society.

In the canton of Kobanê further to the east, there has been heavy fighting between the Kurdish YPG and the "Islamic State" for several weeks. You are lucky in that so far you have no border with the "Islamic State." Is the situation at the borders of your canton quiet?

It is comparatively quiet. Compared to Kobanê, we are indeed in the lucky situation not to be under the siege of the "Islamic State." All the same, the fighters of IS are approaching the borders of our canton from the east and are thus also a threat to us. But we have been able to beat those attacks back so far. In January, there were also attacks by Jabhat al-Nusra. These groups also try to stir conflicts among the Kurds.

With the units of the Free Syrian Army that are at present active south of the canton, things are less problematic. In January, Jabhat al-Akrad and the FSA jointly expelled "Islamic State" from Azaz. We have by now some sort of coexistence with both the FSA and the government troops stationed in [the Shiite enclave] Nubl. As long as they don't attack us, we also don't attack them.

How is the situation at the border with Turkey? Is the canton of Efrîn also cut off there, or is there a border crossing?

Unfortunately, Turkey has closed the border to all of Rojava and thus there is also no legal border crossing between Turkey and the canton of Efrîn. While the jihadist groups do dispose of border crossings, we have to cross the border illegally by night or use the border crossing near Azaz, which is under the control of the FSA. Thus our canton, too, suffers from a blockade by Turkey.

How do you see the policy of Europe vis-à-vis Syria and Rojava? What would you want Europe to do?

The European Parliament actually recognized the autonomy of Rojava indirectly already two months ago. This was an important step for us. But it would also help us very much if pressure were exerted on Turkey to cease its support for the Islamist opposition and to end the economic blockade against Rojava.

But please allow me to use the opportunity to also tell the Europeans that they should support our revolution here. By fighting the terrorists of "Islamic State," we also fight for them, and we want a democratic development in Syria. We are the only ones here who are still able to put up effective military resistance against this Fascist movement. But we don't have experience with democracy and in this realm, we also need the assistance of Europe to refine our democracy. It is very important for Europe not to leave us hanging dry and not to forget Syria. We still wage a daily fight for survival. At the same time, we have achieved much, even though we are still at the beginning of our revolution. Our goal is a democratic and autonomous Rojava in a democratic Syria. We need international support to achieve it.

SA'UD AL-MULLA

Secretary General of the new PDKS (Partiya Demokrat a Kurdistanê li Sûriyê), 1 August 2014

Why did the two Azadî parties, the el Partî and Abdulbasit Hemo's Partyiya Yekîtî Kurdistani, merge into a joint party at the beginning of April?

The party landscape of the Syrian Kurds has been much too splintered for far too long. For many years, we were occupied with splits, which was hard to accept for the Kurdish population and has done severe damage to our political cause. Therefore, in the current situation it was necessary for us to merge, which we finally did at our unification party congress on 3 April 2014. Now we can deploy our energies and competencies in aid of our children and our Kurdish people, and institutionalize a mass party that is competent and works in all areas.

What are the political goals of the new party PDKS?

We stand in the tradition of the PDKS founded on 14 June 1957, and our work is based on a platform of nonviolent struggle for democracy in all its forms. We have a clear political vision. The political programme of our party aims not only at joining the national struggle for democracy in Syria, but also at winning the rights of the Kurdish nation in a secular federal state that represents all religious, confessional, and national groups of Syria. We want equality for women and men in all areas of life. As a party, we put a particular emphasis on women, who make up half of the Kurdish people and are the nurturers of our sons. Thus, we have also reserved half of the leading positions in our party for women.

*The unification party congress did not take place in Rojava, but in Arbil,
under the protection of Masud Barzani. Is the new party a sister party of
the PDK in Iraq or is it just a branch of the latter?*

The Democratic Party of Kurdistan – Iraq has a clear policy towards
the parties and political movements of the Syrian Kurds. We work
with it on an equal footing and both sides always respect each other's
national sovereignty. This must be seen as brotherly cooperation and
as an integration on the basis of mutual respect that corresponds to the
national interests of the Kurdish people in all four parts of Kurdistan.
President Masud Barzani looks back on a very honourable and successful
record and is in many respects the guardian of the unity of the Kurdish
people in all of Kurdistan. He was the patron of both the agreement
of 11 July 2012,[9] and the unification of our parties, and he has always
focused on the unity and strength of the Kurds. There is no doubt that
our parties have a close connection with each other and work together
well, but are simultaneously independent in their political decision
making and mutually respect each other. We respect, however, the
immortal achievements of Masud Barzani for the Kurdish nation and
see ourselves in his tradition.

*After the founding of the party, most members of the new party leadership
left Rojava and went into exile in Iraqi Kurdistan. How is the conflict
between your party and the ruling party in Rojava, the PYD, developing?*

The PYD has so far not allowed any political pluralism and instead
cracks down on rival parties. By now, many of our activists have fled
from Rojava, both to the Kurdistan Region in Iraq and to other areas.
The PYD has so far not kept to the agreements that we reached in the
negotiations with it. We don't believe in cooperation with the PYD
anymore, because it constantly tries to prevent political pluralism and
supresses political activities that are completely peaceful. The PYD tries
to intimidate us through the arrest of activists and cadres of the parties
and uses its influence on the armed militias of the YPG in order to
pressurize and terrorize us.

What are your party's points of criticism of the PYD?

The PYD tries to assert itself by the force of arms and instrumentalizes
the situation of the Kurds to pursue its own power interests. Because of
this policy of the PYD, the Kurdish population of Syria experiences one

of the most difficult phases of its history. The PYD makes all decisions alone and in close cooperation with the regime and the Syrian Army. With this, the PYD has become part of the repression of the regime. Despite the agreements between the PYD and the Kurdish National Council, the political persecution of members of our party has not ended. Many of our activists have been arrested by the PYD and are now in prison.

Does your party also have its own armed forces and if so, of what size?

The Democratic Party of Kurdistan – Syria is a political party and not a militia. Since the founding of the historical PDKS in 1957, it has only used pen and thought as weapons in the political struggle. We condemn the tyrannical regime, but we also condemn the terrorist groups that fight by means of violence, murder, and destruction, and that cut other people's heads off. In such a violent situation, it is even more important for us to refrain from having our own military forces.

The PYD often reproaches your party for cooperating with Turkey. What is the relation between the PDKS and Turkey?

We know of the cooperation of the PYD with the secret services in the region. Salih Muslim flies from capital to capital in the region, where he meets with members of the security apparatuses of these states in open daylight. We as the PDKS are interested in good, friendly relations with our neighbour countries as long as these are based on mutual respect and the common interests of our peoples. We are glad about the interest of Turkey and the role of that country in Syria, and also about the fact that in Turkey itself, ignorance about and denial of the existence of the Kurdish people has come to an end. The bloodshed between the sons of the Kurdish and Turkish peoples must be halted. There will only ever be peace, security, and well-being for Turkey if it also respects the national rights of the Kurdish population in North Kurdistan. Then there will be no more barriers to the cooperation of all peoples in the region.

Has the conquest of Mosul and central Iraq by the "Islamic State in Iraq and Sham" in June led to a rapprochement between the Kurdistan Regional Government in Iraq and the PYD in Rojava, and what does this development mean for your party?

The attack by ISIS is deliberately directed against the democratic experiences of the Kurds. In the end, all representatives of the Kurdish liberation movement must unite brotherly against this threat on the basis of a common minimal programme. I am convinced that we can do the most for the Kurdish people through a national dialogue and a serious and responsible policy.

How do you judge the reaction of Europe to the civil war in Syria and the situation in Rojava?

Europe has not reacted to the struggles of the Syrian people and its revolution in a very positive manner and has remained indifferent to both the violence of the regime and the extremist terror groups. Even the use of chemical weapons has at best led to condemnation by the European Union, but not to any substantial aid for the Syrian people. The regime even exploits the aid deliveries of European NGOs, which it withholds to either sell or distribute them to its own followers. None of this aid really reaches the Kurdish people.

SIAMEND HAJO

Spokesman for the Future Movement in Europe, 10 August 2014

How does the Future Movement see the current development in Syria in general and in Rojava in particular?

In the predominantly Kurdish areas, the situation is generally much quieter than in most other parts of Syria; there are no carpet bombardments and, so far, Islamist groups have much less influence – even though the "Islamic State" is currently coming closer to the Kurdish areas, particularly near Kobanê, but also near al-Hassaka. Unfortunately, the cause of this is too rarely analysed: It is a fact that this relative quiet goes back to the cooperation of the PYD, the Syrian arm of the PKK, with the regime. From mid-2012 on, the Ba'ath regime successively handed the predominantly Kurdish areas over to the PYD, and there was no fighting. As a reward, the PYD has radically suppressed any demonstrations critical of the regime – particularly in Efrîn, but also in the Jezira. Today, the PYD exerts the control over most of the towns in the Jezira, with the exception of Qamişlo and al-Hasaka, where the regime is still strong. In Qamişlo, the PYD and the regime divided the administration among themselves, while in al-Hasaka, right now a change is going on: Faced with the advance of the "Islamic State," the regime has handed its control over the Arab districts to the PYD. The towns of Efrîn and Kobanê are also controlled by the PYD, whereas the surrounding villages are in part under the control of the Islamists, particularly, as already mentioned, those near Kobanê.

When we talk about the Kurdish areas and the danger posed by the Islamists, we must not forget that the YPG has repeatedly *provoked* conflicts with Islamist groups – particularly when the PYD had come under political pressure. Thus, briefly after the attack of the PYD/YPG in Amûdê at the end of July, all of a sudden there was again fighting with Jabhat al-Nusra in Sêrê Kaniyê – even though the PYD, according to Salih Muslim, had allegedly already expelled this group from the town in March of the same year. It stands to reason that the YPG provoked these battles to muzzle criticism of the massacre it had perpetrated in Amûdê. Actually, in mid-July the very same Kurdish parties whose members were expelled, abducted, and tortured by the PYD at the end of June 2013 declared their willingness to fight jointly with the YPG against Jabhat al-Nusra. The strategy of the PYD to present itself as the only effective force against the Islamists has fully succeeded and is still taken at face value by many to this very day.

As far as relationships between the PYD, the "Islamic State", and the regime are concerned, there are generally more questions than answers. Why, for example, did the "Islamic State" cease fighting in Kobanê at the beginning of the offensive in Iraq? Has the offensive in Iraq to do with the fact that the Iraqi Kurds had discussed independence? We don't know.

What points of criticism does your movement have with regards to the ruling PYD and the proclamation of autonomous cantons by the PYD?

The PYD is a totalitarian party with a claim to sole representation. The present government – or rather, the present governments – are not the results of elections, but were put in charge by the PYD. There is always talk about the purported fact that the transitional government is backed by more than 50 groups. The few of these that we even know of are either close to the PYD, like the party's women's organization, Yekîtîya Star, or are totally obscure. None of the groups of the Kurdish National Council, the largest alliance of Kurdish parties in Syria, is a member – only the two leftist parties that formerly used to be in the KNC have affiliated themselves with the PYD. Neither the Yekîtî nor the KDP-S nor the Kurdish Progressive Party – just to mention the most important Kurdish parties – have participated in the formation of the governments. The same is true for the Asayish and the People's Protection Units: The PYD claims that these security organs are independent – but in reality, they are PYD forces that are responsible only to the PYD and the leadership of the PKK. These units don't become any more democratic by virtue of the fact that the YPG increasingly drafts young men by force. The PYD mercilessly exploits its militarily dominant position: Dissenters, whether independent activists or members of other parties, are persecuted unrelentingly. And here, I am not talking about regrettable individual cases, as the PYD would portray such events, because this approach to handling things is rather systematic. Since 2012, at least 30 PYD critics have been killed by members of the PYD or the PYD's security forces, and more than 400 were kidnapped and, in many cases, tortured. Just recently, a young man from Efrîn, Hanan Khalil Hamdusch, died in the custody of the Asayish. In the aftermath of a car crash, there was a dispute, and among other things, Hamdusch berated Abdullah Öcalan. The next day, he was dead. They claimed it was suicide. Hamdusch allegedly banged his head against the wall until he died. But in reality, his body didn't show any corresponding injuries on his skull. Instead of this, a photo of the body unequivocally shows the signs of severe torture. So far, there has been no investigation and none of the Asayish employees has been suspended from work even temporarily, which in such a case would be the very least to be done. In the end, the PYD has replaced the dictatorship of the Ba'ath regime with its own dictatorship, and today, the situation in the Kurdish areas is no better than in 2009 and 2010. Even the proclamation of three cantons, of three transitional governments, is a concession to the regime. Why three? Why this totally inflated structure? Why not a single region administered by Kurds, consisting of the predominantly Kurdish parts of the Jezira, Efrîn, and Kobanê? Because the PYD does not want to convey the impression that it strives for the establishment of a single region administered by Kurds in Syria – even though the establishment of such a region has absolutely nothing to do with separatism. In short, the PYD is totalitarian, undemocratic, and closely synchronizes its policy with the regime.

The murder of the popular party leader of the Future Movement Mishal at-Tammu on 7 October 2011 was one of the most important triggers for the spread of the mass protests from the south of Syria to the Kurdish regions. Is there by now reliable information on the question of who murdered Mishal at-Tammu, and on whose orders?

What do you mean by reliable information? Reliable information would be possible only if an independent commission of inquiry had investigated the murder. But there was no investigation whatsoever. Actually, the circumstances before, during, and after Mishal's murder unequivocally indicate that the PYD, or rather the PKK, murdered him on the order of the regime. We have to ask ourselves: Who had an interest in the death of Mishal? The answer is clear: The regime. Mishal was dangerous because he, as the only Kurdish party chairman, took a clear position for the revolution right from the beginning. Moreover, he wanted to bring Kurds and Arabs together against the regime – and he had enough persuasiveness and support even within the Arab population to reach this goal. Therefore, the regime wanted to get rid of him. And it employed the PKK, or rather, the PYD, for the purpose. Some weeks before Mishal's death, there had already been a first assassination attempt. Mishal himself told me that he recognized the assassin, and that it was a PYD guy. He didn't want to repeat that in public because he hoped the Kurds could fight together against the regime; he hoped to somehow bring the PYD into the boat. This was clearly a miscalculation. Another miscalculation by Mishal was that the Kurds would join the revolution as soon as a single Kurd was killed in the course of the revolution. Mishal was killed, but unlike what your question seems to suggest, this led neither to a situation where the revolution spread to the Kurdish areas, nor to mass protests in these areas. There were one or two big demonstrations, including the one on the occasion of Mishal's funeral – and that was it. At the time, after the failed assassination attempt against Mishal, members of the Future Movement such as Hevrin Ose and Rezan Sheikhmus went to the other Kurdish parties and said that they needed help against the PYD – but the other parties didn't want to have anything to do with it. Today, it is known that there was a PYD, or rather, PKK kill team that killed on the orders of the regime – apart from Mishal al-Tammu, Nasruddin Birhik, a central committee member of the former el-Partî, was among its victims. The existence of this hit squad is confirmed by various sources, for example, by former Syrian secret service officers such as Mahmud an-Nasir, who was officially in charge of the Kurdish question, but also by former PYD members who have left the party and now live abroad because they fear retaliation.

Be that as it may, the murder of Mishal at-Tammu was a severe blow for the Future Movement. There is still no real successor in the party leadership, and locally, in Rojava itself, the Future Movement is hardly detectable. How will things go on with the party?

It is quite correct that after Mishal's murder, the Future Movement lost its direction for a while. That is normal, it would have been similar with any other party. But starting with the European wing, it found its way back to a clear political line relatively quickly. One important part of this line was the decision to cooperate with the Arab opposition and to join the Syrian National Council. Moreover, the Future Movement has understood and publicly proclaimed that a cooperation with the PYD is impossible. At the beginning, the other Kurdish parties sharply criticized us for both positions. They argued that the Arab opposition was anti-Kurdish and chauvinistic. Furthermore, one shouldn't criticize other Kurdish forces because the Kurds had to form a united front. But by now, our line has fully succeeded among the parties of the Kurdish National Council. Now, the KNC is also a member of the Coalition. And the leading members of parties such as the PDKS or the Azadî are telling us very clearly that we were right, that it is impossible to work with the PYD. Today, the PDKS joins our protests against the PYD in Europe.

While we were considered undesirables in the Kurdish National Council after Mishal's death, this has now changed. Now we are the ones who say, we don't want to be members. We want to determine our policy independently, not just from Qandil,[10] but also from Erbil[11] and Sulemaniya.[12] This stance has consequences: Unlike the other parties, we are financed neither by the PKK nor by the KDP nor by the PUK, nor, for obvious reasons, does the Kurdish National Council give us any funds. At least in Syria, where there is a war going on and the economic situation is becoming increasingly tense by the day, this is a big problem, especially since all the other parties are financially in a better situation. Given these circumstances, we are losing members in Syria. On the one hand, that is regrettable, on the other, it is more important that our political line wins the day – and it does. We are by now regarded by many, including forces in Syria, as a "party of the third way," as an alternative to both the PYD and the KNC. Many independent Kurdish intellectuals are politically close to us and support our policy. In addition, we can point to quite concrete successes: The first ambassador of the Syrian Coalition in Berlin, Bassam Abdullah, is a member of the Future Movement.

Your party was the only Kurdish group to play an active part within the Syrian National Council right from the outset. To this day, the Future

Movement is regarded as the force that works most closely with the Arab opposition against the regime. Why do you cooperate so tightly with the Arab and Islamic opposition?

The main goal of the Future Movement was and is the overthrow of the Syrian regime. If we want to achieve that goal, we have to cooperate with the Arab opposition. We can reach this goal only together. We can't expect the Arab population to fight for freedom and democracy while we just quietly and comfortably lean back. Moreover, we simply do not pursue a chauvinist or Kurdish-nationalist policy. The positions should be the litmus test, not whether a party or a politician is Arab or Kurdish. At the time, the Syrian National Council went further in its recognition of specifically Kurdish rights than many of the Kurdish parties in their own party programmes – what would we then want to reproach it for from a Kurdish point of view? But we have never cooperated with any Islamist group. Of course, in the Syrian National Council or in today's Coalition, there are also parties or groups that are close to the Muslim Brotherhood or advocate moderate Islamic positions. But there are no representatives of radical Islamist positions. There is thus no reason not to cooperate with the National Council or the Coalition – even though we, as a party, advocate the separation of state and religion. And let me add: As I have already said, the KNC now is also a member of the Coalition.

What ideas does your party have for the future of Syria and the role of the Kurds in Syria?

Anyone who wants to democratize Syria must begin by advocating a decentralization of the country. For one thing, that means that political responsibilities have to be shifted from the central level to the provinces. But this alone is not sufficient: Nothing is gained when, instead of the president, individual governors take on the role of the little dictator. Power must also be shared *within* the provinces – many decisions concerning daily life can be taken much better on the municipal level than on the provincial one. The fundamental guideline is: Decisions ought to be taken as close to the bottom as possible and as near to the top as necessary. It is very important that the municipalities are not restricted to the right to make certain decisions, but that they can also dispose of their own guaranteed budgets – otherwise, they can make the decisions, but aren't able to realize them. Particularly important is the question of how the security forces will be organized in the future. For one thing, the powers of the secret services must be massively curtailed. But it is also important that the individual provinces are able to exercise control over certain police units. All Syrians, not just the Kurds, have terrible experiences with the – centrally controlled – police. Here, changes are necessary; here, the responsibility must move to the provinces or even to the municipalities.

With regard to the partition of the provinces, we advocate the establishment of a single Kurdish province that includes the predominantly Kurdish areas of the province al-Hasaka and the province Aleppo (that is, the regions of Efrîn and Kobanê). The fact that these areas are not geographically connected does not pose an obstacle for a joint administration and the election of a joint provincial council. Of course, there will be difficulties in the exact delineation of this new province, and this will very likely necessitate plebiscites. The Kurdish province will, in principle, have the same responsibilities as the Arab provinces – this should be an automatic result of decentralization. But additionally, we envision making Arabic and Kurdish the official languages in the Kurdish province. The schools should be allowed to decide for themselves whether Arabic, Kurdish, or Assyrian[13] is their main language. But in any case, the students have to learn Kurdish and Arabic. We think it would be wrong for the Kurds to lose their bilingualism like they did in Iraq. Arabic is a world language, and to master it is an advantage. Beyond that, we envision some sort of quota for all official state posts: Something like 70 per cent of all positions ought to be occupied by speakers of Kurdish. But note, by Kurdish *speakers*, not by Kurds. Language competency can be evaluated objectively, ethnicity cannot. In this way, Kurdish will be promoted in the Kurdish province – and without discriminating against other ethnic groups. Whoever wants to learn Kurdish can do so. Both in the cultural realm or in the realm of education, the Kurdish region should also have special powers. Thus it should be possible to have specific holidays – we are thinking of Newroz and the Halabja commemoration day. In addition, it should also be possible to design separate curricula even beyond the topic of language – why shouldn't we also have a school subject of "Kurdish history" in addition to the regular Syrian history lessons? But if, as is our plan, educational questions are generally decentralized, special regulations would actually be unnecessary, because the schools in all of Syria would get enough room to allow for the creation of additional subjects. The important thing is that no contents with a racist or sexist connotation are taught. The subject of Kurdish history must not be misused for any agitation against Arabs – to mention just one example.

At the moment, however, it looks as if the regime might even win the civil war. Moreover, the secular opposition against jihadist groups such as Jabhat al-Nusra or "Islamic State in Iraq and Sham" has grown weaker. What scenario threatens to be realized if the regime wins?

Has there ever been a secular opposition worthy of note? Most Kurdish parties would define themselves as secular, but actually, they have no real idea what that means. The Free Syrian Army also doesn't really exist anymore – it had always been no more than a loose alliance of armed units, which was later increasingly ground down by the regime on the one hand and the Islamists on the other. The Islamist scene has also changed: Jabhat al-Nusra, for example, doesn't play any role anymore – it has been superseded by "Islamic State." At the moment, I don't see how the regime can win the civil war – at least, not in the sense that it can succeed in pushing back the "Islamic State". To me, it seems more likely that both the regime and IS will control certain areas and will in effect divide the country among themselves. But the regime cannot be sure that IS will be content with the areas it has captured by now. There is strong evidence that the regime is partially cooperating with "Islamic State," for example, by consciously ceding certain areas to it, similar to its stance towards the PYD. It does so in order to show that the "alternative" to the regime is either chaos or rule by the Islamists. The difference is probably that the regime can assume that the PYD will confine itself to the Kurdish territories, while such a "restraint" cannot be assumed for IS. Should the regime manage to clearly win in strength in the Kurdish areas, it is quite possible that it will order the PYD to retreat, and that the PYD will follow that order, similar to the situation in 1998, when Abdullah Öcalan was expelled from Syria. At the time, the PKK was strong in Syria – but even so, there were no protests, let alone armed attacks, against the regime. A further question is whether IS will, in the foreseeable future, make any serious attempts to capture the Kurdish areas of Syria. Watching the difficulty that the Iraqi Kurds are having in pushing back the Islamists makes clear that it would not be too hard for the "Islamic State" to make a clean sweep through the Kurdish regions in Syria. The YPG has a core group of well-trained cadres at its disposal, people from the PKK who are ready to fight and have the necessary training. At the same time, many of its members have been in their ranks for only a short while; they were in part drafted, and in part they do it for the money or out of fear. Their military training was often extremely brief, and they have no fighting experience at all. This outfit is strong enough to browbeat the other Kurdish parties, especially since these do not have their own militias. It is strong enough to terrorize the civilian population. But it is not an outfit that would be able to seriously impede the Islamists – and given the tense situation in Iraq, help from that country is not to be expected.

How do you judge the behaviour of the international community, particularly the European Union, in the Syria conflict?

Europe and the US should have sided with the revolution much earlier. If they had supported the Free Syrian Army as early as 2011 – logistically, by training, and with arms – the Islamists wouldn't have become as strong as they are now. The humanitarian catastrophe that we now face could have been at least limited through the establishment of a safe area – which of course would have had to have been secured militarily. Knocking out the Syrian airforce would have been another important step. None of this has happened, and instead, Europe and the US have essentially waited. But the Syrian conflict very neatly illustrates that "waiting" is by no means always the better or even the more peaceful alternative. Even now, there would still be possibilities to intervene sensibly – both in the military and humanitarian realms. Both the regime and IS could be seriously weakened – namely, by targeted bombardments. Why do the Americans only consider a bombardment of "Islamic State" in Iraq, but not in Syria? That is wrong – particularly because the present problem in Iraq wouldn't even exist had the Islamists been confronted in time in Syria. The important thing is to weaken both sides – it would be a mistake to again see the Ba'ath regime as a possible cooperation partner just because of the crimes of the Islamists. Moreover, the European refugee policy is anything but humane. Europe could and should accept many more refugees than it has up to now – giving, among other things, a reprieve to Syria's neighbour states.

ENWER MUSLIM

Prime Minister of the Canton of Kobanê, 22 September 2014

Since last week, Kobanê has been under massive attacks by IS. Reportedly, the Islamists have conquered half of the canton in the course of the last few days. How is the local situation there?

The situation is very serious. In the last few days, the terrorists have indeed captured half of our canton, triggering a wave of refugees. But we are firmly determined to defend Kobanê. Kobanê must not fall! Otherwise, we Kurds will be threatened with genocide. The jihadists would kidnap our women and sell them, as they have already done with the Êzîdî in Iraq.

> *KRG president Barzani has trained a few thousand Peshmerga in Iraq who were recruited from Syrian-Kurdish refugees. Have any of these so far come to your help?*

No, so far only Kurdish volunteers from Turkey have come here to support us. But Turkey tries to prevent them from crossing the border and is thus actually supporting IS in its fight against the Kurds. On the other hand, we get solidarity from democratic movements in Turkey. A delegation of members of the Democratic Society Congress, of the Peoples' Democratic Party (HDP) and the Democratic Regions Party has visited us. Close to the border, there is a solidarity camp of young Kurds from Turkey.

> *But the town Kobanê itself is still under your control?*

The town itself is still under the control of the YPG. But it is encircled from all sides. Kobanê is of enormous strategic importance for all of Rojava.

> *What would you want from Europe?*

If you in Europe could at long last cut off the support of IS by Turkey and prevent jihadists from Europe from fighting here as mercenaries for IS, we would certainly manage to defend ourselves. But in the present acutely threatening situation, we need the support of NATO, the European Union, and the international institutions to stop the impending massacre.

SALAH AMMO

Musician, 28 September 2014

> *You were already a recognized musician in Syria under the Ba'ath regime. You performed with your orchestra in the Damascus Opera House, you won prizes, you performed internationally, and you were really among the top musicians of your country. How was life as a Kurdish musician in*

a country ruled by Arab nationalists who rejected every form of Kurdish identity?

I could be successful in Syria so long as I performed as a *Syrian* musician and, specifically, *not* as a Kurdish one. It was not prohibited for Kurds to be musicians and I was able to work in Syria really successfully. But in order to do so, I had to set my Kurdish identity aside. I always racked my brain to find out how it might be possible to gain publicity for Kurdish music in places such as Damascus. With that goal in mind, I founded the group "Joussour" for music and song, in which almost all ethnic groups in Syria were represented: Arabs, Kurds, Syro-Arameans, Armenians, Assyrians, and Turkmens. All the same, it was difficult to stage Kurdish music. On one occasion, I had a concert in the Damascus Opera House in which I also presented Kurdish music, which I embedded within the most varied music by different ethnic groups from all over Syria. At the time, the Syrian press wrote about Armenian, Assyrian, and Turkmen music, as well as the music of "other regional cultures." Kurds were not even mentioned.

But that was simply government policy. On the personal and social level, things looked quite different. In Syria, I have always also worked with Arab musicians. There were never any problems and the Arab musicians always also liked to play Kurdish music and always showed interest in it. There have never been any problems among us artists in that regard.

In Syria, at times even the mere public performance of Kurdish music was prohibited. How was the situation at, for example, Kurdish weddings?

Kurdish music was always played at our weddings. One could even say that weddings were *the* place of refuge for Kurdish culture, the opportunity for Kurdish songs to be sung and Kurdish poems to be recited. There is this poem by Mahmoud Darwish, "The Kurd has nothing but the wind," and one of our writers once transformed this into "The Kurd has nothing but the wedding." Weddings were really the single semi-public sanctuary for the Kurdish culture. But it was not possible to play Kurdish music in the cultural centres of Qamişlo, Amûdê, or Efrîn. There, the authorities really saw to it that no Kurdish culture was present.

But now the Kurdish areas in Syria have been under Kurdish control since 2012. Has that led to a change for Kurdish cultural workers? Has the status of Kurdish music changed?

I think the decisive question is not whether or not Rojava is controlled by Kurdish parties. Art and culture need certain social preconditions. If we want to enjoy music or literature in their purest form, we need peace and not a situation in which everyone fights for their survival. Given the situation in all of Syria today, music can also only be thought of in this context of war. At the moment, we are living in a culture of violence, and that also has its effects on music, literature, and the fine arts. Today, we have a lot of Kurdish art in Rojava. But what's being produced are mainly propaganda and war songs. There is no room for any other music. In such a situation, there are only a few opportunities for classical or experimental Kurdish or Arabic music. Add to this the fact that more and more people are fleeing from the war or from political repression. Cultural life suffers from this.

By now, ever larger parts of Syria are under the control of the so-called "Islamic State," unfortunately including many areas immediately adjacent to Rojava. IS destroys century-old cultural assets like mosques, statues, churches, and even prohibits music. Is that also a reason for the flight of many musicians?

Yes, of course. This "Islamic State" is literally the antithesis of culture. With these people, there is no culture. But the reason of the flight of many musicians is not just IS. In a society in which everything turns around the basic foundations of life, there is no place for professional art. This is also true of areas not under the rule of IS. Apart from a few artists very loyal to the regime in Damascus, almost all the artists have fled in the course of the last few months.

Do you think that these artists will return after the end of the war, or will that be a lasting loss for the Syrian society? Have Syria and Rojava lost a whole generation of artists?

I don't know whether one can say that in such a general form. I can only speak for myself. I don't want to go back. I see being here in Europe as a new challenge, and also as an artistic challenge. To begin a new life in exile now, after 35 years in Syria, is a very incisive experience, and I'm still occupied with learning elementary things such as the language. But I also see it as a challenge, and as an opportunity to be in a place where there is a greater interest in and respect for culture. I came to Vienna because of the war. But I brought the music of the Kurds, the Arabs, and the other ethnic minorities in Syria with whom I used to live with me. I took my passion and my musical dreams with me. This is my new life in my new homeland. Here, I have also already recorded, in a duet with the percussionist Peter Gabis, my first CD, given concerts, and made friends. But I miss Syria. I miss my family, my friends; at some point I would like to return there for a while. But at the moment, that is impossible, and when I watch the news from Syria, I am afraid that the Syria I once knew no longer exists. When I check all the news on Facebook from friends of mine who stayed behind, I get very, very sad. Therefore, I simply haven't looked it up for the last few months. It is incredibly terrible to have to watch and follow all this. And it keeps getting worse and worse. The songs I taped for my CD still carry some hope for freedom. But these moments of hope are getting rarer and rarer.

Is there, here in exile, cooperation between Syrian or Kurdish artists? Are there any points of contact where you can fit in?

At the moment, people are very much concerned with themselves. Many of them don't even know their own status, haven't been able to bring their families to Austria etc. But at least we know about each other, and it is quite possible that something like that will happen in the future.

SILÊMAN CEEFER

Foreign Minister of the Canton Efrîn, 2 February 2015

More than a year ago, the three Kurdish cantons proclaimed their autonomy. Do you see any progress since then with regard to the international recognition of these cantons?

So far, we have been recognized neither by the Syrian government nor by any other government. But even so, we are increasingly perceived as a contact partner internationally. We have also already been to Europe with delegations, and I can see that we are being taken more and more seriously and that people understand that we are one of the few secular and democratic forces in Syria that are worthy of support.

You are the foreign minister of an entity that is not recognized. How do you fulfil your tasks? How is it to be the foreign minister of a canton that is largely cut off from the external world?

It is of course totally different from being the foreign minister of an internationally recognized state. I simply try to do my best to build contacts to states and governments. But you are absolutely right in pointing out that it is difficult if one is, in the final analysis, recognized by no one, has no embassies and even has a hard time travelling to foreign countries.

You are yourself a member of the Êzîdî, your prime minister is an Alevi. The strong presence of religious minorities in the government here is surprising at first glance.

For us, that is totally normal. In Efrîn, the Muslims have never been fanatics. Actually, we have always lived together well here. Before I became minister, I was the chairman of a Êzîdî umbrella organization, the Mala Êzîdîya. Everybody here knows that I am a Êzîdî and I have actually never had any problems here because of that.

What, in your view, are the biggest problems in the canton?

One of the biggest problems is certainly the isolation. The fact that we, despite our long border with Turkey, do not have a single border crossing with this neighbour state of ours and can leave our area only through Azaz, which is controlled by the Islamic Front, or across the green border into Turkey, severely hampers us. Because of Jabhat al-Nusra, it has also become increasingly difficult to get to Aleppo, our traditional urban centre. We are increasingly isolated, and this also has a negative impact on the economy of our cantons.

IDRISS NASSAN

Vice Foreign Minister of the Canton of Kobanê, 24 April 2015

How is the current situation in Kobanê after the liberation of the town and the canton?

It has of course become much better after we were able to liberate almost the whole canton. The IS has retreated and thus the security situation has become much better. But from a humanitarian point of view, the situation is still very difficult. The town is destroyed to a very large extent. Many vital goods are impossible to get. We have no construction material.

That is, from the Turkish side the border is still closed?

Yes, sometimes they allow refugees to return home, but no one can travel in the other direction, into Turkey. Occasionally and on some days,

Turkey also allows relief supplies to pass. But this always depends on the whim of the Turkish authorities, something we can do nothing about. At the moment, we have 50,000 to 60,000 persons in the canton of Kobanê who must be fed and supplied. We have rebuilt the mill and the bakery and produce 20 tons of bread there every day. We are trying to repair the water and power supplies and are getting assistance for this from the Kurdish communities in Turkey. But their aid deliveries also often get stuck because the border is closed. At the moment, we are clearing the city of mines and unexploded ordnance. But to do that, we would also need more equipment, which we are unable to get across the border.

What do you think Europe should do?

Europe must exert pressure on Turkey to open the border to Kobanê. We need open borders for humanitarian deliveries, construction material, and trade. Here, Europe, the United States, and all democratic states can do something to support our democratic system in Rojava. It is time for Europe to support us.

NASSAN AHMAD

Health Minister of the Canton of Kobanê, 24 April 2015

Kobanê is free but in ruins. How do things stand with regard to medical care in Kobanê?

Of the four hospitals of the town, we were able to restore two in a provisional manner. But we can guarantee health care only in the town of Kobanê and not, at present, in the surrounding villages. If refugees return to these, they must come to the town if they have medical problems.

What about the supply of medicine?

We have thousands of children as well as pregnant women, all of whom can't get any vaccination or medicine. We will soon be in summer and we have no clean water. The old water supply of Kobanê used to come from Jarābulus, which is still in the hands of IS. At present, we can only use ground water that is partially poisoned. This will have a very negative impact on the health of our population.

Do you fear an outbreak of cholera and other diseases?

Yes, that is a real possibility.

Where does the medicine that does get through to Kobanê come from?

From Turkey, but it often doesn't reach us in time. Here, we are totally dependent on the whims of the Turkish authorities. Should there really be an outbreak of disease, we would have a serious problem.

What should Europe do for the reconstruction of Kobanê?

The most important thing is the opening of the border to Turkey. We need a humanitarian corridor, as well as aid for the reconstruction of hospitals and health institutions. Here, the EU could really help us. What we urgently need is a conference for the reconstruction of Kobanê where funders can commit themselves to concrete projects.

RUKEN AHMED

Women's Minister of the Canton of Kobanê, 5 November 2015

The new system in Rojava is known for the important role that women occupy here. What positions do women have in Kobanê?

Just like everywhere in Rojava, in Kobanê, too, we have a system of gendered leadership positions. That is, we have a female and a male in each important position. We find it important that all leading positions in society are shared by women and men. Without the participation of women in society, there can be no social change. Therefore, we, as women, need a leading role in all social realms.

In the past, we have repeatedly seen how women participated in both resistance and revolution, but weren't allowed to play any leading role afterwards. But we are realizing our programme by immediately taking over a part of the leading roles, which enables us to actually change the existing society.

In many areas, we are told again and again that this is not women's area of competence. But we are showing that women are present in all realms of society and are also able to take over leading roles, even in the military. In this way, we demonstrate that we can play a leading role everywhere.

But patriarchy is not just a Kurdish problem.

The oppression of women is something that has existed not only in all of the Middle East, but also in Europe, for a very long time. Women are now organizing to finally break this oppression. We've been leading a struggle against the oppression of women for 5,000 years. One might say that IS is the organization that robs the women of any rights whatsoever. But we, as women, are against this whole system that oppresses women, and we are fighting for a democratic society.

How important is the role that women played in the defence of Kobanê against IS?

In Kobanê, women made a significant contribution to the military struggle against IS. They are thus both an example and a model for our women.

How is the access of women to education in Kobanê?

Before 2014, we had a women's academy here, which was, just like the whole infrastructure of Kobanê, destroyed. But we are already reorganizing ourselves and are rebuilding everything. Society, parenting, the educational system, and the economy are all areas in which the role of women is particularly important. But there are also everyday problems in society where we have to be active in order to solve them.

Can the Kurdish women's movement also influence other parts of Syria?

We are fighting not just for Kurdish women, but against 5,000 years of patriarchy. We are fighting for the liberation of all women and we have now also created a Syrian Women's Association for *all* women. This includes not just Kurdish women, but also Arab and Assyrian ones. Under the Ba'ath regime, there were no possibilities to create an NGO. But now we see more and more Arab and Assyrian women join us and start to regard all this as a model. Thus, the creation of the YPG, the Women's Defence Army, has become a model for other women. Today, more and more Arab, Assyrian, and Armenian women are participating in the YPJ and fight, together with us, against IS.

IBRAHIM BIRO

President of the Kurdish National Council, 20 February 2016

Four years after the withdrawal of the Syrian army and two years after the proclamation of autonomous cantons by the PYD, how are relations between the PYD, or the canton administration it has created, and the KNC today?

The relationship between us is very difficult. We have never accepted each other as partners. It is like it is with all Syrians: One part is with the regime and another part is with the opposition. The PYD has never ended its relations with the regime. We had several agreements with each other, but they have all been completely inconsequential. The PYD still entertains good relations with the regime and for that reason, it can't work with us as a partner. The PYD is a part of the PKK and doesn't accept any other party besides itself.

We don't accept the self-administration of the PYD because it adopts laws that are against the interests of the Kurds.

Which laws do you mean by that?

For example, the draft for the YPG. They decided to forcibly draft all young men into the YPG. At the same time, our Rojava-Pêşmerge[14] are not allowed to cross the border even though they are ready to fight.

Or take the reform of the school system. We have long suffered in the prisons of the regime and were persecuted for our commitment to the Kurdish language. But the fact that the PYD is now closing down all the state schools and is opening its own Kurdish language schools, which are recognized by no one, will harm our children because they will no longer get official certificates.

But actually, there are schools in Rojava and the mere fact that students are taught in Kurdish doesn't mean that they don't learn anything anymore.

In the first three grades, there is a separate school system that is not recognized by the government and therefore, the regime has closed down all schools for the Kurds. These are not official schools and the quality is often very bad.

You still live in Rojava. Can you, as the leader of the oppositional Kurdish National Council, move around and work freely in Rojava, or are there any constraints or even repressive measures against the KNC or your party, the Yekîtî, on the part of the ruling PYD and its self-administration structures?

Everyone in Rojava who does not cooperate with the PYD will get into trouble, but this is particularly true of our party's politicians. The PYD would probably prefer for me to go into exile, like many other politicians did. But I will remain in Rojava as long as I can.

Were you represented at the peace talks in Geneva?

Yes, I was present at Geneva II, and at other negotiations other representatives of our alliance were present. We participate in these negotiations.

How are things within the Kurdish National Council? After the proclamation of the autonomous cantons by the PYD, two smaller parties, the Kurdish Leftist Democratic Party of Muhammad Salih Gado and the Kurdish Left Party resigned from the National Council and – probably more importantly – in October 2015, Abdulhamid Hadji Darwish's Kurdish Democratic Progressive Party, the sister party of the Iraqi PUK, also left the KNC. Since that time, the PDK and your Yekîtî Party seem to be the only relevant parties left on the National Council.

There had been tensions in the Kurdish National Council before 2015, but after the resignation of these parties, the situation stabilized. In place of the parties that resigned, the Future Movement has joined the KNC. Since then, cooperation within the National Council has worked better than before.

The PYD always accuses the Kurdish National Council of simply being a branch of Barzani's Kurdistan Regional Government in Iraq.

The PYD has relations with the regime, the Arab opposition has relations with Turkey, Qatar, or Saudi Arabia. We have only the Kurdistan Regional Government in Iraq. Why should we reject support that is offered to us? We would love to have more support from the Kurdistan Regional Government.

What would have to happen for the KNC or your party to participate in the self-administration in Rojava and to reconcile with the PYD?

Our party is a part of the National Council. We will participate in every decision of the Council and will certainly not go our own ways. The last agreement was the agreement in Dohuk. At the time, it was clear that the two sides would work as partners and we would not simply join the structures of the PYD. Unfortunately, the agreement was never put into practice. A settlement is possible only on the basis of this agreement, that is, on the basis of a cooperation on an equal footing.

What future visions does the Kurdish National Council have for a political solution for Syria after the civil war?

The first thing that is needed for such a solution is international pressure against the regime. Until now, real pressure was only exerted in connection with the chemical weapons, and the regime did indeed react. If the regime does not relent, nothing will happen, and it *will* only relent if there is international pressure.

But in which direction should a solution go?

We still want a federal and democratic system.

But the PYD says it wants the same thing.

The PYD is not a democratic party and is not ready to share power.

What do you expect from Europe and the international public with regard to the future of Syria?

They should exert pressure on the regime, but those who currently support the PYD should also pressure it to keep to the Dohuk agreement and share power with us. We thus expect Europe to also take a more critical stance towards the PYD.

IBRAHÎM KURDO

Foreign Minister of the Canton of Kobanê, 4 September 2016

The day before yesterday, two people from the camp here at the border who protested against the construction of a Turkish border fortification were killed. How is the current situation at the border with Turkey?

The Kurds in Syria and in Turkey are a single family. Turkey has wanted to split this family into two parts for a long time. We have never accepted that there should be a border between the Kurds. But if they have to have such a border at all, they have to build their wall on Turkish state territory. Instead, they crossed the border to do so.

That is, Turkey erected the border wall on Syrian national territory.

Turkey wanted to build the border wall 20 metres from the border on the Syrian side.

Since when have there been protests against this?

The protest at the border has now been going on for seven days.

How did this lead to these two people getting killed?

I was present at this myself. At first, we Kurds demonstrated. Then Turkey deployed tear gas, then smoke bombs, and at 12 o'clock noon, they used firearms against us. But that also failed to impress the demonstrators, and they simply continued. Then two demonstrators were deliberately shot dead. By evening, the fighting came to a standstill. We wanted an end to this, to the senseless sacrifice of our people. We don't see Turkey as an enemy. We seek friendship with all peoples and hope that the situation will quieten down again.

Will the protests continue?

Turkey has already withdrawn and will now indeed build the wall on Turkish territory. This is accepted by both sides.

But how is the current situation further to the west? On 24 August, Turkey capured Jarābulus, and it is now advancing further to the south. There have also already been clashes with units of the Syrian Democratic Forces.

After IS had fled from Manbij and Jarābulus, the jihadists first shaved their beards in Turkey and then came back together with the Turkish army. The Turkish army and their allies now stand about 15 to 20 kilometres south of the Turkish border. The whole thing was a piece of theatre. Turkey capured Jarābulus within an hour, even though the Americans and the Iraqis have failed to capture Falluja for months. It took Turkey just an hour to conquer Jarābulus.

Is there still fighting between Turkey and the Kurdish units?

In the beginning, there were a few clashes; three tanks were scorched and a couple of people were killed, but by now, there is no fighting anymore.

Does that mean you have a ceasefire now? Turkey has explicitly denied this.

Yes, there is a ceasefire. Turkey is now allowed to advance 20 kilometres to the west, but if they advance further to the south in the direction of Manbi, we will defend ourselves.

That means that the Kurds will continue to try to establish a corridor in the direction of Efrîn?

Yes, we need a connection between Kobanê and Efrîn, and we will not give up that goal.

ABDULHAMID HADJI DARWISH

Chairman of the Kurdish Democratic Progressive Party in Syria, 3 October 2016

Your party was one of the founding members of the Kurdish National Council. Why did you withdraw from it in 2015?

On its fourteenth congress in October 2015, our party decided to leave the KNC because of the hegemony and unilateralism of the Kurdistan Democratic Party, the PDK. Before our decision, the PDK had unilaterally dominated the National Council. The Council did not do any of the things for the Kurds that the situation demanded.

What position does your party have today regarding the self-administration of Syrian Kurdistan as created by the Democratic Unity Party PYD?

It is true that the self-administration in Rojava was created by the PYD. The other parties were not enlisted in this, and the most important parties in Syria, including our own, were never part of this self-administration. Despite many negotiations and despite an agreement between the KNC and the PYD in Dohuk, we were never enlisted in these structures. The PYD didn't comply with the Dohuk agreement. The self-administration of Rojava thus does not reflect the wishes of the masses of the Kurdish people in Syria and only insufficiently includes the various components of the population of the region.

Has your party, after the withdrawal from the KNC, decided to participate in the structures of self-administration in Rojava created by the PYD?

Our party is not involved in the administration of any of the three cantons. The PYD has not invited us to participate in the administration and exerts exclusive control in the region.

Your party has traditionally entertained close relationships with the Iraqi PUK, which in turn has now developed better contacts to the sister parties of PKK. Couldn't your party, after its withdrawal from the Kurdish National Council, play a mediating role in the intra-Kurdish conflict between the PYD and the parties that have remained in the KNC?

Since its withdrawal from the KNC, our party has tried to bring about some form of cooperation and coordination between both sides to create a situation where political decisions for the Kurds in Syria can be made in a healthy political atmosphere. Unfortunately, neither side has taken this to heart; rather, they have insisted on their very negative views of each other instead. From our perspective, a reconciliation of both sides is now more necessary than ever to enable the representation of the interests of the Kurds on a Syrian and an all-Kurdish plane.

The future of Syria is very uncertain. For five years, a civil war has been raging whose end is not yet in sight. The various parties to the war have very different ideas about Syria's political future. What are your party's plans for the future of the Kurds in Syria?

Our primary goal is to establish a democratic Syria, and we also regard this as the only way to secure the national rights of the Kurds. This is the only way for the sons of the Kurdish people and for the other components of Syrian society such as the Assyrians and Chaldeans to live in Syria without injustice, oppression, and national or religious discrimination.

RÊDÛR XELÎL

Spokesperson of the People's Protection Units (YPG), 14 February 2017

The YPG and their allies in the Syrian Democratic Forces (SDF) are militarily stronger than ever before. But even though they were successful against the so-called "Islamic State", they seem to have failed in establishing a corridor between Kobanê and Efrîn. Does this have political or military reasons?

The decision not to advance in the direction of Efrîn was made for political reasons.

What role is the YPG supposed to play in the liberation of ar-Raqqa?

The YPG is a part of the Syrian Democratic Forces and has the same responsibilities in this regard as the other groups and factions within this alliance. The only difference is that the YPG has more experience in fighting IS and is passing this experience on to the other groups within the coalition.

Will the YPG remain in Raqqa after its capture, just as it has remained in Tal Abyad, or will it hand the town over to Arab forces?

One cannot compare Tal Abyad to Raqqa. Raqqa has its own civil council in exile and an administrator of the urban affairs. After the conquest of the town, the SDF will take care of the security situation outside of the town until it is completely safe.

Since 2015, the US army has played an increasingly important role for the YPG. Many observers are afraid that the new administration under Donald Trump could withdraw its support from the SDF. Have there been any local changes since the ascension of the new US president to power?

No, there have been no such changes.

A while ago, US soldiers began to train the Rojava Peshmerga of the PDK to enable them, as they said, to participate "in the struggle against IS." Considering the problematic relations between the PYD and the PDK, and the YPG and the Peshmerga, the Rojava Peshmerga have for now remained in Iraq. Can you imagine a cooperation with them, and if so, what could it look like?

We have no information about any US training for these forces or plans for the latter to come to Rojava. What we do know is that there are no armed forces under this name. Furthermore, we will tolerate no military forces whatsoever apart from the YPG, which is the official military force of the democratic self-administration.

Finally, a few questions about the situation in Aleppo. The battle of Aleppo ended in December 2016. At the beginning of that battle, the Kurdish district, which was located in the Kurdish neighbourhood Şêxmeqsûd, functioned as a neutral zone between the government and the rebels. At the end, the YPG found itself on the side of the regime. What led to this development?

There was no strategic or tactical cooperation between our units and the Syrian regime. Militant groups in the east of Aleppo had threatened our forces in Şêxmeqsûd for four years. Therefore, we attacked these militants and kept them away from Şêxmeqsûd. In the end, the areas under the control of these groups were liberated.

Since the defeat of the rebels, Şêxmeqsûd has been surrounded by areas under the control of the Syrian Arabic Army of the government and its allies. How is the situation in Şêxmeqsûd itself? How is the population supplied with goods, or the YPG/YPJ with arms? Is there any agreement with the regime for the supply of Şêxmeqsûd?

As I said, there is no military agreement between us and the regime. There is, however, freedom of movement for civilians, for relief aid, and for administrative purposes. Things concerning the military supply of the YPG and the YPJ are secrets I cannot disclose. But we have our ways to ensure this supply.

It is hard to imagine that the Syrian regime will accept the existence of a self-administered Kurdish district in Aleppo on a permanent basis. What scenarios and plans do you have for the future of Şêxmeqsûd?

We still have a different vision of the future of Syria and we expect this future to be characterized by a democratic system that will guarantee all Syrians their rights, among them the right to the self-administration of their respective affairs. Once this is the case, and we are optimistic that it will be, there will be no problem anymore.

ABDULHAKIM BASHAR

Negotiator of the Kurdish National Council at the 2017 Astana ceasefire negotiations, 16 February 2017[15]

You were one of the three Kurdish delegates at the ceasefire negotiations in Astana. While the YPG/PYD and the SDF were not invited to Astana, you represented the Kurdish National Council there, which opposes the forces that control Rojava. But what was the role of the KNC in Astana? What could you achieve for the Syrian Kurds in Astana?

The Kurdish National Council is an important part of the Syrian opposition and a partner of the opposition in the Syrian revolution and in the struggle for a new Syria. The invitation to Astana was also a confirmation that this cooperation is continuing. The PYD has so far acted as an ally of the regime and was therefore not invited to Astana. We advocate a real partnership between the Kurds and all representatives of the political and military revolution. Our demands are thus part of the demands of the Syrian opposition.

The UN-sponsored peace talks in Geneva planned for 8 February have been postponed, but are supposed to go into the next round soon. Will the Kurdish National Council participate in these negotiations about Syria's future?

Yes, we were invited and are planning to participate. The Kurdish National Council will be an important partner for the future and the reorganization of Syria.

But at the moment, it is not the Kurdish National Council that exercises the control over the Kurdish areas in Syria, but the YPG, that is, the SDF. Would you support the participation of these forces in the peace negotiations?

That is not our decision but was decided by the US special envoy for Syria.[16] I think everyone can see that the PYD is an important ally of the regime, and the regime itself has been invited to the negotiations.

The conflict between the PYD and the KNC has intensified even more already since the arrest and expulsion of Ibrahîm Biro in August 2016. What does the present relationship between the KNC on the one hand and the PYD and its self-administration structures on the other look like?

The PYD has built a totalitarian and anti-democratic system in its regions, which oppresses the freedom of speech and cracks down on all oppositionist politicians with repression, including arrests, banishments, abductions, and murders. The PYD doesn't want any partnership with other Kurdish parties, but demands absolute fealty. With this ideology and practice, the PYD is unable to establish a collaborative cooperation with other Kurdish parties.

Don't you fear that the Kurds will again lose everything they have achieved so far because of their disunity?

The PYD is not a part of the revolution, but of the counterrevolution. It has pushed the Kurds into a relation of dependency with the regime. But a solution to the conflict in Syria without safeguarding the Kurdish rights will be impossible anyway.

What should the solution to this conflict look like from your point of view? What goals is the Kurdish National Council pursuing in Geneva?

There are basically two possibilities. Either we fight, together with the opposition, for a new Syria, or we reach a transition to a negotiated peace through dialogue and talk. In both cases, our goal is a democracy for the new Syria with all its inhabitants, groups, and components. We want a federal state with a separation of religion and state, with equality of men and women and with religious freedom.

HEDIYE YUSUF

Co-president of the Democratic Federation Northern Syria – Rojava, 2 March 2017

You are, together with the Arab Mansur Selum, who comes from Tal Abyad, the co-president of the Democratic Federation of Northern Syria – Rojava, which was proclaimed in March 2016 and presently exercises control over 17 per cent of the Syrian national territory. Were you part of the Geneva peace talks in any form?

Six years since the beginning of the Rojava revolution, our armed forces, which include not just Kurdish, but also Arab, Assyrian, and Turkmen fighters, exert control over even more than 17 per cent of Syria. They protect the society there and take care of the daily needs of the population. Despite all difficulties and after thousands of martyrs, one year ago our population proclaimed the Democratic Federation of Northern Syria – Rojava. Despite these successes and even though we promote a federal project for all of Syria, so far legitimization and recognition by the international community has eluded us. So far, the UN has been unable to make any genuine steps towards a solution to the Syrian conflict because the will of the Syrian people has been ignored. Therefore, we were marginalized in the peace talks and have so far not been represented at the talks in Geneva.

The area of the Democratic Federation of Northern Syria – Rojava doesn't include only Kurdish areas, but also regions that have an Arab and Assyrian majority. In some cities, there is also an Armenian minority. In what form does the political system, particularly the educational system, take the languages of the minorities into account?

When we established the self-administration of the cantons, in our social contract in the canton of Cizîrê we laid down that there would be three official languages: Kurdish, Arabic, and Syro-Aramaic. Correspondingly, all ethnic groups have a right to education in their own language and to carry out cultural and political activities in their own language. As a first step, we have changed the Ba'athist curriculum and replaced it with a curriculum based on our democratic national philosophy. The new curriculum was translated into all three official languages and starts with the entry to school. We are developing the new educational system step by step. It is a totally new system. As you probably know, the Syrian state never developed an educational system in languages other than Arabic. At the moment, we have the problem that, for that reason, we also have too few qualified academics for instruction in the various local languages. Teachers and academic personnel first have to be trained by the authorities of the self-administration. But we hope that we can overcome these difficulties step by step.

One of the decisive questions for the future development of Rojava will be the economic development of the region. But here, a leftist party must also ask what economic system it wants to institute. What kind of economic system is being built in Rojava?

In our federal framework, we are building a system that combines ecological awareness with environmentally-friendly industry. This system aims at having society participate actively in the economic process and at raising the living standard of the poor. For that purpose, cooperatives were established and, despite our minimal resources, cultivated with the support of the democratic self-administration. But apart from an ecological industry, we also aim at the development of agriculture. We work against exploitation and monopolization. But we have also adopted laws that allow for private investments and private enterprises, provided that these don't exploit society for the benefit of their own profit.

That is, you want a certain amount of private entrepreneurship in Rojava?

Our economic departments are striving for a balance between the interests of society and a particular socio-economic system. All segments of society, particularly women, participate in the development of economic projects on the basis of cooperatives.

MIZGIN YUSUF

President of the Êzîdî Council of Syria (Encûmena Êzidiyên Sûrî, E.Ê.S.), 13 August 2017

How do you see the situation of the Êzîdî in Syria?

The Syrian Êzîdî became victims of Islamist terrorist attacks several times in the last six years. With the support of Turkey and Qatar, these groups attacked Êzîdî villages near Serê Kaniyê. They killed and deported a lot of Êzîdî civilians and robbed them of their property. We repeatedly appealed to the Syrian opposition that the Êzîdî of Efrîn are endangered as well. But the extremists within the Syrian Opposition still conceive of the Êzîdî as nonbelievers. Although we have repeatedly tried to get a representative in the opposition, the National Coalition for Syrian Revolution and Opposition Forces has always refused to accept a Êzîdî delegate.

How do you see the general development of Syria since 2011?

When we established the EÊS on 10 March 2012, we established a non-violent organization. We, the Êzîdî, are peaceful people and we considered it a mistake to militarize the Syrian revolution. It is this militarization that has led to such extreme developments ...

... and of course small religious minorities like the Êzîdî suffer the most in a civil war like this.

The Êzîdî became an easy target for extremist groups, who were supported by a number of states. These groups have nothing to do with humanity and civilization. But this is not only the fault of the Syrian opposition, but also a result of wrong political and military decisions by the PYD ...

... which controls most of the Êzîdî villages in Syria. But how is the situation in the Êzîdî villages outside the territory controlled by the PYD, YPG, and YPJ? Your organization recently made the case of the village of Elî Qîno public. What happened to the villagers of Elî Qîno?

The village of Elî Qîno near the town of Azaz was already under the control of Turkish-backed "Euphrates Shield" rebels. On 12 June 2017, these Islamist rebels told the people of the village that they had only one hour to leave the village. After that, property, including olive groves, livestock, and furniture was reportedly confiscated. We strongly protest against these irresponsible practices and we demand these forces withdraw from the Kurdish area and stop such acts, and immediately allow the civilians to return to their villages and their properties. We also call on all humanitarian organizations and countries involved in the humanitarian and military situation in Syria to intervene to put pressure on these groups to stop their acts against the Êzîdî villagers.

Your organization has its centre in German exile. How strong are you inside Syria?

We used to have a lot of members inside Syria as well, but then the PYD isolated and threatened our members. This is why many of them left Syria and went into exile. But we still have members in Efrîn and Hesîçe (al-Hasaka).

What is the difference between your organization and the other Êzîdî organizations in Syria, the Hevbendiya Êzîdiyên Suriyê (HÊS) and Komela Êzdiyên Rojavayê Kurdistanê û Sûriye (KÊRKS)?

When we established our organization in March 2012, we intended to organize an independent, strong, and centralized organization of all Êzîdî in Syria. The Komela Êzdiyên Rojavayê Kurdistanê û Sûriye (KÊRKS) was, right from the beginning, no more than a PKK-organization, and when they realized that our organization really became strong, they tried to split our EÊS by establishing the Hevbendiya Êzîdiyên Suriyê (HÊS). This organization is completely in the hands of the PKK, with the sole purpose of paying homage to the PYD and PKK. Their main goal is to destroy our image by means of the PKK media.

In September 2016, you left both the Kurdish National Council (KNC) and the National Coalition for Syrian Revolution and Opposition Forces. In May 2017 you returned to both organizations. Why did you leave and why did you return to these umbrella organizations of the Kurdish and the Syrian opposition?

In 2016, many members of the leadership of the National Coalition were anti-Kurdish and dominated by Islamists. They did not include us in negotiations with other states and ignored the Êzîdî. But even the Kurdish National Council partly ignored us. We were never included in the negotiations in Geneva. Each member organization of the Kurdish National Council got financial support by the Kurdish Regional

Government in Erbil. We were the only organization that did not get any support. We even didn't get any information about how much money they got from the Kurdistan Regional Government, and we were never included in any negotiations with the Kurdish Regional Government.

But then at the new conference of the KNC some of our key demands were met. They agreed to support a secular state. They agreed that the Êzîdî religion should be officially recognized by the new Syrian constitution, and to support the principle to have a Êzîdî member in the council of the National Coalition. With these decisions we re-entered the Kurdish National Council, and as the KNC is a member of the National Coalition, this also meant that we became a part of the National Coalition as well.

MOHAMED ŞAIXO (SHAIKHO)

Co-President of the Movement for a Democratic Society (TEV-DEM) in Aleppo, 26 December 2017

The Kurdish district of Aleppo is outside Rojava. However, in 2012 you managed to take over the quarter of Şêxmeqsûd (Sheikh Maqsoud) as a kind of neutral zone between the areas held by the rebels and the regime in Aleppo, the second largest city of Syria. What political structures did you create in Şêxmeqsûd? Who exactly rules this part of Aleppo?

Following the revolutionary movement in Syria in 2011, the people of the Şêxmeqsûd neighbourhood began to organize themselves and protect themselves by placing barriers at the entrance of the neighbourhood to prevent the entry of armed gangs. The Şêxmeqsûd neighbourhood is located in Aleppo and is very strategic because of its position on a hill that overlooks the city centre of Aleppo. It is one of the largest neighbourhoods in the city and is inhabited by different ethnic groups such as the Arabs, Kurds, and Turkmens. Following the establishment of the Council of Western Kurdistan and TEV DEM in 2012, TEV DEM started to establish many institutions to protect society, such as the Asayîş (local police), the People's Protection Units (YPG) and the Women's Protection Units (YPJ). In addition, a local council was formed to provide public services, as well as the Council of Martyrs' Families to take care of the martyrs' families and children. Furthermore, the following institutions were established: The Kurdish Language

Institute to teach the Kurdish language, the Kurdish Red Crescent, the Centre for Social Reconciliation, the Justice Centre, the Centre of Culture and Art, the Centre of Social Protection Forces, the Centre of the Democratic Union Party (PYD), the Centre of the National Syrian Democratic Coalition, the Centre of the Syrian Democratic Council.

However, Şêxmeqsûd did not become part of the Democratic Federation of Northern Syria, did it?

So far, the Şêxmeqsûd neighbourhood is not part of the Northern Syria Federation, because it is not geographically connected to the north of Syria. It is run by the Democratic Self-Administration. It governs itself autonomously, through democratic self-administration.

Astonishingly, Şêxmeqsûd was able to maintain its autonomous status even after the Syrian regime recaptured the east of Aleppo in December 2016. For one year, Şêxmeqsûd has been surrounded solely by regime forces and is a kind of island within a city controlled by the regime. How did you manage that and what is the relationship with the regime like?

The neighbourhood has been under siege for the last six years, and not just one year – sometimes by the armed groups, and sometimes by the regime. But the regime started to prevent the entry of basic goods into the neighbourhood after it had gained control of the rest of Aleppo. This situation has caused great difficulties, especially as far as the removal of the rubble from the streets, the repair of the sewage infrastructure, and similar things are concerned. There are no relationships with the regime. There are, however, some local civil committees that mediate between the regime and the local residents to solve problems and prevent clashes between both sides.

What are the consequences of the regime's blockade for the infrastructure and the supply of the population with necessary goods?

The current situation in the district is very difficult. There has, for example, been no electricity since 2012 and the residents rely on electric generators. In addition, there is no fuel because of the siege imposed by the regime.

In the Democratic Federation of Northern Syria, schools started to teach in Kurdish in 2015. What is the language of education in Şêxmeqsûd?

There are schools in the neighbourhood that teach in both Kurdish and Arabic.

Are there any plans for the future? Should Şêxmeqsûd become part of the Democratic Federation of Northern Syria or do you have any other plans with regard to the future of the Kurdish quarter of Aleppo?

We believe that the future of the neighbourhood is linked to our struggle on the ground, as well as to the final political solution of the crisis in Syria.

EBDO IBRAHIM

Minister of Defence of the Canton of Efrîn, 26 March 2018

After more than two months of fierce fighting YPG and YPJ had to withdraw from Efrîn. Are you a minister of a canton that does not exist anymore?

We have withdrawn our forces because we wanted to save the lives of civilians in the city of Efrîn. We could have fought inside the city as we did it against ISIS in Kobanê, but the result would have been the destruction of the city and a loss of many human lives, including many civilians. In coordination with our elected councils we decided to save the lives of these civilians, including women and children, and stopped the fighting in the city of Efrîn to enable them to flee the fighting zone. However, that does not mean that we stopped the struggle for Efrîn. Until now there are some villages in the southeast of the canton still under control of YPG and YPJ and we decided to start a guerrilla war against the occupation by Turkey and its jihadist allies.

So there are still fighters of YPG and YPJ behind the Turkish lines?

Yes there are and they also did successfully attack the occupying forces several times. However, for security reasons I cannot give you any details about our forces who are still in Efrîn.

Where is the government of Efrîn now?

We regathered in Shahba Canton and recently gave a press conference there. But of course I cannot give you details about our present residence.

Why did you not hand over Efrîn to the government of Syria when Turkey started to conquer the city of Efrîn?

We did negotiate with the Syrian army. We would have handed the city over to them, but it seems that the Syrian regime was not allowed to do that. You have to ask them why they did not defend Efrîn. We do not know it.

German tanks were used to occupy Efrîn. How do you judge the international reactions on the war against Efrîn?

Not only German tanks were used. Most of the arms used by the Turkish Army come from their NATO allies. But they also had the support of Russia. We, the Kurds were good enough to fight against ISIS, but now the international community has completely neglected us. Moreover, some of the European states even helped Turkey to attack us. They helped to destroy a peaceful part of Syria that was ruled by a secular and democratic self-administration. They completely ignored it when hundred thousands of new refugees were sent to exile and they still keep silent about attempts to ethnically cleanse the whole region.

What happened to the displaced persons?

They live under very difficult circumstances either in Shahba Canton, which is still under control of our forces or have fled to regions around Aleppo that are under control of the Syrian regime. We do the best for the civilians who live in our territory. We reorganized them and the Kurdish Red Crescent helps them the best way they can. However, until now they are the only organization that helps them and there is no international humanitarian aid at all.

19

Conclusion
Rojava, Quo Vadis?

Nearly six years after the withdrawal of the Syrian army, it is still too early to arrive at a definite record of the autonomy of Syrian Kurdistan. However, this attempt to present different internal perspectives will hopefully encourage readers to develop their own picture and to take a close look at developments in the region. Rojava still faces enormous challenges. While I was finishing the English version of this book, Efrîn, the most western region of Rojava was occupied by the Turkish Army and allied Islamist militias. Furthermore, Turkey has openly announced its intention to attack the rest of Rojava as well.

The blockade by Turkey and, in part, also by Iraq has severe economic and social consequences. Parts of Kobanê are still a field of rubble. So far, neither the regime nor the opposition has recognized the autonomy of Rojava, and the only Kurdish actors who are allowed to participate in the negotiations in Geneva are those who are hostile to the PYD. On the other hand, today the area under the control of the Kurdish armed forces and their allies is much larger than in 2012 and also includes areas with few or no Kurdish inhabitants. The Democratic Federation of Northern Syria – Rojava proclaimed in March 2016 also comprises predominantly Arab towns and villages.

The hope that emerged with the ceasefire between important – but by no means all – actors in the civil war that was pressed home by Russia and Turkey in January 2017, did not lead to a political solution to the Syrian civil war. Moreover, by February 2018 fighting had intensified not only in Efrîn, but also in East Ghouta, the eastern suburb of Syria's capital Damascus. For now it seems that the Syrian civil war has arrived at another, maybe final round in which the regime will try to gain back the last rebel-held territories in its mainland, and try to consolidate its power over the Arab heartland of Syria. At the same time there is a deal between Russia and Turkey that allowed Turkey to occupy Efrîn. This deal was solely negotiated between Russia and Turkey. Both, the Syrian government and the pro-Turkish opposition militias did not take any part in it. This demonstrates how much of its sovereignty Syria lost. By 2018 Syria had become a battlefield for international actors and their proxies. Syrians of all sides of the political spectrum are sidelined by Russia, Turkey, Iran, Saudi-Arabia, Qatar, and the US.

Russia has become the major player in the future of Syria. The regime owes its victory in large part to the military, and especially aerial support of Putin's Russia. Without Russian and Iranian help, Assad would not be in power now and much of Syria would not be directly controlled by the regime but rather by pro-regime militias, parties from Iran, Iraq, and Lebanon (Hizbullah).

There are also strong indications that Russia and the US have divided Syria into two spheres of influence along the line of the Euphrates. While Russia accepts the presence of US troops to the northeast of the Euphrates, the US administration under President Trump accepts Russian dominance in the rest of Syria. This complicates the position of the Syrian Kurds. While the eastern parts of the Democratic Federation of Northern Syria – mainly the former cantons (and now regions, Kurdish: Herêm) of Cizîrê and Kobanê, plus the territories taken over from "Islamic State" in 2017 – have become a kind of US-protectorate, the Trump administration has made it very clear that it will not help the Kurds to the west of the Euphrates.

Turkey, still a member of NATO, started to play its NATO partners and Russia against each other, threatening to change allegiance to Russia if the US continued to support the Syrian Democratic Forces, respectively the Kurdish YPG and YPJ. This silenced western criticism about the recent Turkish attack against Efrîn and left the most western region of the Democratic Federation of Northern Syria at the mercy of Russia.

Months passed between the first minor artillery attacks of summer 2017 and the start of a ground invasion on 20 January 2018. We can still only speculate what happened between Russia and Turkey in the weeks before this. However, we do know about several meetings between Turkish and Russian officials in autumn 2017 ahead of the Turkish invasion, including several meetings between President Putin and President Erdoğan himself. Putin and Erdoğan met on 28 September in

Ankara, on 13 November in Sochi and again in Ankara on 11 December. It does not take much imagination to believe that in these meetings the fate of Efrîn was also decided.

What we definitely see is the result of these negotiations: Russia withdrew its own troops from Efrîn in the days before the Turkish invasion and neither defended, nor protested the Turkish attack against Efrîn. In effect Putin gave Erdoğan a green light for the attack against Efrîn that started on 20 January 2018.

The close coordination between Turkey and Russia continued after the beginning of the Turkish attack against Efrîn. After a phone call between President Putin and President Erdoğan on 8 February 2018 the Kremlin issued a statement that Russia and Turkey had agreed to strengthen coordination between the countries' military and security services in Syria.

Russia's goal in its cooperation with Turkey was to force the YPG/YPJ to cooperate with the regime and to accept a return to the rule of Assad. For Turkey the main strategic goal was to remove at least a part of its Kurdish enemies from the Turkish border. Additional Turkish officials openly announced that they wanted to use Efrîn for the return of Syrian refugees. Emine Erdoğan, the wife of President Recep Tayyip Erdoğan, publicly announced in a statement promoted by many Turkish media that some 500,000 Syrians would be expected "to go back to the northwestern Syrian district of Afrin", after Turkey had "liberated" the area from the YPG.[1]

Thus, the Turkish attempt to conquer Efrîn has also a connection with the EU–Turkey refugee deal. Turkey wants to get rid of at least a part of the 3.5 million refugees from Syria and as Europe has closed its doors, Turkey needs space to return them to Syria. Nevertheless, most of them would certainly not be "returning" to Efrîn because they never came from there. A relatively small number of Arabs fled from the Tal Rifaat region when the Syrian Democratic Forces (SDF) conquered that town and region in February 2016. However, this region did not include 100,000 inhabitants in total. To "return" 500,000 Arab Syrian refugees to Efrîn is rather a declaration of ethnic cleansing. The idea behind such a plan might be to "transfer" the Kurds of Efrîn – including its most vulnerable Êzîdî minority – to Kobanê and Cizîrê and to resettle Sunni-Arab Erdoğan loyalists near the Turkish border. This has already partly happened in Azaz and Jarâbulus, towns to the east of Efrîn that are have bee under the control of pro-Turkish forces since summer 2016. In fact

Turkey already started to settle Arab Syrians and Sunni Turkmens from Iraq in Efrîn even during the fights with YPG and YPJ. Displaced Kurds from Efrîn report that they were refused by the Turkish army and their Islamist allies to return to their homes. While I was finishing the English version of this book, the forced demographic change of Efrîn by Turkey continued.

The Turkish invasion of Efrîn also has consequences for the autonomy of the Kurdish quarter of Aleppo called Sheikh Maqsood (Kurdish: Şêxmeqsûd) and the presence of YPG and Jabhat al-Akrad forces in Aleppo. While the YPG was able to hold that quarter after the fall of the opposition in December 2016, it had to raise the Syrian flag and accept a partial return of the regime at the end of December 2017. On 22 February 2018 the YPG Aleppo Commander Fırat Xelil finally made the following statement about the deployment of Syrian regime forces in eastern neighborhoods of Aleppo:

> As YPG and YPJ forces in Aleppo, we have acted with the awareness of our responsibility since the first day of the attacks against Afrin. We have taken our place in the Resistance of the Age against the attacks of the invading Turkish state. Due to the silence of all world powers on the barbaric attacks, all the YPG and YPJ forces in Aleppo went to Afrin and participated in the defense. For this reason, the neighborhoods east of Aleppo have come under the control of regime forces.[2]

The YPG and YPJ completely withdrew from the city of Aleppo. This meant that by the end of February the whole city of Aleppo, including Şêxmeqsûd, was under the control of regime forces.

By the time of the printing of this book a similar development was taking place in Tal Rifaat, a town with about 20,000 predominantly Arab inhabitants that was conquered by the Syrian Democratic Forces (SDF) in February 2016. It is – or was – one of the headquarters of the Army of Revolutionaries (Jaysh al-Thuwar), the main Arab ally of the YPG/YPJ in the SDF. Negotiations led to a return of the regime's Syrian Arab Army on 23 February to Tal Rifaat and the nearby Menagh airbase.

An agreement between the regime and the YPG on 18 February led to the support of some Shiite militia but not regular Syrian troops. The support of Shiite militias did not prevent Turkey from taking the city of Efrîn. Although it took the large and well equipped NATO army of Turkey two months to take the small region of Efrîn, the YPG and YPJ decided to leave the city on 18 March 2018 to enable the civilians to flee the city. However, this does not mean that the YPG and YPJ stopped their resistance. The same day a declaration of the YPG announced that they will continue their resistance as a guerilla war all over Efrîn.

The disunity of the Kurds still plays into the hands of both Turkey and the Syrian regime. Although the Kurdish National Concil (ENKS) did issue a statement against the invasion of Turkey and for the defence of Efrîn[3] this did not lead to any practical cooperation between YPG/YPJ and the Rojava Peshmerga. Moreover, Turkey is using some minor Kurdish groups, made up of Kurdish Islamists and Turkish-Kurdish village guards[4] to fight in Efrîn as well. Although these groups – such as the Mashaal Tammo Brigade, the Kurdish Front or the Saladin Brigade – were small in numbers and did not have a strong military impact, they were useful for Turkish propaganda to demonstrate that Turkey isn't fighting the Kurds, but a "terrorist organization".

Although the region of Efrîn is highly now under occupation and threatened by ethnic cleansing, it is also remarkable that Turkey has not had a quick success there. While Erdoğan originally announced that Efrîn would fall into Turkish hands within a few hours, the Turkish army and its Syrian allies did not even reach the outskirts of the city of Efrîn after a month of fighting. Keeping in mind that this is a fight between a well-trained and -equipped NATO army that also uses German tanks and American planes to attack its enemy, this is an astonishing success for YPG/YPJ. Turkey seemed to have hesitated in using its own soldiers and overestimated the combat strength of its Syrian allies.

After the first month of fighting it turned out that Turkey's Syrian allies were badly trained and poorly motivated and that the Turkish army was afraid to use its own soldiers. War might be popular in Turkey for now, but it could become much less popular if the number of fallen soldiers drastically increased. Although the well-equipped and -trained Turkish army would surely be able to win a war against a lightly armed militia like the YPG, the political costs for such a full-scale war could be high for President Erdoğan.

Measured by Erdoğan's own propaganda, the war against Efrîn was a failure for Turkey. However, with the occupation of Efrîn city on 18 March, with censorship of critical media and a strong propaganda machinery, the Turkish government managed to gain internal support not only by supporters of the ruling AKP, but also of the nationalist MHP and the Kemalist opposition party CHP. Maybe winning this support was even one of the main goals of an otherwise weak president. The war allowed him to use nationalist feelings and oppress the remaining opposition even more than he already did before.

The fights in Syria could increase again during 2018. However, these are the battles of a second stage of the Syrian civil war. Since the end of 2016, when the regime reconquered East Aleppo, it has been clear that the regime will stay in power. After a partly respected ceasefire in 2017 the regime has tried to take over remaining opposition pockets in Syria's heartland and Turkey has tried to get rid of its enemies on the border. These fights are already struggles for the future map of Syria and might finally lead to a negotiated peace in the next stage.

However, a Syria ruled by the regime after a negotiated peace would not be a return to the situation as it was before 2011. Such a Syria will be an unstable state.

If a negotiated peace were possible, it would need some kind of federalization of Syria. Such a federalization would be a chance for the establishment and recognition of the autonomy of the Democratic Federation of Northern Syria. At the same time, it would also create extremely bad conditions for a real democratization of the region. What it would make much more likely is the division of the region among authoritarian regional rulers who, even though they no longer wage war against each other, are also not interested in a democratization of their societies.

Even in Rojava itself, such a solution would, under conditions of continuing instability, probably strengthen the forces that primarily act according to a military logic. This could also multiply the tensions among the Kurds. The fighting in Şingal in Iraq at the beginning of March 2017 and the subsequent abuses and arrests directed against members of the KNC in Syria; and the killing of the 16-year-old Êzîdi Nazê Naif Qaval on 14 March 2017 and the subsequent closure of party offices of the PDKS in Rojava all show how closely intermingled the developments in the Iraqi and Syrian parts of Kurdistan have become.

The authoritarianism of the PDK in the Iraqi part of Kurdistan is countered by a similar authoritarianism against the PDKS and its allies on the part of the PYD/YPG in the Syrian part of Kurdistan. At the moment, neither the PDK that rules in Iraqi Kurdistan nor the PYD that governs Syrian Kurdistan appear to be willing to share their power with rival currents within the Kurdish movement. Especially in view of the party militias of both sides, which receive their arms in no small measure from Europe and the US, there is a danger that the intra-Kurdish *conflict* could escalate into a Kurdish *civil war*. Those who would bear the brunt in such a development would probably be the small minorities such as the Êzîdî in Şingal, and civilians in the region generally.

Since the failure of Barzani's attempts to achieve the independence of Iraqi Kurdistan from Iraq and the ensuing retreat of the Kurdish Peshmerga in Iraqi Kurdistan in October 2017, the two Kurdish entities no longer share a border. The fate of both autonomies also depends on the development of their respective national states. In the Syrian case, the security of the region higly depends on the alliance of the Syrian Democratic Forces with the US. The growing threat of a Turkish military intervention against Efrîn pushed the Kurds of Efrîn and Aleppo into the arms of the Syrian regime. At the end of 2017, the Kurdish district of Aleppo, Şêxmeqsûd publicly put the Syrian banner on display for the first time since 2012. After a months-long economic blockade, the administration of the quarter agreed to accept a certain degree of regime control in exchange for the return of basic services to the district. In February 2018 the Kurds had to hand it over to the regime because they needed their forces to defend Efrîn. By the end of March 2018 the YPG and YPJ and their allies within the SDF also handed over the remaining rest of Efrîn – the villages in the extreme southeast of the Canton Efrîn and the region around Tal Rifaat (Shahba Canton) – to the regime. The other parts of the Democratic Federation of Northern Syria depend on the continuing support of the US. A public statement by US president Trump at the end of March 2018 that he would like to withdraw from Syria as soon as possible alarmed many Kurds. While the French president Macron declared his support for the Kurds, including his willingness to send French troops to the Kurdish territories of Syria, it is hard to imagine that France would replace the US completely.

So far, however, the Kurdish autonomous regions in Iraq and Syria continue to exist. There is still a historical chance that the Kurds, who in the course of the twentieth century became the victims of the order carrying the names of Sykes and Picot, will in the future be able to play an autonomous political role in the Middle East. It will depend not only on the policies of the hegemonic powers, but also on the Kurdish actors themselves whether this historical opportunity will be realized.

Bibliography

Acıkıyıldız, Birgül (2010): *The Yezidis: The History of a Community, Culture and Religion*. London: I. B. Tauris.

Allsopp, Harriet (2014): *The Kurds of Syria: Political Parties and Identity in the Middle East*. London: I. B. Tauris.

Ammann, Birgit (1991): Kurdische Juden in Israel. In: Berliner Institut für vergleichende Sozialforschung, Haus der Kulturen der Welt, and medico international (eds.): *Kurden im Exil: Ein Handbuch kurdischer Kultur, Politik und Wissenschaft*. Berlin: Edition Parabolis, 1–23.

Barfield, Thomas J. (2002): Turk, Persian and Arab: Changing Relationships between Tribes and State in Iran and along its Frontiers. In: Keddie, Nikki R. and Mathee, Rudi (eds.): *Iran and the Surrounding World: Interactions in Culture and Cultural Politics*. Baltimore: University of Washington Press.

Brentjes, Burchard and Günther, Siegwart-Horst (2001): *Die Kurden: Ein Abriss zur Geschichte und Erfahrungsberichte zur aktuellen humanitären Situation*. Vienna: Braumüller.

Bruinessen, Martin van (1989): *Agha, Scheich und Staat: Politik und Gesellschaft Kurdistans*. Berlin: Edition Parabolis.

Bruinessen, Martin van (1992): *Agha, Shaikh and State: The Social and Political Structures of Kurdistan*. London: Zed Books. Translation of Bruinessen (1989).

Bunzl, John (1989): *Juden im Orient. Jüdische Gemeinschaften in der islamischen Welt und orientalische Juden in Israel*. Vienna: Junius.

Cigerxwîn (1995): *Jînenîgariya min*. Spånga: Apec-Förlag.

Commins, David and Lesch, David W. (2014): *Historical Dictionary of Syria*. Lanham, MD: Scarecrow Press.

Desai, Raj M., Olofsgård, Anders, and Yousef, Tarik M. (2009): The Logic of Authoritarian Bargains. *Economics & Politics*, Vol. 21, March 2009, 93–125.

Dillemann, Lois (1979): Les Français en haute-Djezireh 1929–1939. *Revue Française d'Histoire d'Outre-Mer*, Vol. 66, 33–58.

Dirik, Dilar (2015): Die Frauenrevolution in Rojava. In: Küpeli, Ismail (ed.): *Kampf um Kobanê: Kampf um die Zukunft des Nahen Ostens*. Münster: edition assemblage, 38–50.

Flach, Anja, Ayboğa, Ercan, and Knapp, Michael (2015): *Revolution in Rojava. Frauenbewegung und Kommunalismus zwischen Krieg und Embargo*. Hamburg: VSA Verlag.

Fuccaro, Nelida (1997): Die Kurden Syriens: Anfänge der nationalen Mobilisierung unter französischer Herrschaft. In: Borck, Carsten, Savelsberg,

Eva, and Hajo, Siamend (eds.): *Ethnizität, Nationalismus, Religion und Politik in Kurdistan*. Münster: LIT Verlag, 301–326.

Fuccaro, Nelida (2004): Minorities and Ethnic Mobilisation: The Kurds in Northern Iraq and Syria. In: Méouchy, Nadine and Sluglett, Peter (eds.): *The British and French Mandates in Comparative Perspectives – Les mandats français et anglais dans une perspective comparative*. Leiden: Brill, 579–596.

Galehr, Joel (2011): KurdInnen in der Syrisch-Arabischen Republik. In: Schmidinger, Thomas (ed.): *Kurdistan im Wandel: Konflikte, Staatlichkeit, Gesellschaft und Religion zwischen Nahem Osten und Diaspora*. Frankfurt am Main: Peter Lang, 197–208.

Gaster, Moses (1925): Die samaritanische Literatur. In: Dexinger, Ferdinand and Pummer, Reinhard (eds.) (1992): *Die Samaritaner*. Darmstadt: Wissenschaftliche Buchgesellschaft, 141–186. Eng. translation as Third Lecture: Literature. In: *The Samaritans: Their History, Doctrines and Literature*. London: Oxford University Press, 96–158. Online at: http://sammlungen. ub.uni-frankfurt.de/freimann/urn/urn:nbn:de:hebis:30:1-149481 (Last access: December 2017).

Gunes, Cengiz (2012): *The Kurdish National Movement in Turkey: From Protest to Resistance*. Abingdon: Routledge.

Gunter, Michael M. (2014): *Out of Nowhere: The Kurds of Syria in Peace and War*. London: C. Hurst & Co.

Hamelink, Wendelmoet and Barış, Hanifi (2014): Dengbêjs on Borderlands: Borders and the State as seen through the Eyes of Kurdish Singer-poets. *Kurdish Studies*, Vol. 2, No. 1, 34–60.

Henderson, Ebenezer (1826): *Biblical Researches and Travels in Russia Including a Tour in the Crimea and the Passage of the Caucasus. With Observations on the State of the Rabbinical and Karaite Jews, and the Mohammedan and Pagan Tribes, Inhabiting the Southern Provinces of the Russian Empire*. London: James Nisbet.

Hinnebusch, Raymond (2011): *Syria: Revolution from Above*. Abingdon: Routledge.

Hochmüller, Wolfgang (2011): Die PKK in Syrien. In: Schmidinger, Thomas (ed.): *Kurdistan im Wandel: Konflikte, Staatlichkeit, Gesellschaft und Religion zwischen Nahem Osten und Diaspora*. Frankfurt am Main: Peter Lang, 217–224.

HRW: Human Rights Watch (1996): *Syria: The Silenced Kurds*. Online at: http:// www.hrw.org/sites/default/files/reports/SYRIA96.pdf (Last access: August 2014).

HRW: Human Rights Watch (2009): *Group Denial: Repression of Kurdish Political and Cultural Rights in Syria*. Online at: http://www.hrw.org/sites/ default/files/reports/syria1109webwcover_0.pdf (Last access: August 2014).

HRW: Human Rights Watch (2014): *Under Kurdish Rule: Abuses in PYD-run Enclaves of Syria*. Online at: http://www.hrw.org/sites/default/files/reports/ syriakudrs0614webwcover.pdf (Last access: August 2014).

Ismael, Tarq Y. and Ismael, Jacqueline S. (1998): *The Communist Movement in Syria and Lebanon*. Gainsville, Tallahassee: University Press of Florida.

Joseph, John (1983): *Muslim-Christian Relations and Inter-Christian Rivalries in the Middle East: The Case of the Jacobites in an Age of Transition.* Albany, NY: State University of New York Press.

Jweideh, Wadie (2006): *Kurdish National Movement: Its Origins and Development.* Syracuse: Syracuse University Press.

Knapp, Michael, Flach, Anja, and Ayboğa, Ercan (2016): *Revolution in Rojava: Democratic Autonomy and Women's Liberation in Syrian Kurdistan.* London: Pluto Press. A revised and updated translation of Flach et al. (2015).

Kurdwatch (2009): *Die Kurdenpolitik der syrischen Regierung und die Entwicklung der kurdischen Bewegung seit 1920: Ein Überblick.* Online at: http://www. kurdwatch.org/pdf/kurdwatch_einfuehrung_de.pdf (Last access: August 2014). Eng. translation as *The Kurdish Policy of the Syrian Government and the Development of the Kurdish Movement since 1920: An Overview.* Online at: http://www.kurdwatch.org/pdf/kurdwatch_einfuehrung_en.pdf (Last access: December 2017).

Kurdwatch (2010): *Staatenlose Kurden in Syrien. Illegale Eindringlinge oder Opfer nationalistischer Politik.* Online at: http://www.kurdwatch.org/pdf/kurdwatch_ staatenlose_de.pdf (Last access: August 2014). Eng. translation as *Stateless Kurds in Syria: Illegal Invaders or Victims of a Nationalistic Policy?* Online at: http://www. kurdwatch.org/pdf/kurdwatch_staatenlose_en.pdf (Last access: December 2017).

Kurdwatch (2011): *Wer ist die syrischkurdische Opposition? Die Entwicklung kurdischer Parteien 1956–2011.* Online at: http://www.kurdwatch.org/pdf/ kurdwatch_parteien_de.pdf (Last access: August 2014). Eng. translation as *Who Is the Syrian-Kurdish Opposition? The Development of Kurdish Parties, 1956–2011.* Online at: http://www.kurdwatch.org/pdf/kurdwatch_parteien_ en.pdf, http://www.kurdwatch.org/pdf/kurdwatch_parteien_en_2.pdf (Last access: December 2017).

Lescot, Roger (1938): *Enquête sur les Yézidis de Syrie et du Djebel Sindjar.* Beirut: Institut Français de Damas.

McDowall, David (1998): *The Kurds of Syria.* London: Kurdish Human Rights Project.

McDowall, David (2004): *A Modern History of the Kurds.* London: I. B. Tauris.

McGee, Thomas (2016): Mapping Action and Identity in the Kobani Crisis Response. *Kurdish Studies,* Vol. 4, No. 1, 51–77.

Mahr, Horst (1971): *Die Ba'th-Partei: Porträt einer panarabischen Bewegung.* Munich: Olzog.

Maisel, Sebastian (2017): *Yezidis in Syria: Identity Building among a Double Minority.* Lanham, MD: Lexington Books.

Marcus, Aliza (2007): *Blood and Belief: The PKK and the Kurdish Fight for Independence.* New York: New York University Press.

Matras, Yaron (2012): *A Grammar of Domari.* Berlin and Boston: Walter de Gruyter.

Moubayed, Sami (2006): *Steel and Silk: Men and Women Who Shaped Syria 1900–2000.* Seattle: Cune Press.

Niebuhr, Carsten (1778): *C. Niebuhrs Reisebeschreibung nach Arabien und anderen umliegenden Ländern.* Band 2. Copenhagen: Nicolaus Möller.

Olszowy-Schlager, Judith (1997): *Karaite Marriage Documents from the Cairo Geniza: Legal Tradition and Community Live in Mediaeval Egypt and Palestine.* Leiden, New York, and Cologne: Brill.

Oron, Yitzkhak (ed.) (1961): *Middle East Record 1961.* Volume 2. Jerusalem: Tel Aviv University.

Osztovics, Christoph (2011): Die jüdische Bevölkerung Kurdistans. In: Schmidinger, Thomas (ed.): *Kurdistan im Wandel. Konflikte, Staatlichkeit, Gesellschaft und Religion zwischen Nahem Osten und Diaspora.* Frankfurt am Main: Peter Lang, 77–86.

Phillips, Christopher (2016): *The Battle for Syria: International Rivalry in the New Middle East.* New Haven and London: Yale University Press.

Pierret, Thomas (2013): *Religion and State in Syria: The Sunni Ulama under the Ba'th.* Cambridge and New York: Cambridge University Press.

Rabinovich, Itamar (1972): *Syria under the Ba'th 1963–66: The Army–Party Symbiosis.* Jerusalem: Tel Aviv University.

Rezvani, Babak (2013): *Ethno-Territorial Conflict and Coexistence in the Caucasus, Central-Asia and Fereydan.* Amsterdam: Amsterdam University Press.

Röpke, Andrea and Schröm, Oliver (2002): *Stille Hilfe für braune Kameraden: Das geheime Netzwerk der Alt- und Neonazis.* 2nd edition. Berlin: Ch. Links.

Said, Edward (1978): *Orientalism.* New York: Pantheon Books.

Schur, Nathan (2008): *The Return of the Diaspora Samaritans to Nablus at the End of the Middle Ages.* Online at: http://shomrono.tripod.com/articles/thereturnofthediaspora.pdf (Last access: August 2014).

Schmidinger, Thomas (2014): The Haqqa Community: A Heterodox Movement with Sufi Origins. In: Omarkhali, Khanna (ed.): *Religious Minorities in Kurdistan: Beyond the Mainstream.* Wiesbaden: Harrassowitz, 227–234.

Schmidinger, Thomas (2016a): Syrien: Kurden im Zangengriff. *Blätter für Deutsche und Internationale Politik,* Vol. 10, 25–28.

Schmidinger, Thomas (2016b): Şingal nach dem Genozid: Die politische und militärische Entwicklung in der Region seit 2014. In: Brizić, Katharina, Grond, Agnes, Osztovics, Christoph, Schmidinger, Thomas, and Six-Hohenbalken, Maria (eds.): *Wiener Jahrbuch für Kurdische Studien 2016,* Band 4, *Şingal 2014: Der Angriff des "Islamischen Staates", der Genozid an den Êzîdî und die Folgen.* Wien: Ceasarpress, 33–55.

Social Contract in Rojava (2014): Online at: http://www.kedistan.net/2017/08/11/document-constitution-rojava-social-contract/ (Last access: December 2017).

Tachjian, Vahé (2003): Khoybun und Daschnaktsutiun: Eine ungewöhnliche kurdisch-armenische Allianz. *Kurdische Studien,* Vol. 3, Nos. 1–2, 55–78.

Takla, Youssef S. (2004): Corpus juris du mandat français. In: Méouchy, Nadine and Sluglett, Peter (eds.): *The British and French Mandates in Comparative Perspectives – Les mandats français et anglais dans une perspective comparative.* Leiden: Brill, 63–100.

Tejel, Jordi (2009): *Syria's Kurds: History, Politics and Society.* London and New York: Routledge.

Vanly, Ismet Chérif (1968): *The Syrian "Mein Kampf" against the Kurds: Ba'th Thinking Reviewed.* Amsterdam: J.S.K.

Vanly, Ismet Chérif (1992): The Kurds in Syria and Lebanon. In: Kreyenbroek, Phillip G. (ed.): *The Kurds: A Contemporary Overview*. London and New York: Routledge.

Velud, Christian (2000): French Mandate Policy in the Syrian Steppe. In: Mundy, Martha and Musallam, Basim (eds.): *The Transformation of Nomadic Society in the Arab East*. Cambridge: Cambridge University Press, 79–81.

Weismann, Itzchak (2007a): *The Naqshbandiyya: Orthodoxy and Activism in a Worldwide Sufi Tradition*. London and New York: Routledge.

Weismann, Itzchak (2007b): Sufi Fundamentalism between India and the Middle East. In: Van Bruinessen, Martin and Howell, Julia Day (eds.): *Sufism and the "Modern" in Islam*. London: I. B. Tauris, 115–128.

Wierzbicka, Aleksandra (2011): Staatenlose KurdInnen in Syrien. In: Schmidinger, Thomas (ed.): *Kurdistan im Wandel. Konflikte, Staatlichkeit, Gesellschaft und Religion zwischen Nahem Osten und Diaspora*. Frankfurt am Main: Peter Lang, 209–216.

Yalçın-Heckmann/Strohmeier (2000): *Die Kurden. Geschichte – Politik – Kultur*. Munich: C. H. Beck.

Yildiz, Kerim (2005): *The Kurds in Syria: The Forgotten People*. London: Pluto Press.

Zaza, Noureddine (1982): *Ma vie de Kurde, ou, Le cri du peuple kurde*. Lausanne: Favre.

Interviews

Kheredin Murad, 22 January, 2006, Vienna.
Hassan Muhammad Ali, 20 October, 2012, Vienna.
Abdulbaset Sieda, 10 January, 2013, Istanbul.
Hassan Salih, 11 January, 2013, Amûdê.
Hisham Sheikho, 11 January, 2013, Amûdê.
Manal Husseini, 11 January, 2013, Amûdê.
Dilowan an-Nuri, 11 January, 2013, Amûdê.
Zerdaşt Muhammed, 12 January, 2013, Amûdê.
Muhammed Weli, 12 January, 2013, Amûdê.
Group interview with the activists of the Tansiqiya Amûdê, 12 January, 2013, Amûdê.
Munzur Eskan, 12 January, 2013, Amûdê.
Mehemed Eli Mosa, 12 January, 2013, Amûdê.
Sabri Rasol, 12 January, 2013, Amûdê.
Hassan Draieî und Hla Draieî, 12 January, 2013, Amûdê.
Mufid al-Khaznawi, 21 November, 2013, Vienna.
Salih Muslim, 30 December, 2013, Vienna.
Mustafa Khidr Osso, 18 February, 2014, Erbil.
Mustafa Abdelaziz, 19 February, 2014, border post Semalka.
Ahlam Rammu, 19 February, 2014, Ger Balad.
Fadi Yakub, 19 February, 2014, Dêrik.
Kamil Kurie, 19 February, 2014, Dêrik.
Naeem Youssef, 19 February 2014, Dêrik.
Abjar Musa, 19 February, 2014, Dêrik.
Murad Murad, 19 February, 2014, Dêrik.
Dajad Akobian, 19 February, 2014, Dêrik.
Akram Kamal Hasu, 20 February, 2014, Qamişlo.
Taha Xelîl, 20 February, 2014, Qamişlo.
Group interview with activists of the association Duat al-Hayr, 20 February, 2014, Amûdê.
Group interview with activists of the Kurdish Unity Party in Syria and the Tansiqiya Amûdê, 20 February, 2014, Amûdê.
Shahida Adalat, 21 February, 2014, in a YPG camp near Qamişlo.
Thomas Thomasian, 21 February, 2014, Qamişlo.
Sheikh Ibrahim, 21 February, 2014, Qizla Cox.
Asya Abdullah, 21 February, 2014, Qamişlo.
Barzan Iso, Journalist in Kobanê, 13 July, 2014, Kobanê.

Hevi Ibrahim Mustefa, 30 July, 2014, Efrîn.
Sa'ud al Mulla, 1 August, 2014, Qamişlo.
Siamend Hajo, 10 August, 2014, Berlin.
Hisen Ibrahim Salih, 25 August, 2014, Vienna.
Enwer Muslim, 22 September, 2014, Kobanê.
Salah Ammo, 28 September, 2014, Vienna.
Hevi Ibrahim Mustefa, 2 February, 2015, Efrîn.
Silêman Ceefer, 2 February, 2015, Efrîn.
Ebdo Ibrahim, 3 February, 2015, Efrîn.
Aisha Afandi, 4 February, 2015, Kobanê.
Nassan Ahmad, 24 April, 2015, Vienna.
Idriss Nassan, 24 April, 2015, Vienna.
Enwer Muslim, 5 November, 2015, Kobanê.
Ruken Ahmed, 5 November, 2015, Kobanê.
Idriss Nassan, 5 November, 2015, Kobanê.
Ibrahim Kurdo, 5 November, 2015, Kobanê.
Ibrahîm Biro, 20 February, 2016, Vienna.
Ibrahîm Kurdo, 4 September 2016, Kobanê.
Group interview with the women of the Women's Centre Kolîşîna, 5 September, 2016, Amûdê.
Abdulhamid Hadji Darwish, 3 October, 2016, Qamişlo.
Rêdûr Xelîl, 14 February, 2017, Qamişlo.
Abdulhakim Bashar, 16 February, 2017, Erbil.
Hediye Yusuf, 2 March, 2017, Qamişlo.
Mizgin Yusuf, 13 August, 2017, Berlin.
Mohamed Şaixo (Shaikho), 26 December 2017, Aleppo.
Ebdo Ibrahi, 26 March, 2018, Tal Rifaat.

Notes

1   In some European languages, "Islamic State in Iraq and Greater Syria" (ad-Dawla al-Islāmiyya fi al-'Irāq wa-sh-Shām) has often been translated as "Islamic State in Iraq and the Levant," with the accompanying abbreviations ISIS, or ISIL. In this, ISIS is supposed to be the abbreviation of "Islamic State of Iraq and Sham." But "Sham" does not mean Levant, but rather, historical Arab Syria. Whereas the term "Levant" denotes the whole coastal area of the Eastern Mediterranean, including the Turkish Mediterranean coast, the Greek islands, Cyprus, and occasionally even the Egyptian Mediterranean coast, historic Syria comprises, in addition to today's Syrian state, the territory of Lebanon, Jordan, Israel/Palestine, and the Arab-speaking region Hatay/Antakya in Turkey, and sometimes still other Arab-speaking cities in Turkey near the border, such as Urfa and Mardin – but certainly not Cyprus, Egypt, or the Turkish and Greek Mediterranean coast. There is a programmatic meaning in the fact that the organization in question, which is generally abbreviated as DAASH in the region, refers to "Sham" and not to today's Syria. For that reason, the author of the present book has come to the conclusion that the translation "Islamic State in Iraq and Greater Syria" is the one closest to the Arabic original. Since the proclamation of the "Caliphate" on 29 June 2014, the group refers to itself only as "Islamic State," reflecting, among other things, the goal to extend its territory to the whole Islamic world. Yet in addition, IS has published maps of the "Caliphate" that also include Spain, Southeastern Europe, and Austria.

CHAPTER 3

1   The Mandaeans practise a syncretist monotheist religion based, inter alia, on Judaism. Its adherents regard themselves as followers of John the Baptist. This religious community was able to hold forth as a minority in the south of Iraq and in the Iranian province of Ahvaz. Because they were repeatedly subjected to attacks by jihadi militias during the Iraqi civil war, today many more Mandaeans live in the diaspora in the USA, Sweden, and Australia, where new exile communities have developed. Today, their variety of Aramaic, Mandaean, is almost exclusively used only in sacred contexts.

Classical Mandaean (ISO 639-3: mid) is still used as a language of the sacred in religious contexts and is also taught to children, but it is not spoken in daily life. However, older members of the Mandaean communities of Shûshtar, Khorramshahar, and Dezful in the southwestern province of Khūzestān still speak New Mandaean dialects (ISO 639-3: mid). Given the small number of dispersed communities, however, it is questionable whether it is being passed on to the younger generation.

2 All maps in the book are modified versions of those which appeared in the original German-language edition.

CHAPTER 4

1 These descendants of those adherents of the Yahweh religion who were not deported during the great Assyrian deportation in 722 BC developed their own autonomous religion after that time.

CHAPTER 8

1 The literature on the event cites many different numbers. While most sources give the number of 152 dead children, the website www.diekurden. de talks about 283 children. The Kurdish encyclopedia *Kurdica* mentions 180 to 300 victims (http://www.kurdica.com/News-sid-Der-Kinobrand-von-Am%C3%BBde-920.html), but the highest number is given by Birgit Cerha of *IFAMO* (*Information. Forschung. Analyse. Mittlerer Osten.*), who talks about "almost 300 Kurdish schoolchildren who died behind locked doors" (http://ifamo-blog.blogspot.com.tr/2012/08/syriens-kurden-zwischen-allen-fronten.html).

2 http://www.diekurden.de/news/die-wunde-von-52-jahren-der-kinobrand-von-Amûdê-3317457/ (last accessed: August 2014).

3 Even so, the historical relationship between Zakī al-Arsūzī and the Ba'ath Party remained very volatile and al-Arsūzī did not become part of the leadership of the new party. It was only after the split of the party into Iraqi and Syrian wings in 1966 that al-Arsūzī became the chief ideologist of the Syrian wing, while Aflaq became the chief ideologist of the latter's Iraqi counterpart, and al-Bitar went into exile in France.

CHAPTER 9

1 Peshmerga (Kurdish: Pêşmerge) is the traditional Kurdish name for guerrilla fighters and was used primarily in Iraq for the fighters of the PDK and the PUK. Yet the term itself has existed since the 1920s and was also used in Iran

and in Turkey. A close to literal translation would be "those who look death in the eye" (*pêş* – in forward direction, *merg* – death). Since the former guerrilla units of the PUK and the PDK continued to exist after the establishment of an autonomous Kurdistan Region (Iraq) in 1991 and were, at least formally, even merged after the overthrow of Saddam Hussein, the military forces of the Kurdistan Regional Government are still called Pêşmerge today. To dissociate themselves from the PDK and the PUK, the PKK parties today normally do not describe their fighters as Peshmerga, but as guerrillas.

CHAPTER 10

1   While the regime claimed that he was killed by a bomb planted by members of Jabhat al-Nusra, this was denied by some oppositionists and Western journalists such as the BBC journalist Jim Muir. They hold that the regime itself was responsible for the murder of al-Būtī, because – or so the speculation goes – he might have been planning to switch sides.

2   The party, whose original name was the League for Communist Action, was renamed as the Communist Workers' Party in 1981. Since this oppositional party had numerous Alawi members and was therefore regarded as particularly dangerous by the Alawi-dominated regime, the latter's repression at the beginning of the 1990s was particularly directed against this group, which was de facto destroyed in 1992, but rebuilt in 2003. The party was also active in the protest movement of 2011–12, but was opposed to the militarization of the opposition. The Arab website of the organization is www.ahewar.org.

CHAPTER 11

1   In Kurdish, *tirej* means "muzzle flash."

CHAPTER 12

1   With the exception of the hilly area of the Kurd Dagh, Rojava is largely a flat area without mountain refuges. Its separation into three enclaves makes it even more unsuitable for guerrilla activities. While the guerrillas in Turkey, Iran, and Iraq always had the possibility of retreating into barely accessible mountain regions, this would be impossible in Syria.

CHAPTER 13

1   This decree was actually put into practice. In the following months, the *ajānib* were indeed able to get Syrian passports when they applied for them.

Yet that also meant that young men became eligible for the draft right in the midst of the unfolding civil war, whereas the *maktūmīn* remain excluded from citizenship to this day.

2 Apart from the PYD, the NCC included the Nasserist Democratic-Arab Socialist Union, the Marxist-Ba'athist splinter group Arab Revolutionary Workers Party led by Yasin al-Hafiz, the Leninist Communist Workers Party, the Left-Ba'athist Arab Socialist Movement founded by the erstwhile co-sponsor of the Ba'ath Party, Akram al-Hawrānī, the Marxist Left Assembly, the Christian-Aramaic Syriac Unity Party, the Left-Ba'athist Democratic Socialist Arab Ba'ath Party, and the Syrian Democratic Popular Party founded by the long-term political prisoner Riyad al-Turk, which until 2005 had acted under the name Syrian Communist Party (Political Bureau). But this last party was not represented in the executive bureau of the NCC and simultaneously became a member of the Syrian National Council (SNC); it should thus only be regarded as a "corresponding" member of the NCC. It seems that with the continuing Syrian civil war, the Syrian Democratic Popular Party has allied itself more with the Syrian National Council than with the NCC. Indeed, its member George Sabra became president of the SNC at the end of 2012 and was president of the Syrian National Coalition from April to July 2013.

3 Oppositional Syrians regard the release of these jihadist prisoners as a strategy of the regime, which they suspect of using this practice to split and discredit the opposition. The motives of the regime for releasing hundreds of jihadis who often had fighting experience from the Iraqi civil war will probably not be definitely clarified anytime soon. It is, however, remarkable that in the first phase of the civil war the government army rarely attacked these groups in any serious way, but directed its attacks almost exclusively against more moderate units of the Free Syrian Army. Because of the mounting influence of the jihadist groups, the opposition did indeed become discredited in the international arena, in addition to being unable to overcome its own splits.

4 The founding of the Free Syrian Army (al-Jaiš as-Sūrī al-hurr, FSA) was announced in July 2011. Although it was never a real army in the sense of a central command structure, but rather an umbrella association of different armed groupings, during the first phase of the civil war it represented the most important armed challenge to the regime. In December 2011, the FSA declared its readiness to coordinate with the SNC, but it was never able to prevent a certain autonomy of its various brigades. By its own account, in February 2012 the FSA had 50,000 to 60,000 soldiers under its command and controlled a number of territories in North and South Syria. Apart from deserters from the Syrian army, many volunteers fought in the ranks of the FSA. Many of its commanders were recruited from the Muslim Brotherhood. But the FSA lost many of its brigades after the founding of the Saudi-supported Islamic Front on 22 November 2013, which was joined not only by the most important brigades of the Syrian Islamic Liberation Front (SILF), the Salafist Syrian Islamic Front (SIF), and the Kurdish Islamic Front led by Abu Abdullah al-Kurdi, but also by several brigades of the FSA. Since the end

of 2013, the FSA has been in a state of dissolution in large areas of Syria, a fact that also expressed itself in the replacement of its chief of general staff, Selim Idriss. But his successor, Ilah al-Bashir, was also unable to stop both the disintegration of the FSA and the advance of the "Islamic State," which fights against not just the FSA, but also the Islamic Front and Jabhat al-Nusra.

CHAPTER 14

1 https://twitter.com/YPGRJAVA/status/393983929729830912

2 http://www.theguardian.com/world/2014/jun/26/186-kurdish-students-kidnapped-isis-syria

3 Until the beginning of August 2014, the Çiyayê Şingal was the largest settlement area of the Êzîdî. In June, after the conquest of Mosul by IS, Kurdish Peshmerga had secured both the town and the region. On 2 August, however, they retreated in the face of the onslaught by the "Islamic State" and left the civilians of the area to their fate. Tens of thousands of Êzîdî sought refuge in the mountains of the Çiyayê Şingal, fleeing IS, which openly threatened to murder the members of this minority whom it denounced as devil worshippers. Even before the Peshmerga of the PUK could reinvade the area, fighters of the YPG from Syria crossed the border into Iraq and secured exit routes for the Êzîdî civilians.

4 Aishe Afandi is both the wife of the PYD party chairman Salih Muslim and the sister of Ezzat Afandi, the surgeon living in Vienna who, in 2014, made an important contribution to health care in Kobanê by means of the Vienna Hospital, which was unfortunately largely destroyed during the fighting with IS.

5 The towns al-Zahraa with its 13,000 inhabitants and Nubl with its approximately 21,000 inhabitants represent a Twelver Shia enclave in a Sunni environment. From July 2012 to February 2016, the enclave was under the siege of Sunni rebels, including the jihadist Jabhat al-Nusra, and was thus accessible only via Efrîn. It was only in February 2016 that a government offensive in the surroundings of Aleppo succeeded in establishing a corridor to Nubl and al-Zahraa.

6 https://www.basnews.com/index.php/en/news/middle-east/272869

7 https://www.washingtonpost.com/news/checkpoint/wp/2017/03/08/marines-have-arrived-in-syria-to-fire-artillery-in-the-fight-for-raqqa/?hpid=hp_hp-more-top-stories_raqqa-230pm%3Ahomepage%2Fstory&utm_term=.9b867d88fd42

8 http://www.spiegel.de/politik/ausland/syrien-bundesregierung-dementiert-einsatz-deutscher-soldaten-a-1097730.html

9 http://www.rudaw.net/english/middleeast/syria/270520164

10 http://kurdishquestion.com/article/3643-first-us-soldier-dies-in-rojava-syria-brett-mcgurk

11 http://www.reuters.com/article/us-mideast-crisis-syria-russia-idUSKBN16R1H4

12 The Russian Reconciliation Centre in Syria tries to negotiate local ceasefires between the regime and moderate opposition groups.
13 https://de.sputniknews.com/politik/20170322314985442-russland-tuerkei-offensive-gegen-kurden-stopp/
14 http://aranews.net/2016/11/kurds-clash-pro-assad-forces-syrias-qamishli-casualties-reported/
15 The name for Halabja in Kurmancî.

CHAPTER 15

1 Not only have I seen this "border station" of Mabrouka with my own eyes, but returnees from IS, that is, former jihadist fighters, have corroborated in conversations with me that this trade indeed exists and that trucks are allowed to pass through IS areas unimpeded, provided the ransom they pay for this is considered sufficient.
2 http://www.leeza.at
3 http://www.medico.de/themen/aktion/dokumente/hilfe-fuer-rojava/4605/

CHAPTER 16

1 https://twitter.com/irevolt9/status/594449000411099136
2 http://aranews.net/2016/11/syrian-islamists-launch-chemical-attack-on-kurdish-district-in-aleppo/
3 http://aranews.net/2016/12/islamists-bomb-kurdish-district-amid-mounting-violence-in-syrias-aleppo/

CHAPTER 17

1 For the English translation of the "Social Contract in Rojava," see http://www.kedistan.net/2017/08/11/document-constitution-rojava-social-contract/.
2 These are, however, by no means the only Arabs in the region! All cantons, particularly the Jezira, contain Arab tribes, some of which have lived there for centuries, but also Arabs who were settled there in the course of the policy of creating an "Arab Belt."
3 http://www.fides.org/en/news/35357-ASIA_SYRIA_Archbishop_Hindo_Christians_do_not_support_the_Kurdish_autonomous_entity#.WfuLftDiaUk
4 http://www.kurdistan24.net/en/news/0251c0a-3aea-4b59-9d45-6d8a74b0c8bb/Kurdish-National-Council-excluded-from-Turkey-based-Syrian-opposition
5 http://ezidimedia.com/en/the-yezidi-council-of-syria-announced-its-whithdrawal-from-kurdish-national-council-and-syrian-national-council/

6   http://aranews.net/2017/03/post-sinjar-tensions-continue-40-pyd-rivals-arrested-syria-knc-offices-burned/

CHAPTER 18

1   In the summer of 2012, in Hewlêr (Arbil), the capital of Iraqi-Kurdistan, an agreement was hammered out between the Kurdish National Council and the PYD that led to the founding of the Supreme Kurdish Committee, but which otherwise didn't really work very well.

2   Mahmoud Darwish (1941–2008) was the best-known Palestinian poet of the twentieth century. As a child he fled with his family to Lebanon in 1948, but then returned, again with his family, as an "illegal intruder." In 1969, he went to Moscow to study and later on lived in Egypt, Lebanon, Cyprus, France, and Tunisia. He returned to Palestine only after the beginning of the "peace process" and then, from 1996, commuted between Ramallah and Amman. Beyond writing his world-famous poems, Darwish also edited a literary magazine, worked as director of the Palestine Research Center of the PLO and was an MP in the Palestinian National Council from 1987 to 1993. His poems were translated into more than 30 languages.

3   Mohammad Sheikho, in Kurdish Mihemed Şêxo, aka Mihemed Şêxmûs Salih (1948–1989), was born in Qamişlo. As a Kurdish nationalist and cultural activist he went into exile in Lebanon in 1969 and then worked among the followers of Mulla Mustafa Barzani in Iraqi Kurdistan in the early 1970s. In 1983, he returned to Syria, where he died in 1989. He developed his own musical style with very political lyrics, a style that is still characteristic for many Kurdish musicians today.

4   The colours of the Kurdish flag.

5   Andrei Alexandrovich Zhdanov (1896–1948) was Regional and City Secretary of the party organization of the CPSU in Leningrad from 1934 to 1944. In this position, he gained notoriety as a merciless "purger." During the 900-day blockade of Leningrad by the German Wehrmacht, he was Colonel-General in the War Soviet of the town. From 1945 to 1948, he was the main force behind the repressive cultural policy that was named after him, the "Zhdanovshchina." Even well-known and actually politically loyal Soviet writers, filmmakers, and musicians such as Pasternak, Eisenstein, or Shostakovich were attacked by Zhdanov. In this way, Zhdanov succeeded in securing socialist realism as the only legitimate artistic style in the Soviet Union for good.

6   Abdullah Öcalan, founder and leader of the PKK.

7   Synonym for the PKK guerrilla fighters.

8   A collection of holy texts of the Êzîdî that is probably a later textualization of religious chants that were handed down orally.

9   This agreement between the Kurdish National Council (KNC) and the People's Council of West Kurdistan/PYD created the Supreme Kurdish

Committee, which was to function as the transitional administration in Rojava.

10 The headquarters of the PKK is located in the Qandil Mountains in Kurdish Northern Iraq.

11 Capital of the Kurdish Regional Government; the reference here is to the PDK, or Barzani.

12 Traditional stronghold of Jalal Talabani's PUK; today, the stronghold of the PUK breakaway Goran.

13 Many Christians with a New-East-Aramaic mother tongue refer to themselves as Assyrians. So the reference in the main text is to these two New-East-Aramaic varieties in Rojava and not to the historic Assyrian, which hasn't been spoken as a mother tongue by anyone for more than 2,000 years.

14 The military units created by the Kurdish National Council with the support of Barzani, which were trained in the Iraqi part of Kurdistan.

15 Between 2007 and the fusion of the party with three other parties into the new PDKS in 2014, Abdulhakim Bashar was the chairman of the PDKS (el-Partî), which, until 2014, was the Syrian sister party of Barzani's PDK in Iraq. He is still regarded as one of the most powerful politicians in the new PDKS, and is a close confidant of Barzani.

16 Staffan de Mistura.

CHAPTER 19

1 http://www.hurriyetdailynews.com/500-000-expected-to-go-back-to-syria-after-afrin-operation-turkeys-first-lady-127450

2 https://anfenglish.com/features/ypg-statement-on-aleppo-25083

3 https://ara.yekiti-media.org/

4 The village guards (Korucular) were set up in Kurdish parts of Turkey to use Kurdish villagers to fight the PKK. For the fight in Efrîn Turkey mainly mobilized village guards from Şırnak, Diyarbakır, and Mardin.

Index

secret service 52, 57, 64, 65, 67, 68, 76,
    77, 80, 81–2, 144, 220, 226–7
Sekban, Mehmet Şükrü 43
self-administration 41, 42, 130, 136,
    149, 177, 179, 193, 209, 238, 242,
    245, 252
Selim, Memduh 43
Selum, Mansur 139, 247
Semalka 151
semi-autonomous principalities 30,
    34
Semile 15
semi-nomadic people 32, 33, 45
separation wall 142, 240–1
separatist movements 48, 63, 160, 179
Serê Kaniyê (Arabic: Ra's al-'Ain) 13,
    15, 21, 45, 75, 86, 89, 98, 101–2, 116,
    168, 181
Şeşo, Haydar 104
Shabak people 32
Shadala, Sheik Ebdulkerîm 23
shadow diplomacy 116
shadow economies 8, 116
Shahin, Bozan bey 43
Shammar tribe 45–7, 101, 103, 111
Sharabiyya tribe 101, 103
Sharia courts 109
Sheikan tribe 36
Sheikh Maqsoud (Kurdish:
    Şêxmeqsûd), Aleppo 8, 92–3,
    125–8, 244–5, 251–3, 257–8
Sheikho, Hisham 162–3
Sheiks, Kurdish 23–4, 32, 33, 39, 52,
    176
Shekhe, Lukman 70, 71
Shia 19, 33–4, 41, 108
Shiite religion 19, 26–7, 33–4, 64
Shikakan tribe 36
Sieda, Abdulbaset 90, 155–7, 182
sieges 103, 162, 195, 214–16, 229–30,
    252
Siirt, Turkey 70
Silo, Talal Ali 139, 144
Şingal 20, 22, 104, 105, 136–7, 260
Six Day War (1967) 26
Slejuk Brigade 139

smuggling 8, 28–9, 121, 124, 210, 214
social contract of Rojava 129, 130–1
socialist ideologies 6, 7, 55–6,
    211; see also Marxist-Leninist
    revolutionaries
"Socialist Party of the Arab
    Reawakening" (Hizb al-ba'th
    al-'arabī al-ištirākī) 55–6; see also
    Ba'ath regime
socialist realism 202
Social Nationalist Party, Syrian 49,
    54, 55
social science research methods 10–12
Soran, principality of 34
Soranî 13, 35, 197
Southeast Anatolia Project
    (Güneydoğu Anadolu Projesi,
    GAP) 69, 72
Soviet Union 43, 65, 68
Stalinism 50
statelessness 60–2, 86, 154, 158, 161
State of Aleppo (État d'Alep) 41–2, 45
State of Damascus (État de
    Damas) 41
state of emergency 65
Strohmeier, Martin 70
Sufism 23
suicide attacks 119
Sulemaniya 225
sun, in Kurdish culture 2
Sunni Islam 16, 19, 22, 23, 26–7, 32, 41,
    42–3, 46, 64, 66, 191, 216
supply routes 110, 126, 128, 138, 151,
    235, 245, 252
Supreme Kurdish Committee 91, 157,
    161, 168
Suq al-Saruja, Damascus 8
surface-to-surface missiles 119
Suruç (Serugh), Turkey 37
Suryoye people 188–9
Sutoro/Sootoro (Christian-Aramaic
    police unit) 118, 186–7, 188
Sykes-Picot Agreement 38, 261
synagogues 28, 29, 94, 117
Syria, constitution as a national
    state 5